Odyssey Dima Hasao & Autonomous Council

RAMU UPADHAYA

ZORBA BOOKS

ZORBA BOOKS

Published by Zorba Books, September 2024
Website: www.zorbabooks.com
Email: info@zorbabooks.com
Author Name: Ramu Upadhaya
Copyright ©: Ramu Upadhaya

Title: Odyssey Dima Hasao & Autonomous Council

Printbook ISBN: 978-93-5896-188-1
Ebook ISBN: 978-93-5896-968-9

Zorba Books Pvt. Ltd. (opc)
Sushant Arcade,
Next to Courtyard Marriot,
Sushant Lok 1, Gurgaon – 122009, India

Printed by Manipal Technologies Limited
A1 & A2 Shivalli Industrial Area Manipal Udupi, Karnataka – 576104

Contents

My Note   *ix*

Gratitude   *xi*

Prologue   *xv*

Chapter-I: Features – Geographical & Topographical   1

Structure & Content   2

Imaginative parody   5

Blue hills, green valleys, white and cloudy skies &
people's language   9

The earliest Dimasa Kingdom and its subsequent
establishment in Maibang   11

How did the hilly area of Assam shape into an entity?   13

Dima Hasao's successive growth and development   17

An onlooker of Haflong's growth   22

A Short Landscape of Dima Hasao   24

Chapter-II: History-Heros & Reformers   29

Transactional gesture   30

Freedom fighters from the tribesmen   31

Veer Sambudhan Phonglo & lieutenants   32

Dimalik Kemprai   34

Senapati Tularam Thaosen   39

Joya Thaosen in Golden Letters   43

Chengjapao Doungel   47

Haipou Jadunang & Rani Gaindinliu   48

J.B. Hagjer, J. N. Thaosen, H. M. Haflongbar   48

Durga Malla & Ram Singh Thakuri	50
A Cultural Icon - Princess Disru	52
Alaidao Khersa as a Seer	55

**Chapter-III: Direction & Administration	58**

Satire of positive development	59
How does the NCHAC get modelled?	60
Cabinet Mission; Advisory, and Bordoloi
Sub Committees	62
Recommendations	62
Actual Approval & inauguration	65
Body, strength and terms of the Council	65
District or Autonomous Council as a political
entity or body	67
Dima Hasao Autonomous Council's Role	68
Executive Power	68
Dima Hasao Autonomous Council's Managed
Major Subjects	71
Dima Hasao Autonomous Council's Entrusted/
Transferred State Subjects/Departments	72
Financial Power	76
Another aspect of Financial Ethics	77
Council's Sources of Revenue & Receipt	79
Judicial Power	85
Justice Delivery & Development Systems minus
Panchayat Raj	86
Legislative Power	89
Office of the Chairman and Governor's role	90
Governor's intervention in the Council's matters	91
Additional role of Chairman, Dy. Chairman &
Member of Autonomous Council	92

Council Session — 93
Stipulations — 94
Members of Autonomous Council & Blender — 95
Aspect of discretions-I — 96
Aspect of discretions-II — 98
Executive following bureaucracy — 99
State bureaucracy accepting the DHAC as Administrative Authority — 101
Ministerial posts creation in Transferred Subjects — 103
State employees' recruitment, promotion & transfer under Council — 105
Public Accounts Committee — 108
Encroachment of Council's administrative authority (Case-I) — 109
Transactional ethics (Case-II) — 111
Child Care Leave Sanction (Case-III) — 112
Inconsistencies in Transferred Subjects (Case-IV) — 114
Plugging the loopholes — 114

Chapter-IV: Etymological Alignment — 116

Colourful tribe members, their stocks and identities — 117
Stocks' likeness, lenience and language & analogy between Dimasa and Tripuri — 118
A Good Samaritan! — 123
Dimasa monarchs & their rapport — 123
Transactional relationship — 124
How do we have the Dimasas, the descendants of Bhim in Mahabharata? — 125
Generosity & Secular propensity — 126
Titbit on man and matters — 127

Chapter-V: Republic & Ethos   **131**

How does the division of people get fostered?   132

Tear-jerking regional force growing up   133

Sixth Schedule unrelated schemes not harmful in
Dima Hasao   135

Panchayat Raj haunting in Dima Hasao.   138

SSPC, hunger strike, Autonomous State issue   143

More power uprising & After   149

The 125th Amendment Bill, 2019   155

Panchayat Raj and Autonomous Council's Difference   160

GI Tag syndrome of land encroachment   164

Separate Electoral Roll for NCHAC   169

Whither any encroachment of tribals land?   172

Election trends   174

Electorates' arbitration   175

Electorates in exercising their choices -I   177

Chapter-VI: Managerial Acuity   **181**

Pastille of Unity   182

Reflection in work execution.   185

District HOD of Transferred Subjects' role   186

District HOD's provided Services   188

Encountering Approaches   189

Grievance redressal mechanism with clients   190

An adverse effect of changing farming   191

Government entities' objectives   191

Affect & remedy on eulogy.   192

Development entity's significant parody   192

Fund transfer and ethical proposition   194

Eagle-eyed view   197

Stumbling Blocks in Council administering ... 200
Honouring emotion! ... 201
Visible Remedies Sought ... 202
Peace ensures the ray of light ... 204
Rancorous Tale ... 205

Chapter-VII: Traditional and Religious Perceptions ... **208**

Contributions after Conversion ... 209
The practice of worshipping deities ... 210
Brahmanical Traditions ... 214
Dimasa tradition & rituals ... 216
The spiritual development in retrospection ... 217

Chapter-VIII: Strategic Development ... **222**

Denizens' footstep ... 223
Yearning Workforce ... 225
Propelling the Kopili River! ... 231
Cross-examination ... 237
Luring efforts ... 238
Entrusted Subjects' Administrative Establishment ... 238
Ornamental & Tunnel Tree Plantations; Religious
and Cultural Tourism ... 240
Post-Harvest Bonanza to lure tourists ... 242
Different development entities' functional approaches ... 244
Other approaches towards the development ... 247
An egalitarian structure of development proposition ... 248
Handloom potentials ... 250
Strategizing further Development of Dima Hasao ... 251
Administrative future of Dima Hasao ... 254
Development plan extension ... 258

All about the self-sufficiency cord   260
Tap Ethnic Power, Ensure Peace by Awards!   262
Towards a Bi-cameral solution   264
In support of scrapping SIU and other.   267
An Account of Distasteful Support   270

Chapter-IX: Culture & Creases   **275**

Negotiating the social changes   276
Post-Harvest Bonanza   277
Busu   279
Chavang Kut   282
Hega-Ngi   283
Hacha Kekan & Ok Kepru   284
Nulding Kut   285
Parsem Kut   286
Ruolsafak   287
Sikpui Ruoi   288
Sngi Lumlang   288
Other published works of the same author: 296

Epilogue   *291*
Selected Bibliographies   *295*

My Note

My book, *Odyssey, Dima Hasao & Autonomous Council,* is the second attempt to dwell on the hilly region of Assam; presented at this moment in the hands of esteemed readers, it tells the tale of the countryside right from the days of North Cachar Hills to the present Dima Hasao. It consists of 9(nine) chapters, aiming to make the experience I gained as one of the commoners of Haflong handy! It is somewhat historical and challenging to interpret every whit of intricacy about the administration of a political entity. What I honestly feel is the growth of education, or political consciousness does not expectedly produce more liberals than obscurantists everywhere in the world. People's pride in being different from each other augurs well for the region inhabited by several groups of people, as long as the task to ensure unity in diversity rests with all stakeholders of the greater Dima Hasao society when everyone requires dwelling on cementing the human relationship among different groups inhabited locality or between the Council and the officials of the Transferred Subjects of the State.

However complex the subject may be, I have made every human effort to accommodate the aspirations of the readers without undercutting the authority of any individuals or institutions involved in rendering services to the people of this locality, thinking such a task, when undertaken, turns somewhat herculean to execute amidst conflicting claims and counter-claims of the stakeholders. In working out the modalities for ensuring a solution to the unforeseen crisis that emerged from my writing conscience, I have made several suggestions, including achieving self-sufficiency in Chapter-VIII. All these may not be acceptable to all. Nevertheless, these are for educative value, not evil-willed ones, which may be treated as unwanted glitches if found distasteful. Further, no ethics can copy-paste and claim to be original. Besides being blessed to be an onlooker of rapid changes, I studied several historical texts and books by prominent authors. Having updated, I have presented the narrative in my language. Hence, please bear with any unintentional shortcomings. The story sticks out the process adopted and some loopholes in Chapter III – illustrating Cases I, II, III & IV– visible in the implementation of the rules of the Autonomous Council from time to time.

Everybody knows the Dima Hasao Autonomous Council is one of the oldest self-governing entities in Northeastern India. Many desire to know and must be familiar with how a State Department functions under the administrative control of the Council. One hopes the book, which speaks of my truth about the parody of North Cachar Hills under the Sixth Schedule to the Constitution of India, will serve the purpose of having the written records of expression made by somebody reflecting the past and present Dima Hasao. At the same time, I can not claim to be hundred per cent perfect in the presentation, though it is the first of the kind. The issue I present is older than me because I was born in 1965 at Bhanjang (aka Bhunjung), in Haflong, where the people of the erstwhile North Cachar Hills got the District Council in 1952.

In the end, I want to clarify that any errors cropped herein the book are not intentional but coincidental; the attempt to present the narrative is to make the issue accessible while enjoying an exercise of freedom of expression with the utmost restriction.

Gratitude

The writer is delighted to record his gratitude to all who have made it possible to present the second book in a nonfiction series from a place like Dima Hasao. It was impossible to utilise the opportunity to publish under the Zorba Book team's guidance. He first and foremost feels grateful to Nandita Gorlosa, Hon'ble Minister and local Member of Legislative Assembly, who termed this presentation a kaleidoscope of information. Then, some items of useful information found walled in the residential complex of Debolal Gorlosa, Chief Executive Member of the Dima Hasao Autonomous Council about a few historical characters in the book, which the author of the book has inserted, and is indebted to him. Next, he is deeply thankful to Mohit Hojai, Chairman of the autonomous body whose help in procuring and inserting some items of useful information into the book, has brightened the presentation.

Also, he feels glad to the district administration of Dima Hasao, North Cachar Hills Autonomous Council, and other persons like Tai Tsho Daw Daulagupu, Debanon Daulagupu, Debojeet Thaosen, Mukut Kemprai, Saindesh Ardao, Ringpendra Nunisa, Shringdao Langthasa, Khupjang Doungel, Purabi Phonglo, Dr. Monali Longmailai, Dr. Vandana Thaosen, Maipal Kemprai, Subita Kemprai, Sylvia Suchiang, Ritesh Nunisa, Raju Joishi, Lutlal Chongloi, Sanaba Singha, Surya Kumar Singha and Omi Paul. Some are in politics or another profession, some are still working in the autonomous body, and others are serving elsewhere or under the administrative control of the North Cachar Hills Autonomous Council. They stood by him whenever he required their help tackling issues in this narrative. They deserve a special mention of thanks.

Next, he remains indebted to Dr. Mohanta Langthasa, Dr. Motilal Nunisa, Bikash Roy Debbarman, Sunil Ranjan Nunisa, Samarjit Haflongbar, Prokanta Warisa; Holiram Terang, Golon Daulagupu, Indranil Dutta, Bankim Phonglo, Biswajyoti Daulagajau Barman, Karan Chetri, Sarthamjit Daulagupu, Anup Biswas, L.K. Hengna & Sanjib Parbosa. He had gone through their publicly aired views or published materials several times, which helped him immensely in regaling the story, for which he recorded his heartfelt thanks.

Then, he consulted several published titles of prominent authors, namely Edward Gait, E.T. Delton, C.A. Soppitt, B.P. Singh and Amar Krishna Paul, Sonaram Thaosen, and N.K. Barman, which helped him accomplish the project with few hitches, unfortunately, except for A.K. Paul and N.K. Barman's updates about others are not available with the author, but their works helped him entertain the narrative to esteemed readers. Therefore, he inwardly feels thankful to them from his heart's core.

The author is especially thankful to Dr. Dhruba Hojai for immensely feeding the former on regaling several historical accounts of the Dima Hasao. Likewise, he acknowledges the help of Mihir (Joel) Gorlosa, who spent sometimes of his busy life to dwell on the burning issues of the people of Dima Hasao, with a bouquet of thanks.

Moreover, he would feel his emotional head and heart smoothened when Meena, Barsha, Sandhya, Pratiksha, Pratibha, Priyamvada, Shreya, and Sristi always stood by him, with their occasional tea, coffee, snack and fruit services. Along with these caring ladies, the two adoring kids at home – Pankshi and Prahant – would help him get those things in time. Besides Gobinda, Dr Rishikesh Upadhyay and Gokul's moral support smacked of the strength of their blood relationship. The author is incredibly thankful to Bharat Upadhaya, the owner of M/s Bharat News Agency, who helped him procure some books by the above writers.

Likewise, he feels grateful to all those individuals or organisations, including Rahul Roy-Chowdhury & his team members, whose suggestions and tautological alerts for improving the glitches, proofreading and criticisms have found some places in the book and turned valuable in shaping the presentation into the hands of esteemed readers.

Lastly, the author feels pleased to thank Isaac Thiek who set the photographs in the book's cover designed by Sithesh. Likewise, Pailian Hrangkhol beautifully clicked some photographs of the cover. He profusely thanks the District Information and Public Relations Department, Dima Hasao, for having kindly helped him get the beautiful snaps for the book's cover.

Prologue

Everything impresses some. When things are commonly visible, they do not always make a lasting impression in our minds. Instead, some uncommon things attract deeper than common ones! Let it be clear that the mindset of the people, as that of the participating athletes in the game of life, subtly defines the structure and content of their needs. The necessity that brings about an inevitable change seems competitive. It sometimes reflects emotions rather than reasons that take place in their environment.

The blue hills, green valleys and white and cloudy skies of the hilly region of Assam – namely, Dima Hasao – are the breath-taking bounties Nature has invested here, of which everybody hardly feels proud because not all enjoy the conspicuous presence of beauties of Nature. But the locality has the potential to give many muses to creative minds.

Hence, the features of the locality above are exciting for those who adore the bounties of Nature. However, those who rejoice in their happiness may have questions: What is the countryside's history? Was the area under any monarchy in ancient times? Were there any participants in the country's freedom struggle? Where does the place exist? When did it come into existence? How did the stalwarts of the countryside conceive the idea of the place? Who were those freedom fighters from Dima Hasao who fought against the British? How have the present tribal leaderships given respect to other freedom fighters? Who are the permanent settlers of the hilly region of Assam? How severe is the breeder of loathing and suspicion? How do the minor entities want to get significant? How does the feeling of treating other elders of the locality exist? To which religion do the people practice? Which are their festivals? How are their cherished goal, ethos, stocks and identities? How does the division of people get fostered? How did the tear-jerking regional force grow up?

Having answered all the questions above, everyone can understand the place enjoys autonomy under the Sixth Schedule to the Constitution of India. The narrative aims to answer several other questions: Can we not meet up the ethnic aspiration by introducing a bi-cameral legislature? How does the District or Autonomous Council stand as a political entity or body? How generous and secular were the elders of Dima Hasao? How do the hill people exercise rights over the land under the jurisdictional areas of the North Cachar Hills Autonomous Council? Does the need to introduce Panchayat Raj in the autonomy schemes presently available still exist in Dima Hasao? How is the prospect of Direct Central Funding? Is there scope for any outsiders to encroach upon the land? What is the GI Tag encroachment of council land? How does the administrative authority of the Council get encroached? How best can they introduce a separate electoral roll for the North Cachar Hills Autonomous Council?

What led to the birth of the Autonomous State movement? Is there any incremental scope for enhancing the strength of elected representatives from Dima Hasao? How can we streamline the employment generation sectors? How do the electorates exercise their choice? How does the informal reservation of people's representatives exist?

In dwelling on the particular Schedule of the Constitution, *Odyssey, Dima Hasao & Autonomous Council* begins with an onlooker of Haflong's growth; it sticks out a short landscape of Dima Hasao. Also, it highlights the Bordoloi Sub-Committee Report based on the Cabinet Mission and recommendation of the Sub-Sub Committee, actual approval and inauguration, formation of the District Council, its powers & functions, including those of the Public Accounts Committee, and the conduct of Council Session, as well as financial aspects of discretion. How does the fund transfer exist? How does the State Finance Commission relate to the institutions of the Sixth Schedule areas vis-à-vis Panchayat Raj? What is its ethical proposition? What benefits an elected representative from going by the bureaucratic suggestion? How does the delay in the fund receipt shape the relationship between the State and Council? The Council's uniqueness, nuances, and responsibilities have also found places in the definition of the role of the Chairman and Elected Member of the Autonomous Council, among other things.

The formation of every political institution brings changes resulting from the administering process. Some issues crop up as a stumbling block, by unlocking which the administrators require to suggest remedial measures. In carrying out such tasks, the role of zonal administrative units becomes significant – How ethical was or is the transaction between the State and Council, from those days of Excluded Area to the present days of the Revenue Receipts, Dao Tax and Expenses management? How does a government official accept the North Cachar Hills Autonomous Council as an Administrative Authority? What is the actual parody of the significant development entity? How can we boost the religious and cultural sectors of tourism? How successfully or fairly does the development entity function to honour people's sentiments? Which outwardly opens Pandora's Box?

The need for a political and administrative unit to preserve the customs and traditions of all ethnic groups, besides ensuring equality, safety and security, stood out – How have the people pledged to honour their cultural icon or observe their festivals, for instance? Secondly, what are the objectives of the development entities? How do the District Heads of Departments of the Council function? How does the Administrative Establishment of the Entrusted Subjects exist? What are the prospects for the North Cachar Hills Autonomous Council to establish a transactional relationship with the newly set Assam's Mini Secretariate at Silchar?

Thirdly, how do the Transferred Subjects provide services to the farming communities by identifying which approaches are needed? How can we further strategize Dima Hasao's development? What are the stumbling blocks and remedial measures in the administration of the Council? Finally, how worthy are the grievance redressal mechanisms with the clients? What is the self-sufficiency cord? To get answers to all such questions from different perspectives, let us slowly turn the pages of the book one after another.

CHAPTER-I

Features – Geographical & Topographical

Structure & Content; Imaginative parody;

Blue hills, green valleys, white and cloudy skies & people's language; The earliest Dimasa Kingdom and its subsequent establishment in Maibang; How did the hilly area of Assam shape into an entity; Dima Hasao's successive growth and development; An onlooker of Haflong's growth; A Short Landscape of Dima Hasao

Structure & Content

The life of a human being is a game in the mystery field. They participate in it as a sportsman the moment they enter their vast existence as an entity. Conquering the temporal world's hurdle is participating in the competition for survival and going ahead of time. The search for individual identity sometimes brings about a blatant involvement in which man does not feel it egregious to weaken the fellow high-spirited for personal gain. The solid tries to shut down justice's door to the weak wherever possible. Why?

Well, everybody knows in competition, there is neither mercy nor relationship. All are friends or foes alike. Neither friend can share their Performance Reports with the other, nor do the assailants often kill their rivals. Individuals can not share their reports with their friends because every portion of such privileges restricts or hampers the growth of donors. Not everybody likes to lose their life or strength to save others.

Hence, the competition is a neutral game. It remains healthy. However, the occasion leaves a note on how an individual as a human being deals with their fellowmen. The dealing reflects an individual's character to get judged by others, whose appreciation becomes a narrative about the former. Though many pretend to care less about it, they appear to move on the wrong path of truth when they realise it later in life. So, the realisation echoes not only the symptom of the experiment but also begins with shaping the story of an individual.

When their struggle is over, men's transactional details get regaled as they visit the mysterious world for a certain period. Man created history like this. If their sequence of events becomes impressive, it becomes a beacon's light for others. But only a few remain present in their minds and accomplish the task in the past. Some persons with a modicum of knowledge try to immortalise their names without physically participating in the game but disappear, sticking out their insincerity to examine for others.

However, in the inspiring part of their stories, man does not protrude to have done anything wrong in life; only their activities that draw appreciation get accounted for. Contextually, everything is something; nothing is anything.

There is an uncanny race to assert individual supremacy between coming and living. Therefore, some complete the journey by fishing in the troubled waters, while others lead their self-centred lives. Because very few are aware of the truth, their unconsciousness drives them into the craziness – knifing one another. Every kind of human is available, from good to evil. Those who are fortunate come in contact with good people; others come across wretched creatures. Therefore, some of them seem lost in selecting the right ones.

One finds the involvement in selecting the right persons, regardless of their sexes, is a tough choice an individual undergoes in life because peace and satisfaction, success and failure – all rest on choosing.

Thus, the choice is a challenging exercise. It may concern anything that relates to the growth and development of an individual, for it always seeks to replace. Generally, replacement does not speak of evil; it favours well. So, every activity that pertains to change brings about hope and aspiration or curiosity, and everybody interested in enjoying the beauty of replacing something longs to possess the new thing. Relatively, the choice for change ignites curiosity. The task becomes simple as long as an individual is in peace of mind. But then, it becomes problematic when it gets obfuscated by the driver of greed, arrogance and self-importance. All these factors emerge from ignorance.

Unawareness does not always lead an individual to the right path, except acting as a dare-devil, because no conscientious person can be more courageous than the ignorant.

Be that as it may, both ignorant and intelligent fight against each other, without which, where is the longevity of humans sticking out being successful or fulfilled?

But honestly, nothing remains permanent in life. As an individual comes from the mother's womb empty-handed, they go alike.

Thus, the temporal world is a mystery. Every individual's visit to it is to create their history. Between incoming and outgoing, if somebody makes some people happy by helping them, the happiness spreads its wings.

On the other hand, when some people follow the excellent footpath of an individual after them, it becomes history. In exercising its role, the contentment or pleasure of man thus regales a memorable journey into the chronological world.

If an individual born into a locality turns evil or greedy, their conscience tells them how to treat other men. In a heterogeneous society, an individual tends to be sectarian because of the spread of a mean-spirited mentality. The dishonesty crops up due to the fear of failure in competition because it is challenging, and everybody does not like to follow the principle.

Then again, man or animal never wants to follow the same path that threatens their life. Every wrong or right gets carried out in complete freedom, without which nothing is attractive in our mind—the attraction factor results from the conditional life of human beings on the earth.

Without expecting anything in return, nothing seems subtly possible in this world.

Thus, I reiterate human life on the planet is conditional.

Some evils feel privileged, and others live deprived. When I say a man is evil, I refer to their greed. How does the relationship between the two exist? It reflects the method of outward reciprocation or transactional business they adopt or hold in the temporal world. If the conscious or privileged treat the commoner, ignorant or backwards well, it cites an example of modern civilisation.

Likewise, the Constitution of India is a written avatar of justice and equality. The founders of the Indian Constitution, who wanted to ensure equal opportunities for all citizens, created specific provisions separately administering the people who appeared disadvantaged under the Sixth Schedule, by which they worked out self-rule to ensure social justice. The people of the erstwhile North Cachar Hills (now Dima Hasao) enjoyed the provision under the scheduled areas.

Imaginative parody

After the people of the erstwhile North Cachar Hills got a separate district, the locality began to change rapidly. The new mindset of the people has no beginning or end. In exceptional cases, the mystery brings about ignorance, which, in turn, breeds wrongdoers. Everybody must agree that all inexperienced turn evil, which eliminates or ruins the innocent or unconscious, though it does not truly define victory over death or destruction. In this sense, all evils are losers, not winners.

After the death or destruction, of whom the wicked feels afraid? Frankly, if there is nobody to praise for somebody, nobody is a hero in their lifetime. Hence, no conscientious or wise person can claim to be a true hero in the real sense of the term. In such a situation, nothing seems perfect, so the true definition of life appears partly acceptable.

Contextually, our destiny seems pre-decided by Nature. She is the actual Creator of humans. But, in fulfilling the fate, we require doing work for our livelihood; for, even if we are more educated or capable than those who get privileges, we do not get justice, or we don't deliberately like to stay and work in our place of birth. We don't want to live or serve in any capacity because of the lack of sense of being and belonging.

The loss of interest in doing any good work for the cause of humanity seems to be Her delicate handiwork. For instance, everybody does not get what they want. Nature does not like everybody to remain mindful of their position. If somebody minds their work, they can not take any hasty action due to fear of an adverse outcome. Our mind and heart seem subtly related to Nature, without whose guidance we can not decide where to go and what to do, though some boast of having defeated us or Nature. But such a victory does not carry any significance.

Thus, I told myself our life is to fulfil the definition of competition, in which both good and evil are equal. However, it turns out to be a bone of contention when we fail to be appreciated and rewarded of what we feel deprived.

However, some exceptions to success in life are due to sheer complex work and labour, based on which most people in modern times make their unstinted efforts to better their prospects of defeating Nature.

Nevertheless, if there are blessings of Nature and we happen to have been tricked by fellow humans, our fate is restored due to our expanded horizons. After acquiring skills, we fought all kinds of injustice in the trade we earned from educational institutions.

Hence, I said the teacher was next to our parents.

Nonetheless, I do not refer to those teachers who get appointed for merely receiving a monthly salary. Some blatantly part with other persons to carry out the former's role and never attend to their duties.

Given the supposition, it hampers realising the main objective of education. It aims to refine our societal living, in which we are inclusive of growth and development. These two aspects shape different kinds of people from various fields of specialisations. The state, district, or locality gets recognised based on the individual's share of their human resources contribution.

Though we claim are advanced, have not been able to root out some diseases. Of course, it does not mean undercutting the efficacy of science. Nor does it mean that Nature does not plan well. Death in some pandemics reminds me of how Nature carries out Her tasks and creates and finishes Her creation according to Her will. We can not be more brilliant every time than Nature. It remains the same in the relationship between man and Nature or between humans. There is a subtle difference, which brings on the way to ensuring peace and unity.

But then, somewhere, the flaw exhibits the human Achilles' heel, which regularises the mode of living in the given society. Some speak harsher than others; some sugar-coated languages damage more than evils in our transactional business. Good and sins are inseparable for all living creatures.

To draw a parallel language to live as humans, we have established laws to abide by to resolve the disputes between two or more warring groups among us (humans). Therefore, we cannot live without the rules that are free from anybody's control but seemingly respected by all as social entities to fulfil the independence of the judiciary.

We all want to do this or that in life, but only some succeed in such an effort. Some say they have much confidence, faith, and belief in themselves and can do whatever they like, but it is only sometimes advantageous for such people.

Of course, once or twice, the wrongdoer may escape from the police dragnet, but they have no permanent freedom from sin or crime. So, our life is unpredictable – It does not matter who is who or what: whether sinner or saint, everybody is to quit the temporal world. Nobody has specific information about who goes where after demise, but there is a hearsay report about the presence of the heavenly abode. As long as an individual is alive, it is their duty to contribute towards the place of their birth.

It is only the unpredictable Nature of life that constantly searches for the light to live as an individual in Dima Hasao's parody of the human race. The unpredictability gets wrapped up in ignorance or arrogance. But the ignorant never admit to lacking knowledge about something other fellowmen do. Why?

As the Sun relates to light, death signifies their darkness for man.

Similarly, if the Sun gives us the strength of fire, the Moon must have been there to supply water.

At the same time, if strength ensures power, the chink in our armour provides peace.

Our life and death always seem wrapped up in mystery. However, Nature has invested stunning beauties in the hilly region of Assam.

Blue hills, green valleys, white and cloudy skies & people's language

The Dima Hasao is a land of blue hills, green valleys and white and cloudy skies, covering Assam's total geographical area of 4890 sq. km and belonging to the jurisdictional scope of the Dima Hasao Autonomous Council, governed under the Sixth Schedule to the Constitution of India. From a writer or poet to a plain traveller, it has a legacy to offer for everybody's choice. Everybody can enjoy Assam's only rugged hilly region and witness the varied flora and fauna.

It has a marvellous world-famous but mysterious phenomenon of birds dying in a place called Jatinga and falcons visiting near the industrial town of the Dima Hasao of Assam – Umrongso– on which I dwelt, crafting a few similar poetic lines published last year, which I would like to reproduce below:

THE WINGED VISITORS OF JATINGA & UMRONGSO.

"Somewhere, it is true,
Somewhere untrue;
Flora & fauna gradually reduced;
So, the winged species seemed to rue:
"Human greed seems irrepressible;"
It's reached its subterfuge;

On the one hand, they fool,
Saying making tools,
Which protect us under their roof;
On the other, they get schooled,
Inwardly thinking of consuming us in full";
They united all,
And left their original cage, as the Hindu Lord Siva Bull
Sometimes, on the road and in different public places;
Turning it out to be true:
'One fool locating another fool!'
When they got toy-gunned by some people,
Unaware of welcoming those two-winged visitors by being humble,
Alarmed by their steady decay and dawdle,
Surfaced the Dima Hasao authority control,
Killing all kinds of animals is an offence punishable;
Then come the Assam Hills region carnivals –
Jatinga and Falcón Festivals!
Making them annual,
Celebrating these to make the local
Hunters not to be cruel
Towards the animals,
Including the two-winged ones by the name – Falcon!
I praise the North Cachar Hills Autonomous Council;
It's annual efforts to contain the cruelty on animals."

It is breathtaking to be among the colourful tribe members.

If somebody has a sense of feeling, Dima Hasao is full of diversity and excitement. Various ethnic communities, their culture, festivals and habits make it an alluring destination.

It has stunning variety; the hilly district of Assam nestles in the Borail Hills, an abode of pretty dwellers with their respective languages, cultures and dialects.

All groups have united by adopting a common link language called Haflong Hindi with peculiar overtones.

There is an adventure in trekking green valleys and hilly tracts. Most of the smaller tribe members have adopted Christianity, while the Dimasa, who hold the majority, follow Hinduism, including non-tribals but excluding the Punjabis, who are Sikhs.

There are also Muslim residents.

Given the presence of the various groups of people, the place is sensitive. To foster the growth of perennial peace and tranquility, the administration of Dima Hasao Autonomous Council would do well to work out some strategies by knowing their truth, on which I have dwelt in Chapter VIII of the book.

The earliest Dimasa Kingdom and its subsequent establishment in Maibang

The Ahoms came from the side of Burma (now Myanmar) and overwhelmed the Dimasas by taking advantage of the tribe members' following their traditions. How?

For instance, the Ahoms, under the cover of cows (Mushu), advanced up to Dimapur, the capital of the Dimasa Kingdom, when the Dimasa army retreated without a fight in fear of harming the bulls drawing the carts of the Ahoms.

In 1523, the Ahom King, Suhungmung, annexed the Chutia Kingdom. Afterwards, he decided to reclaim the lost territory from the Dimasas, who defeated the Ahoms in 1526 but could not succeed in the second battle in the same year, during the reign of their King Khunkhara.

Though the Ahoms lost their territory to the Dimasas, the skirmishes continued between the two.

The Ahoms reportedly murdered the king of the Dimasa Kingdom along with his mother and several royals after the former reached Dimapur. Later, the Ahom General installed Detchung, the son of the earlier king, Khorapa, as the king of the Dimasa Kingdom, with yearly taxes of 20 elephants and 1 lakh rupees (mudras).

The Ahoms settled into the tract between the Chutiya and the Dimasa Kingdoms that the Borahi and Matak people inhabited.

The Dimasa forces entering the Ahom territory after victory brought about an uninterrupted scuffle between the two. And the Ahoms caused the infliction of heavy casualties upon the Dimasa tribe members – at least seventeen thousand soldiers!

In 1536, the Ahoms attacked the Dimasa capital again and sacked the city. After the death of Detchung, Dimapur went under Ahoms, and Marangikhowa Gohain commanded the kingdom.

To dwell more on the details of the conflict, after the subjugation of the Borahis and the Morans, Sutyinpha, the first Hindu Ahom King, demanded the surrender of the Dimasas or the acknowledgement of defeat by paying taxes. The Dimasa king refused the demand and asserted that his people had lived there for three generations and that no outsiders could claim these lands.

The first clash with the Ahom Kingdom occurred in 1490 when the Dimasas defeated the Ahoms, who pursued peace by offering a princess to the Dimasa king. The Dimasas took control of the land beyond the river Dhansiri. The Ahom General, Suhungmung, proceeded west of the Dikhow, where he sent an expedition against the Dimasas once more. At last, the Ahoms were able to lay claim on Marangi. Both sides now agreed to offer sacrifices to the deity at Dergaon. The Dìmasas withdrew to the west of the Dhansiri.

The Dimasas gave up Dimapur and shifted south, setting up their new capital in Maibang ("Mai" means "Paddy" and "bang" means "Plenty or abundance") in the erstwhile North Cachar Hills.

How did the hilly area of Assam shape into an entity?

To begin with, the past of the present Dima Hasao was under the present-day Khaspur in the colonial era. The British annexed the Kachari Kingdom in 1832 under the Doctrine of Lapse. The last king of the people of the Dimasas was Raja Gobinda Chandra. The capital of the Dimasas at that time was Khaspur (now Silchar). He surrendered to the British.

During the British regime, they governed it as an "Excluded area" under the administration of the Governor of Assam since 1937. However, after India's independence, the Government administered it "under the Sixth Schedule of the Constitution of India" by granting a self-ruling political institution called North Cachar Hills District Council to the tribals of the hilly region on 29th April 1952.

It has the boundary surrounded by Manipur and Nagaland on the East, Meghalaya and West Karbi Anglong on the West, Karbi Anglong and Hojai on the North and Cachar district on the South of the Dima Hasao.

Then, Khaspur, situated in the present Cachar district, was under the administrative Centre. However, the internal rift between two or more groups of people led to the division of the erstwhile Cachar Kingdom into North Cachar and (South) Cachar, as reflected in the story of Senapati Tularam.

Be that as it may, the birth of the erstwhile North Cachar Hills paved the way for growth and development, followed by the grant of an Autonomous Council. The present Dima Hasao was born on 2nd February 1970 and possessed 4,890 sq. Km of land. At this juncture, the erstwhile North Cachar Hills and Mikir Hills had a total population of 2 13,529 and got their headquarters in 1985. Before 1832, it was in the Kachari Kingdom. The territory spanned from Jamuna on the North and Mizoram on the South, Nagaland on the East, and the river Kopili on the West.

As mentioned, the Dimasa monarch once made the present Dima Hasao his capital. However, there was bloodshed in the kingdom in 1830 when the faithless General Gambhir Singh killed Gobinda Chandra Hasnusa, the King. Afterwards, on 14th August 1832, the British took control over the southern part of his kingdom. However, it left the rest of the territory to Tularam, the Dimasa General, who ruled it until he died in 1837 when some parts of the kingdom went under them. Subsequently, the General's demise in 1854 led to the British annexation of the whole Dimasa kingdom.

Afterwards, the British established a Sub Division in Asalu, and it functioned till they abolished it in 1867, separating and amalgamating with the erstwhile Cachar District. Besides, the other sub-division areas under the British joined with the districts of Nogaon, Cachar, Jaintia and Khasi Hills. The erstwhile Assam's hilly region under the Cachar district merged with the Civil Sub Division after its headquarters creation at Gunjung in 1880. After that, they shifted the sub-divisional headquarters to Haflong in 1895.

With the growth of population, the Government created a new administrative unit by the name of United Districts of North Cachar and Mikir Hills on 17th November 1951, enacting these two present hilly regions of Assam (Dima Hasao and Karbi Anglong) under the Sixth schedule of the Indian Constitution on 19th April 1952.

Recalling the creation of the hilly regions of Assam, Dr. Dhruva Hojai said, The Constituent Assembly granted the Sixth Schedules to the Constitution of India to both the hill districts in the United Mikir & North Cachar Hills with its headquarters at Diphu and subdivision at Haflong (sic).

Consequently, the Government separated the North Cachar Hills District (now Dima Hasao) from Mikir Hills District in 1969, apart from giving the option to join the newly formed hill state under the provisions of Article 244 of the Constitution of India (a state within a state) or (an autonomous state Meghalaya) (sic)

Meghalaya became a full-fledged state in 1972 under the provisions of the North Eastern States Reorganization Act 1971 along with the States of Manipur and Tripura and the Union territories of Mizoram and Arunachal Pradesh (which later on became full-fledged states) (sic)

As the administration of the two hilly regions of Assam – North Cachar and Mikir Hills – must have become an intricate exercise, the Government divided and created two separate districts named Karbi Anglong and North Cachar Hills in 1970.

Dima Hasao is one of the three hill administrative units of the State of Assam. Karbi Anglong (East) and West Karbi Anglong are other hill districts. Though these two districts fall under the hilly region of the State, Dima Hasao is hillier, with its headquarters at Haflong. Its total geographical area is 4890 Sq.km, which is 6.28% of the entire geographical location of Assam. There are 13 tribes in the district, which constitute 70% of the total population. The district of Dima Hasao is above two lakhs (2 13,529, as per Census of India 2011) with a population density of 44 per sq. km.

The percentage of the area is small; approximately 5-10% of it is flat and low-lying and is adjacent to the plain district of Assam. The topography seems rugged, with elevation ranging from 120m to 1320m and a slope varying from 50 to 300 and above 600. The district's soil varies from sandy loam to fine silt and clays in the Northern and Western parts. The subtropical monsoon dominates the climate. The annual rainfall varies from 1800mm to 3000mm.

Situated at altitudes between 600-900 metres and 1000 – 01866 metres on the North West and South East regions, the present Dima Hasao is one of the three hill districts of Assam. It was a part of the Greater Dimasa Kingdom; has a population of two lakhs, thirteen thousand, five hundred twenty-nine according to the 2011 Census; six hundred ninety-five villages; five development blocks – viz, Diyung Valley Development Block, Diyungbra Development Block, Harangajao Integrated Jumia Development Project (IJDP) Block, Jatinga Development Block. There are nine hundred thirty-two schools – Primary, Upper Primary, High and Higher Secondary; three colleges; ninety-one health centres (popularly known as Community Health Centre, Model Hospital, Primary Health Centre and Sub-Centre) under the administrative control of the North Cachar Hills Autonomous Council. Besides, there is a plan to set up a Sainik School at Mahur – the dream village of one of the founders of the erstwhile North Cachar Hills – Joy Bhadra Hagjer.

Now, let's have a look at how sunnier has Haflong grown!

The transitory cycle of life gets wheeled – some were endearing species, and some unbearable elements were born to give a bumpy ride to innocent and peaceful lovers. I always enjoy and accept both good and evil as though I were aware of the hallmark of societal living.

Because every activity of the State starts in the fledgling stage, shortcomings seem natural, so one must be very compassionate toward everybody in the literary field to carry out.

I was not born in the formative year of the Dima Hasao's headquarters, but I wish to share with the esteemed readers what I have hitherto known in my few simple poetic stanzas for the good of them:

Dima Hasao's successive growth and development

An Uncanny Raven in Man,
Sprouted from the façade of the community,
Appeared as a Goliath to downplay:
The need to preserve the beauty,
Better ensured by the British, subtly rued Sonaram Thaosen!
Hailed as one of Dimasa's literary icons,
He was next to Jatindra Lal Thaosen,
Phanindra Johari, Jatan Kumar Thaosen,
Among others, Sonaram said, "We're the temporary custodians...
And should not indulge in mindless destruction."
From the extraction of natural resources
In the distribution of human resources,
The intelligentsia can well overhaul the present sources,
By taking a clue from the ancestors' Wisdom and intellectual
farsightedness

Of the past to ensure proper checks and balances!
There is oceanic scope for taming the Uncanny Raven
Prepared the North Cachar Hills District Council's parody by
Desondao,
He drafted its resolution after a public meeting, to which Hamdhan
Mohan
led a delegation of all tribes and submitted it to the Bordoloi Sub-
Committee,
Surath Chandra Daulagupu got to be one of the Members!
Nityalal Daulagupu initially set up,
On the advice of Joy Bhadra Hagjer,
The Autonomous Council was fortunate
To have some prominent Chief Executive Members,
Right from Gobinda Chandra Langthasa, who pardoned his sons'
killers!
Acted as the Council's veteran politician,
Gobinda Chandra was the first to empower the women of the
Dimasa tribe!
Appointed Pramila Hojai as the first Executive Member,
Though her hubby could not get the chance!
Gobinda Chandra was also Assam's Minister.
Among those older from top to bottom,
Established educational institutions for broadening our children's
mental horizons were Nityalal Daulagupu, Jatindra Lal Thaosen,
Rajendra Chandra Langthasa, Gobinda Chandra Langthasa, Ajit
Bodo,
Kuladhar Ranjan Hojai, M. Ch. Daulagupu, K.P. Upadhaya & K.L.
Thapa,
Shyam Chand Hojai and
Arun Chandra Haflongbar
Were the most endearingly
Outspoken Chief Executive Members
The Dima Hasao Autonomous Council has ever

Surath Chandra Daulagupu got
All the zonal Heads of Department establishments
Transferred, entrusted & established
To the erstwhile North Cachar Hills Autonomous Council
Formally!
Prokanta Warisa & Samarjit Haflongbar
Led the Autonomous Statement movement,
M.S. Daulagupu, Depolal & Mohet Hojais, K. Sengyung, Rajat M.
Thaosen, R. Dibragede,
J.T. R. Nampui, V. Varte, R. Upadhaya, N. Chongloi, G. Joishi, S. Dey
& Others
They acted as their right hands from erstwhile N.C. Hills' of ASDC
leaders!
Jayanta Rongpi, Holiram Terang & Elwin Teron;
Balaram Thapa, Iswar Nepal and others' names
I have forgotten now
Were the forefront
Leaders in Karbi Anglong led the movement!
S.B. Chavan, then Home Minister,
Government of India,
Supported Jayanta Rongpi
Who was an M.P. from the Assam's Hills areas
We got an MoU (Memorandum of Understanding) signed, granting
more powers!
Uniting together for more autonomy toward the political body
Was not that task easy:
Public humiliation following surveillance
By the Police on suspicion
Supporting outlawed went hand in hand!
However, my expectation of getting a handsome grant of privileges
By supporting the erstwhile ASDC
Without indulging in any wrong
That causes the loss of lives or properties,

It was clear, and they did not go deaf.
Sonaram Thaosen and Kumba Kumar Hojai were friendlier
politicians.
Pabitra and Debojeet ruled as the best-qualified CEMs
Because they were well qualified in the Council's history!
Debolal Gorlosa has hitherto become the best performer
Chief Executive Member.
Nityalal Daulagupu remained
A Secretary Sahib throughout his Career & lifespan
Jatan Kumar Thaosen
They appeared to be next to Nityalal Daulagupu
In my general assessment!
Gokul Chandra Hojai,
Nindu Langthasa & Narendra Kemprai
Were the Sportspersons
Chief Executive Member
And Executive Members!
Chonhau Khotlang
Was the first Chief Executive Member;
While Harimoy Das Barman
Elected & Served
As a Non-tribal Executive Member
Joy Bhadra Hagjer
&Prokanta Warisa
Were the First & Second
Members of Parliament
From Dima Hasao!
Surath Chandra Daulagupu
Was the successor
Of Joy Bhadra Hagjer
In representing
The erstwhile North Cachar Hills!
Established Joy Bhadra Hager

His dream village at Mahur
Called Baojen;
While Palon Chandra Langthasa & Hamdhan Mohon Haflongbar
Set up Gidinpur (Maibang) & Harangajao Kachari (Rangapur)
respectively
Palon Chandra Langthasa
Held the position of the Chief Executive Member,
Of the erstwhile N.C. Hills Autonomous Council;
While Hamdhan Mohon Haflongbar served as Chairman of the
Council!
They represented their respective positions as the first Dimasa Tribe
members.
Arun Chandra Haflongbar,
Palon Chandra Langthasa,
Both held the office
Of the Chief Executive Member,
Were endearingly outspoken politicians in my analytical assessment!
If we take it as a great heritage,
Who and why can it not be protected from any savage?
From maintaining flora and fauna,
And an undying bond
With the Brahmaputra and Barak Valleys,
In the standing flourishing transactional relationships
With the Danguria, Bhadralok and Gedema,
There is an urgent call for minting
The familial wounds
Getting infected severely at home!
Time and tide wait for nobody,
Nor does the arrogance of power
Or somebody!
Nothing can remain
Forever with everybody!
Assuming the entire world

Does not alone move on to science and logic,
I said belief, faith and worship;
They have relieved many entities
From tensions and anxieties!
So, both science and religion.
Work in two different ways
For retaining their respective identities!
Nobody has the power to defeat both besties!
Opposing one for ensuring others' supremacy
It is not the real solution to any difficulties
That crop up in their disparity.
Hence, both are twigs.
Of knowledge and Wisdom!
So, this is the first time anyone seemed involved in acquiring these
entities.

Let us have a look at the kaleidoscopic view of the headquarters of the erstwhile North Cachar Hills (now Dima Hasao).

An onlooker of Haflong's growth

Haflong, where I was born, was full of luxuriant verdure. Nature was the guardian of the greenish beauty. Her beauty appears to cause rainfall, sometimes without the rainy season's onset. I wonder if She understands the need for Her light and dark green creations. Do they call for the liquid to fall from the rampart of Heaven even during the off-season? Otherwise, how do Her luxuriant varieties' desires get rain without Her bowing down upon their wishes? The rainfall has some interaction with the mysterious entities that cause it.

I have always searched inwardly for such bodies to enjoy their interactions. If there is no understanding or living relationship between Nature's green beauty and rain God, I don't think a drop of liquid can come down from the sky. Yet, even the sky's rise in the fog does not appear to occur without reason. It occurs as though the plumber or valve-man of the Public Health Engineering of the Government of Assam has opened the distribution of house tap connection to every household of their particular locality.

By the way, when the issue of water distribution in Haflongtown comes up, one remembers the Executive Engineer named Chanda, during whose tenure he recruited many new staff. The Department executed water supply schemes in the greater Haflong area. After his transfer, his recruited staff Amlal and Homlal Joishis of Upper Bagetar became well-known workers in this Department. The majority of the people would know these two staff of the establishment above. They are no longer among us but were sincere and obedient workers of the Office of the Executive Engineer of the State Department. They included other co-workers and executed the construction of several pipeline connections in and around Haflongtown.

They got the opportunity to carry out many development schemes following the initial establishment of the Department in the District headquarters – Haflong. Until the State Public Health Engineering Department existed in the erstwhile North Cachar Hills in 1973, the Haflong Town Committee used to handle the Water Supply in Haflongtown areas. Many Town Committee employees exercised their options to join the Public Health Engineering.

Nowadays, there is an acute scarcity of water in the dry season. Of course, when Hamjanon Langthasa was holding the charge of Executive Member of the North Cachar Hills Autonomous Council, the people of Haflongtown area would get water timely. So, I have a proposition for new scheme, which I suggested have got a place in Chapter-VIII.

It's time to enjoy the scenic beauty of the hilly region of Assam.

A Short Landscape of Dima Hasao

The greenish beauties of Dima Hasao include various kinds of plants, including ornamental ones, ferns, orchids, bamboos, and thorny shrubs that stand majestically along with the hillocks. The Barail Peak from View Point Boro Haflong looks exciting. Trekking is a thrilling experience in the hills. One can also view the Hekhao Kha peak from there. The Hekhao Kha peak is higher than Hempio Pet. Besides, there are several tea gardens which stick out her green beauty. Driving on the road covered by the luxuriant greenness on both sides excites the tourists. Some find pleasure in calling the situation of Haflong on the Ant Hill.

Besides, significant rivers like the Jatinga, Mahur, Diyung, Kopili, Kayang, and others surround the district of Dima Hasao. If one looks at the headquarters of the borough of the State Assam, which one finds in her Central zone, it seems like an island.

Though the distance between Haflong and these two places is long, the communication exchange between the people of Haflong and Cachar Districts, including Silchar, Karimganj and Hailakandi, seems better. One can reach Silchar from Haflong within three hours, while it takes four and five hours to find Lanka and Nogaon, respectively, from the district headquarters of Dima Hasao–Haflong.

However, there is room for developing road communication between Haflong and Silchar. Due to heavy rains, the runoff water washes the metallic road of the National Highway Authority. Off and on, the people raise their voices against the central road authority of the Government of India over the poor maintenance of National Highway No. 27 between these two places. Indeed, the way the Government incurs losses of public money is debatable. One cannot understand why the Road Authority has not been able to drain off the rainwater yearly.

Mention worthy, several rivers surround the place Dima Hasao. The district literarily is a water land; everywhere there is water, but its headquarters suffer from the shortage of it. Has the plantation of deep-rooted plants caused the water shortage in the locality? Whatever other reasons, one must be the lack of proper planning and development amidst the population growth that sprouted from the rural migration, not the urban one. Because the urban population hardly extends its settlement in rural areas

Everybody knows why the relocation takes place. Because the flocking of goods and services near the thickly populated villages does not cause any exodus of people from one place to another, one can safely say the lack of amenities leads to the movement of people from their original place of inhabitation. And people were also peace-loving, as though they knew it was worthless to indulge in anger. Because violence breeds violence, in the same way, sentiment stokes up sentiment. The lack of awareness of the people always causes problems in society. There is no cry over the shortage of such packages, which the Government of the Council or District Administration could have announced after such grants by Dispur.

At the same time, Dispur can only make grants by receiving a proposal from the people's representatives. So, the people became poor by the wrong choice of their representatives.

Agreeing on it or not, the mass departure from other parts of the countries due to specific favourable provisions damages the original inhabitants. The migration is slowly but steadily stinging the body politics of the Dima Hasao. However, there is nothing to comment on a particular entity for having been responsible for it. The vicious cycle of politics has emanated from the sting of migration.

In the past, some people's representatives got elected for personal growth and development. They took advantage of the lack of political consciousness among their people, who never questioned the efficiency of their representatives, some of whom allegedly threw feasts, distributed cigars and sugarcane cake during the elections and secured votes from some constituencies' voters. However, things have changed now with the growth of literacy. The people have started sending their better representatives, some of whom have been doing excellent jobs. Nevertheless, there is a need for better political awareness among the hoi polloi. Merely dividing people on ethnic lines is not going to ensure any better future; educating them to be free from the clutch of mean-spiritedness is the wealthiest option.

If the people's perception of politics changes and they start electing representatives who can deliver goods, ferocity may turn perilous. Where the contest becomes competitive, selection turns tough. Such a situation may always pave the way for the might to assert their right. Any assertion of exemplary works sans honesty and integrity may encourage violence, apart from facilitating the entry of guns into politics.

Until the percentage of literacy was low, the whims of one or two parties' functionaries carried out political activities. The growth of political and economic consciousness ensured competition, in which the highly educated and the less educated started questioning each other's efficiency or transparency. The assertion or debate over the prominence or significance of the individual led to the birth of another reason for the delivery of violence and mischief-mongers. Because human beings have a similar will to compete against one another, excess rebellion undercuts the objective of healthy political activism.

Hitherto, politics has not succeeded in purifying the spirit of it in every ethnic group. On the contrary, it has developed little consideration, subtly paving the division's growth as quickly as possible. Hence, there is an undying need to nourish unity in diversity. In realizing the objective, our spirit, especially born from the majority, should be able to exhibit its neutral character. Usually, all entities maintained from the head and heart tried for it but failed to realize the goal. Honestly, even the inroads of evils into the more powerful entity in the game of power initially resulted from the fissiparous tendency developed in the smaller ones. Greed also helped the percolation of iniquity in analyzing politics as a whole.

However, implementing the Anti-Defection Law in 2019 has prevented elected members of the Autonomous Council from changing one party to another in the hilly area of the State.

The Sixth Schedule to the Constitution of India has gifted "a State within State" to the people of Dima Hasao to play the game of power well. Sincere efforts are made to highlight the autonomy package in Chapter-III.

CHAPTER-II

History-Heros & Reformers

Transactional Gesture; Freedom fighters from the tribesmen; Veer Sambudhan Phonglo & lieutenants; Dimalik Kemprai; Senapati Tularam Thaosen; Joya Thaosen in Golden Letters; Chengjapao Doungel; Haipou Jadunang & Rani Gaindinliu; J.B. Hagjer, J. N. Thaosen, H. M. Haflongbar; Durga Malla & Ram Singh Thakuri;
A Cultural Icon - Princess Disru

Transactional gesture

Man's true identity speaks of their work after hard labour or because even the undeserving may assert and get it sanctioned to them during their lifetime on different pretexts. As such, people prefer to avoid fishing in troubled waters. Thanks to this, many faintly suffer from the life of hypocrisy – speaking one thing, doing another. Because somebody may claim to be big, and the people may also follow them for fear of reprisal, it says of the acquisition of power by arrogance or coercion, which hardly defines any bigness.

The more man becomes humane, the more they systematise their transactional behaviours in society — custom, tradition and beliefs—no need to feel proud of having better dealing than others because everybody can adapt to any practice.

If the maker or Creator of the course is wise, their creations cite an excellent example for the succeeding generation to imbibe those as their ideals. The tradition ensures that everybody lives fully, without fear, favour or anxiety. It also subtly frees an individual from the need to establish a life-long company.

After demise, nobody knows where our breath, aka soul, travels after getting free from our body. Some religious groups believe there is a resurrection, but none can substantiate the claim with evidence, as already stated.

However, where do our flesh and bone go after death? This becomes the concern of those who remain alive. Man's relationship with their fellowmen, who feel how and when over which activities or actions defines the life of human in the given society. Accordingly, history gets written or created.

To this end, let us dwell on some of our freedom fighters who sacrificed their lives for today's independence of the country's citizens must have witnessed from their rampart of heaven how the people of this locality remember their contribution.

The countryside fondly remembers India's freedom fighters. Mahatma Gandhi, Rabindranath Tagore, Subash Chandra Bose, Durga Malla, Haipou Jadunang and Veer Sambudhan Phonglo, Senapati Tularam and Dimalik Kemprai, Joya Thaosen and Disru every year. The people used to remember Veer Sambudhan Phonglo and Haipou Jadunang prominently. Of course, their celebration comes after Mahatma Gandhi and Subash Chandra Bose. However, neither had their statutes, which the people of the locality have installed now. In the past, the festivity would be informal.

We now turn to dwell on those freedom fighters whose contributions hitherto remained ignored but have been prominently celebrated in this part of India, one after another.

Freedom fighters from the tribesmen

With the installation of their statues in Haflong, the Government has made the contributions of several freedom fighters as above, setting aside others' sacrifices in the narrative because most people of the locality already know about the leaders such as Mahatma Gandhi and Subash Chandra Bose.

Whoever may hold the power of the State or district, paying fitting tributes to all those in history who sacrificed their lives for our country's freedom is a must. But, at the same time, only the selected few could become a Nation's guard. In plain clothes or uniforms, such individuals are unique in every country of their birth. If a country is fortunate to have given birth to such children, it entirely rests on how unbiased her people are in sticking out their deliverance.

Honestly, the delivery of the high-spirited souls or their presence itself ensures the opening of the history page. It is not that they should necessarily remain charismatic; it is their moves that make them immortal. Hence, I told myself immortality gets attached to their birth itself so that it does not get separated under baffling circumstances. What is true is they need to look back to show their novelty for why they come into the temporal world.

Let us begin with Veer Sambudhan Phonglo:

Veer Sambudhan Phonglo & lieutenants

The year 2023 showed light from the tunnel of darkness. The people of Dima Hasao celebrated the 141st Martyr's Day of Veer Sambudhan Phonglo somewhat differently from their past celebrations. I only require a little elaboration about why it was significant because everyone in Dima Hasao knows the State Government even decided to install his statue in Guwahati, preferably in Sankardev Kalakshetra, Guwahati. However, though he was already a hero, he only got recognition in his home district. Because no previous regime ever considered celebrating his heroism necessary, he remained unfamiliar among many outside this locality.

So, let me dwell on them briefly, according to my ordinary conscience.

Deprondao Phonglo and Khasaidi Phonglo parented Sambhudhan Phonglo on the 16th day of March 1850. He was born in a village named Longkhor, somewhere near the present Maibang, in the erstwhile North Cachar Hills, where he subsequently shifted to several places, starting with Gunjung, the former headquarters of Haflong. Then, he moved to Saupra, a tiny but famous hamlet called Nanadisa, which gave birth to two other prominent persons of the hilly region – Joy Bhadra Hagjer and Dr. Madhu Sudan Kachari. Then, Sambhudhan Phonglo moved to Samdikhor, near Mahur, the dream village of Joy Bhadra, where he married Nasadi.

As for Veer Sambudhan Phonglo's participation in India's freedom struggle, he rebelled against the British when they imposed certain restrictions upon his clan members. He was Lord Siva's devotee, virtual spiritual guru, and freedom fighter. However, the British ruthlessly dealt with the tribe members, subtly enslaving the whole community, which he did not tolerate and wanted setting free from their suppression.

Seeing all kinds of injustice done to his people or followers, he took advantage of the support he used to get from them to teach a lesson to the oppressors and intruders; he was about to organise a movement. It aimed to raise the demand for self-rule, for he wanted to restore the old Dimasa tribe members' kingdom.

As mentioned, the British initially issued the summon after a native complained against him to the police.

Meanwhile, the British Government got wind of it and issued an arrest warrant against him, but no one of his followers cooperated with the police.

Subsequently, the official messenger got an order to leave Maibang, where Sambudhan Phonglo established his headquarters.

After that, the Sub-Divisional Officer who issued the arrest warrant sought the help of the Cachar Deputy Commissioner. The British Major Boyd, who went to arrest Sambudhan Phonglo with a force of forty men, could not accomplish the task but lost his life in a fatal injury. Sambudhan Phonglo's supporters carried out attacks against the Major and his boys.

Sambudhan Phonglo died from an injury in his leg on the 12th February 1883. The British killed his adviser, Man Singh and also the Subordinate Commander.

Further, there are reports some political enthusiasts took a leaf from Sambudhan's political Notebook to ignite a similar crusade against the British. Those participants were from the Kuki and Naga groups.

Dimalik Kemprai

Dehmalu's historical place, Dimalik Kemprai, aka Manik Singh's, was similar to Veer Sambudhan Phonglo's. He made his fortune by defeating some wrestlers. He had to take up the gauntlet when they reportedly overthrew two State commanders, namely, Rangadao and Dehgadao, of the Dimasa Kingdom. However, it was a challenge of wrestling competition set forth by those visiting combatants, but it ignited an uncanny wrath in Dehmalu. He defeated the opponents of his country commanders subsequently.

While his victory ensured the reinstating of honour of the Dimasa kingdom, for which he participated in the bounce competition, the downfall ignited resentment.

Mentionable, the visitor wrestlers were reportedly saints who came across those commanders above in the metropolis of the Hidimbapur, situated in Dimapur. They participated in a wrestling session on their way to the pilgrimage of Parsuram Kunda" (in the present State of Arunachal Pradesh), in the

North-eastern region. Hence, as they felt pleased with Dimalik's feat, they taught him the art of Yoga. Thus, he became a Yoga specialist and achieved enough power of yogic endurance.

Besides specialising in Yoga, he was a staunch follower of the Hindu Lord Siva. Once, the Lord felt satisfied with his total devotion to Him. The Lord appeared in his dream, spread out His palm, asking Dimalik to catch hold of any of the fingers so that He would grant him blessings. In contrast, he demanded total boon by holding His whole palm. The Lord did not feel fully satisfied with him and vanished, leaving a simple prophecy which I may cursorily craft in my simple language in the interest of helping the esteemed readers know it:

"Nobody will succeed in defeating you in an open fight. However, you'll have to die a dejected death sans an opportunity to defend".

Dimalik was the son of Dechangdao Kemprai and Rhibangdi Thaosen (Kemprai). He was born on the 15th of August 1215 AD in Dimapur, a historical place once the capital of the Kachari Kingdom. The day was reportedly Saturday. It was during the reign of Raja Makardhwaj Narayan Thaosen. They said there was a big earthquake after his birthday. The Hiramba King felt surprised and went to see Dimalik.

He began his career as a chef of the two commanders of the Dimasa Kingdom above, but King Makardhvaj acknowledged Dimalik as the sober man of his country. In the past, people became virtuous by their sobriety. The king took advantage of the presence of the sturdiest, making all neighbouring rulers, including chieftains, acknowledge the supremacy of the Hiramba ruler, and they paid taxes to the monarch.

According to a source, Dimalik had possessed his arms, apart from the wearing apparel. His two wives ingeniously made it with thick cotton and stitched profusely. It smacked of a magical proof against spear, sword and bullets. The tunic, they said, gave him a better advantage over his enemies. He would strike his adversaries, leaping forward and backward a great distance, let alone his dexterous vaulting with an equal height simultaneously. All his opponents felt like getting hit by the thunderbolt (sic).

By the way, the Naga chieftains were in awe of his mighty strength and cooperated with him in subliming the Manipuri kingdom, binding Manipuris.

The acceptance of the Hiramba king's dominion by its neighbours prompted the king to extend his dominion by defeating the Manipur rulers. To an historian, N.K. Barman, Dimalik bound Manipuris "with oaths and terms, that no Manipuri would, henceforth, construct their dwellings with frontals not wider than twelve cubits and that no betel nuts should be grown in Manipuri soil proper".

In his *Queens of Cachar and the History of Kachhari*", N.K. Barman said Dimalik first defeated Manipur, then headed with his forces to Burma, where he put the Burmese to rout. He made the Burmese wear lungi (shawl) as male cloth, apart from fixing bamboo poles upside down. (*Page 72, para 3*)

King Makardhvaj called for the presence of Dimalik in his country when the latter was in Burma after a perceptible threat posed by the slow but steady advancement of Ahom rulers into the region.

In honour of his Burma victory, the people of Hiramba Kingdom reportedly held a banquet, praising Dimalik by singing

Bai Maijai. Here's the facsimile Dimasa song and its English translation by one Pintu Barman Phonglo of Bodo and Dimasa Heritage Digital Archive. He carried out the task by taking help from the older adults of the village Joypur in the district of Cachar:

Nahorsa and Nahsadi caught a snakefly
The snakefly, which was making guh-guh gang guh-guh sound, was caught.
Our gold and silver sieve,
We danced the dance of the sieve;
Shibarai, Gamadi showed the dance of the sieve;
Taught to dance, knows to dance and showed the dance to people;
Be happy and laugh together,
We danced and enjoyed together;
Come one, friends! Let's wear, drape and get ready,
We will keep the hair as per the wish of the king's son,
We will keep the hair,
Come on, friends! The king and queen are dancing with us,
Look dancing with us;
The gods of heaven will laugh with joy and happiness,
There will be peace in the State, and they will be able to live peacefully;
There will be no illness and no worries;
The world will be beautiful,
Will celebrate Surem together;
Will eat Bushu together;
Will spend days in this world with joy and happiness;
Will weave, enjoy and plant paddy;
If you work, then only your stomach can get filled in this world;
Will be lazy
Deer! Deer! Deer! You!

Will you eat the fruit of the tree?
The small fish is moving in the water, which is not deep.
Young boy and girl gone mad;
The small fish escaped,
The small fish escaped,
Beautiful flower, thin like an onion cover;
If my daughter grows up,
Could watch dancing for once,
Giving brinjal seeds,
Giving Chilly seeds,
With seeds and
Vulture! Vulture! Vulture! You,
Fly high and high,
Fly, fly and look around-
Will a dead animal be visible?

The ruler of Burma (now Myanmar) reportedly presented Dimalik with a white elephant as a token of appreciation.

Given the prevailing practice, the sycophants of King Makardhvaj demanded that Dimalik present the animal to the monarch, which the latter refused, saying it was his hard-earned glory to retain with him. As a result, it brought about inevitable jealousy and resentment among the court ministers. They could not openly challenge Dimalik. The courtiers led a giant elephant to trample him down but to no avail. However, they finished him off by taking the help of his stepmother.

Before his demise, caused by the pouring of a *hot molten lead* into his ear by the overt and covert involvement of the infidel lady as above in the crime, Dimalik reportedly cursed the Kingdom. Let me simplify his feelings in my simple language to help the readers understand them better:

"As treachery and jealousy have drowned their thoughts for other consideration of national interests, some people of the Hiramba Kingdom have exhibited their narrowest tendency in them. Mark the words there shall no longer be a hero born among the Dimasa tribe men" (*Page 74, para 4 – Queens of Cachar or Herambo & the History of the Kachchhari*)

Until the Eleventh North Cachar Hills Autonomous Council formally started exercising its role in 2016, no person in the history of the Dima Hasao ever before appreciated the sacrifice and contributions of Dimalik Kemprai, whose deeds got recognised with the installation of this soberest warrior statue at Maibang and Haflong.

Senapati Tularam Thaosen

If there were no desires smacked of gluttony coupled with favouritism and the arrogance of power in the kings and their subjects, there would be no annexations in the monarchical history of humanity. So, as one comes across the historical records, sticking out the Dimasas' suffering from their ruthless enemies and indulgence, it does not surprise him.

First, as the Burmese were unkind, so were the Ahoms. The Burmese subjugated the Dimasas like the Ahoms annexed the latter's territory in the nineteenth century.

There was internecine rivalry in the question of succession visible among the royal clans in the Dimasa tribe members.

For instance, though Govinda Chandra Hasnu was the last King of the Dimasas, he could not defeat Senapati Tularam, whose domain areas covered the river Mahur and Naga Hills on the south, Doyang River on the West, Jamuna and Doyang on the North, and East, the river Dhansiri.

Tularam secured the kingdom above in the aftermath of his father's death. Kasi Chandra was his father, and the former was a cook but the kin of Krishna Chandra. Although he was a cook's son, Tularam thus belonged to the royal dynasty. Of course, evidence states some did not treat him well because of his father's profession. However, Tularam's parent used to get respect in Krishna Chandra's court, no matter how some people looked down upon the former's kin.

Nevertheless, King Gobinda Chandra did not like Kasi Chandra, and the former reportedly had assassinated the latter. The death of his father ignited anger in Tularam, who now wanted to take revenge, mobilising public opinion against King Gobinda Chandra and the British. Sensing danger, David Scott, the first Commissioner of Assam under British rule in India, caused the grant of a separate Kingdom to Tularam. The kingdom covered an area of 2224 sq. miles.

One of Tularam's heroic battles was against the invading enemy, Baghdad Pathan, from the Muslim-dominated areas of Bengal. He defeated Baghdad and thus saved Cachar from the Muslims, said Dr. Dhruba Hojai.

After the demise of Krishna Chandra, Gobinda Chandra succeeded the throne, but the latter acted as directed by the British. Apprehending the loss of the Dimasa empire at the hand of the British, of whom Tularam reportedly demanded the kingdom above for him so that he could save his community together with his country

"Sengya Tularam Senapati was a recognised Senapati (Military Commander or General of the Army) required for the Dimasa kingdom from the twelfth century Dima Hasao. There was a temporary Cosmic arrangement due to the sudden demise of the Dimasa king Krishna Chandra. The heir to the throne of the Dimasa kingdom, Govinda Chandra, was a minor. The people awaited his coronation; the adventures of Sengya Tularam during his period are complete and heroic deeds for the protection of the Dimasa Kingdom".

He tied his nuptial knots with Dhanavati, a religious lady like her Prince Charming; she even wrote a book of songs named "Dipok". Some said he constructed several Hindu temples. Everybody was in awe of his "determination, mental power, courage, adventure and physical strength". His enemies would feel terrorised at seeing him, saying even the wild elephants feared Tularam.

According to a reliable source, Tularam did not directly belong to the Royal Hasnusa clan and became Senapati, not King. However, available evidence suggests all Sengphongs who ruled the Dimasa kingdom were mainly from the "Bodosa, Thaosensa, Haflangfangsa & Hasnusa".

The Kingdom of the Dimasa Kachari remained independent under Tularam Senapati until the British annexed it to their domain under the Treaty of Budderpore, which came to be known as North Cachar Hills.

As per royal tradition, if the King did not have any child to succeed his throne after him, his ministers with the Sengpongs (Shengphong) or their representatives were to choose a new prince, who was to hail from the Hasnusa clan of the Dimasa. In such a matter, the queen had no power to exercise after the King.

Some historical evidence suggests Tularam used to speak in Assamese, and he was the disciple of an Assamese guru.

Given the affinity between the two groups of people of the Brahmaputra Valley, one feels safe to say the Dimasas, under Tularam's leadership, had a good relationship with the Assamese people of the Brahmaputra Valley. Hence, some intellectuals of this tribal group who now like to remain different from the majority community of the State of Assam, make one wonder: Does it ilk any reasons why the Dimasas fear losing their uniqueness amidst the majority Assamese? The tribe members do not even like any rule under the Provision of Assam Panchayat Raj in Dima Hasao where there is an autonomous entity called North Cachar Hills Autonomous Council exercising its role under the Sixth Schedule to the Constitution of India.

Coming to the central point of discussion, the British appointed Tularam as Senapati based on the findings of an enquiry conducted by Lieutenant Thomas Fisher, who was in charge of Cachar Affairs and submitted his report to David Scot, Agent to the Governor-General, North East Frontier.

In 1832, the British pensioned off Senapati Tularam Thaosen, annexing his region. Subsequently, the former even conquered Govinda Chandra Hasnu's province in 1833, which the British granted him once, as per the Treaty of Yandabo, in 1826.

In memory of Veer Senapati Tularam Hasnusa, in Dima Hasao, the Governments – Central and State – agreed with the leaders of the Dimasa National Liberation Army & Dimasa Peoples' Supreme Council, in a Memorandum of Settlement signed on 28th October 2021, to build a Dimasa Kachari Royal Museum, apart from building a Statue in his name.

Joya Thaosen in Golden Letters

After Princess Disru, who fought for the cause of women's emancipation, the North Cachar Hills Autonomous Council made public another Dimasa woman, Joya Thaosen's participation in India's struggle against the British. There are now two standing statues of women activists from the Dimasa tribe member who fought against the evils. These two of the erstwhile North Cachar Hills represent both assimilatory and dissimilatory symbols in their fight against the evils inflicted upon the Dimasa society. So, Disru holds a pigeon in her hands, subtly meaning the need to ensure freedom from superstition and oppression, gender equality and peace so that society can achieve progress. In contrast, Joya's hands with guns sticking out the women's power seemingly targetting the inimical forces – the mighty British soldiers!

To begin with her story in brief, Sengyajik (equivalent to swordman/commander) Joya Thaosen was born to Jamangdao Thaosen and Baosadi Langthasa (Thaosen) on the 26th of October 1925 at the Jorai Bathari village in the erstwhile North Cachar Hills district of Assam. She needed more education because schooling was not widespread during those days. However, she had enough of her community's sentiment, coupled with an audacious will to uproot the evil designs of the British from her country, which one can gauge from her story presented by some writers.

According to reliable sources, the fight to gain her independence from the British was going on in India amidst the rise of Azad Hind Fauz (Indian National Army), led by Subash Chandra Bose. Joya Thaosen and her co-revolutionary friends, including Arjun Langthasa, her cousin, Jaotedao

Kemprai and other thirty-five to forty nationalists, fused. They would listen to the news on the Radio about their community's illustrious past, dwelling on the existence of the Dimasa/Kachari kingdom, Sengya Tularam Raja, Veer Dimalik Kemprai, Sambudhan Phonglo and so on. The formation of Azad Hind Fauz, followed by the presence of the Rani Jhansi Regiment, developed a longing to join the Rani's army in Joya Thaosen.

At this juncture, she and her young friends, as already stated, got to know about Netaji Subash Chandra Bose's presence in Nagaland, where the freedom fighters experienced the shortage of food staffs following the imposition of a road blockade by the Britishers between Dimapur and Guwahati. Realising the gravity of hunger and deprivation, her group collected rice grains and salt from the households of Haflong, Mahur, Maibang & Gunjung areas. They wanted to transport all foodstuffs to the INA through the porous border of the erstwhile North Cachar Hills with Nagaland.

On reaching Dimapur, after three days and nights of continuous walking on foot via Daotuhaja, Guilung, Shemkherma, Gisimling hading and Dimakro (aka Prasadimdik), they came across the British soldiers against whom they fought tooth and nail, under the Khirem Khowai Range. The fierce battle between Joya & Co and British soldiers brought about heavy casualties, including the receipt of grievous injuries by some of the English forces. Nevertheless, the Britishers overpowered Joya and her friends, and she unfortunately lost her life on the 7th of April 1944.

Mention worthy, her patriotic and courageous zeal shows the bravery of a Dimasa woman to protect her country and people by raising voice against the British, which appears in the writing of her name in golden letters. The present North Cachar Hills Autonomous Council made her contribution known to the new generation by installing a stone statue in Haflong town on the 26th of October, 2023.

By the way, perhaps, it would not have been possible to get such prominent projects physically executed in Dima Hasao without the Chief Minister's regular blessings to the Twelfth Executive Committee to the North Cachar Hills Autonomous Council.

The Chief Executive Member of the Twelfth Executive Committee deserved to be Serial No. 3, a good-performing political leader of Dima Hasao. The first was Surat Chandra Daulagupu, in terms of establishing offices of the Transferred Subjects of the Council, among other things. "Followed by him, Gobinda Chandra Langthasa had caused several major development schemes implemented during his Chief Executive Membership and Ministership of Assam. Of course, it is my assessment; it may not be acceptable to all. I agree others did do well for the Dima Hasao. Different leaders made different contributions towards the good of the hilly area of Assam".

There is no gainsay that the present Chief Minister, Dr Himanta Biswa Sharma, has always treated the people of Dima Hasao well, even inducting a sole Member of the Legislative Assembly into his cabinet.

The North Cachar Hills Autonomous Council stalled Joya's standing statue with a gun in her hands on the triangular point. It is near the Synod Literature Services and the Sarkari Bagan and Lower Haflong Main Road, which passes between the residential complexes of Nityalal Daulagupu, former Principal Secretary, North Cachar Hills District Council and his sibling Nityananda Daulagupu, Ex-Sub- Divisional Officer of the Public Works Department.

For the educated female tribe members searching for equal status to men, the installation of the statues of the two women in recognition of their bravery seems to fit the occasion.

In the past, several members of the Dimasa Mother Association aired their views on ensuring equality for their womenfolk. Given the premise, some members of the Dimasa Women still find room to improve their standing in society. However, a few have achieved worldly success in administrative and political fields recently.

Be that as it may, the installation of the figurines of Princess Disru and the freedom fighter Joya Thaosen by the Chief Executive Member of the present North Cachar Hills Autonomous Council reflected the Dimasa men's honour to their women sentiment.

As mentioned, the Dimasas are in the majority in Dima Hasao. In the hilly region of Assam, all smaller or sub-smaller groups of people follow the path shown by the majority, though it may not be outwardly acceptable to all. Hence, the step taken by the autonomous body will go a long way in inspiring other tribe members.

On the other hand, the autonomous entity already showcased its favourable attitude toward the Dimasa women folk when it arranged a grand felicitation after one Diksha Langthasa, granddaughter of the former Chief Executive Member, Shyam Chand Hojai, recorded her selection into the Indian Police Service as the first Dimasa woman from the Dima Hasao.

Chengjapao Doungel

Chengjapao was the Chief of Aisan, representing the urban Doungel Clan of the Kuki tribe members. He along with other revolutionaries fought against the external aggression in the Anglo-Kuki war during 1917-1919.

According to a reliable source, the record is available at the Historical Museum in Kolkata.

The Kuki tribe members in Dima Hasao have installed the statue of Chengjapao Doungel at Mahadev Tilla.

When Debojeet Thaosen was the Chief Executive Member of the North Cachar Hills Autonomous Council in 1915, he unveiled the statue of Chengjapao on the 28th of August.

There is also information regarding the exhibition of hospitability shown by the Kuki tribe members to the Dimasa King and his subjects. Even Sambudhan Phonglo and his guards reportedly got help from the Kuki tribe members.

To construe about the Dimasa Monarch and his political orders, who entered the erstwhile North Cachar Hills following the annexation of their territory by the Ahom armies, some Kuki tribe members sheltered the former at the Khongsai village, also known as Kuki punji, aka Boro Kumpi, somewhere in the present Cachar district.

Appreciating the Kukis' good gesture, the Dimasa monarchs gifted gold and silver plates and artefacts.

Further, the establishment of villages of different tribe members took place near each other, highlighting the interdependent nature of the tribe people of various types.

Haipou Jadunang & Rani Gaindinliu

"Though the entire Naga tribe population of Dima Hasao was under Haipou Jadunang's leadership, his arrest did not affect the movement against the British, for he seemed to pass it on to a young and energetic freedom fighter, namely Rani Gaidinliu who languished in jail on several occasions. Thus, she led the Zeliangrong movement after him till her last breath.

The Dima Hasao Autonomous Council declared the observance of a Holiday in honour of the Naga tribe freedom fighters on the 29th of August.

His Heraka Movement seemed to originate from an urge to unite all stokes of the Jeme population and defeat the evil designs of the British, which the Britishers noticed, arrested him from the erstwhile North Cachar Hills and took him to Manipur, where he lost his life in gallows Imphal 1931.

The movement of the Naga tribe population of the erstwhile North Cachar Hills (now Dima Hasao) launched by Haipou Jadunang still ensures the unity of all the tribe members.

After Rani Gaindinliu, one Ramkuiwangbe Jeme from Lodi village in Dima Hasao led the movement. The Government of India even nominated Ramkuiwangbe Jeme for the Padma Shri".

J.B. Hagjer, J. N. Thaosen, H. M. Haflongbar

Everybody knows Joy Bhadra was one of the stalwarts of the erstwhile North Cachar Hills (now Dima Hasao). He hailed from the village Nanadisa. The tribe people's hamlet also gave birth to another prominent surgeon, the first person from the erstwhile North Cachar Hills, to qualify for the medical profession. If he could not serve throughout his life, he rendered yeomen services after superannuation in Dima Hasao when it was seething with dissent.

Both contributed a lot towards shaping today's Dima Hasao. I have already dwelt on how the people of the locality should remember those born into the town in another published work.

Additionally, it would be of the fittest tribute to Joy Bhadra Hagjer if the people could extend the development plan to include the more significant areas of Baojen and Nanadisa. The former village was the creation of Joy Bhadra, which many of us know. He returned to Dima Hasao after quitting his job in the Royal Indian Air Force as a sergeant and established his Dream Village in Mahur.

The British imprisoned him because he tried to save his people's lives, but very few still seem to make up their minds to believe that it is not illogical to declare him a freedom fighter without arms. He fought against the evil designs of the British, which wanted him to lead some Dimasa youths in the fight against the Japanese in Mizoram, which he reportedly refused. That led the Britishers inflict punishment upon him under the Defence of India Rules, which were a proof of adding the feather to his cap.

By the way, Jogendra Nath Thaosen also served as the Commander of the Labour Corps of Dimasas for six months in Lushai Hills (Mizoram). But unfortunately, he clashed with the British and lost his job.

Mentionable, the village Nanadisa also gave birth to Surgeon Madhu Sudhan Purusa (Kachari), whose success led many aspirants from Dima Hasao to choose Medical Science as their profession.

We have installed the statues of several historical figures of Dima Hasao. Why do we ignore Joy Bhadra Hagjer, N.L. Daulagupu, Hamdhan Mohon Haflongbar in front of the Dima Hasao Autonomous Council?

To remember such personalities, the Dima Hasao may obtain necessary clues from other places, apart from following the example of Cachar's Civil Hospital if it doesn't find anybody else deserves it.

They may focus more on rural development as a tribute to the producer locality of two prominent persons. It will convey the message of truth that a person interested in achieving worldly glory is not necessarily required to be born in an urban area if they have developed a positive attitude in life.

Moreover, if adopted from the proper perspective, the strategy will go a long way in checking the migration of people from rural to urban areas. But, on the other hand, if the scantly known issue needs to be taken in the proper perspective, the growth of the urban population might create an insurmountable problem in the long run.

Durga Malla & Ram Singh Thakuri

In dwelling on the chronological events in Dima Hasao's history, the name of Durga Malla does not need to be more relevant. However, the presence of a sizeable population of Gorkhas, followed by the Council Chief Executive Member's unveiling of his statue during the Chef Executive Membership of Debojeet Thaosen, makes one feel justified in including this freedom fighter's details in the book.

To this end, "Durga Malla stuck out with steadfast integrity and loyalty to his country India by sacrificing life for her cause, in honour of which the Gorkhas of India, including those of Dima Hasao, observe Balidaan Divas (Martyr Day) on the 24th of August because the British hanged him on this day. He was from Dehradun.

Mention worthy, Malla's title originates from the warrior Thakuri/ Rana clan of the Gorkha. Another person from this clan, Ram Singh Thakuri and his party under Netaji's stewardship first composed the lyrics for the Indian national song, JANA GANA MANA.

Mentionable, the British Government arrested Durga Malla from Nagaland, where he worked for the INA.

In appreciation of an unstinted loyalty and devotion to his duties and responsibilities, the British initially persuaded him to continue working for it, but to no avail. Finally, it sensed the danger of his presence as an officer in the intelligence wing of the Azad Hind Fauj (Indian National Army); the British tried to use him.

On the other hand, his integrity was beyond doubt as he was handsome and out and out a patriot. Moreover, he was a courageous & intelligent Gorkha and did note care the British's pressure. In recognition of his bravery and sacrifice, among other things, the Government of India installed a statue in front of the Parliament House.

Further, the British asked him to give up the idea of working for Subash Chandra Bose through his spouse. They even intimidated and forced her to persuade Prince Charming to give up fighting against the British, which he refused, saying India would surely earn her independence and that his sacrifice would not go unnoticed.

He had served in the British Army already, but a solid allegiance to his country led him to give up the job to join the Azad Hind Fauj (AHF) led by Subhas Chandra Bose. Interestingly, the British pretended to be unaware of it, or their lack of understanding of the mindset with which he was fighting led them to put pressure on him.

While dwelling on the above issue, one finds it justified to reflect on the historical events in which one considers hardly wise ignoring the noble contribution of the above heroes towards the freedom of the country. They opposed the British tooth and nail, which got wind of it and arrested and hanged them.

It's now time to dwell on the mythological heroes of Dima Hasao: -

A Cultural Icon - Princess Disru

At long last, the much orally told story of Princess Disru has become widely known in Dima Hasao and outside. The story started getting popular after the installation of her statue at Harangajao since the ruling BJP party came to power in the Dima Hasao Autonomous Council. Since 2023, even the Dimasa Mothers' Association has started celebrating her birthday as Women's Day at Haflongtown.

Until recently, many outside the Dimasa clan did not know about Princess Disru. However, the celebration of her birthday by the Dimasa Mothers' Day at the Haflong Municipal Board Field in 2023 has made the public aware of who the princess was.

According to my cursory assessment, the princess' celebration picked up for several reasons.

First, a monarch's kin dealt with both good and evil. The Dimasa King, known as Hariram Haflongbar, was the princess's father whose life was full of ups and downs. It smacks of a mythological tale! It was not her fault; Disru seemed innocent, but destiny gave her a hard time. However, she became a torch bearer to the subsequent generation of the tribe women, because she not only faced the cruelty of men upon women but cited an example of overcoming the obstacles in life.

On the other hand, she was courageous and had an opportunity to learn how to make a career in her chosen trades like weaving, knitting, sewing, and other weaving crafts.

Meanwhile, she was the first princess who inspired other women to assert their rights in such circumstances.

In the past, the society seemed riddled with orthodoxy; otherwise, it would not have prompted the King to undercut the importance of his daughter, though he reportedly said already had many female children born and nurtured. Disru, too, could have enjoyed being with her parents, whose discrimination obliterated her whereabouts beyond being present to get help from a Manipuri woman in Manipur.

Of course, some storywriters projected her mom as a kind-hearted queen who fostered Disru for fifteen years and trained her to live by the traditional or independent will or choice.

The capacity of a woman to take a challenge with a man in those days was not accessible. Only the stature of Disru had the courage and conviction with which she prevented the Dimasa King, Hariram, from entering the "woman's land" held by his princess.

Following her mother, Daokadi Haflongbar's footpath, Disru had already started weaving the Dimasa traditional clothes.

By the way, Dimasa clothes got popularised when Indubala Daulagupu took up weaving for the first time in Dima Hasao. She reportedly inherited it from her mom when she was a village girl. Indubala not only conceived the idea of the traditional Dimasa dresses but also popularised among the tribe women far and wide and brought *rijamphain, rikhausa and Rigu* out in the given market.

Secondly, Disru was extremely beautiful by any standard of imagination when a father could not initially agree to accept her as his daughter and wanted to tie nuptial knots, however unethical it may be. Finally, the King could not imagine she was his creation because he once ordered not to rear any female child if born to his queen.

Thirdly, he had to accept the fact that led his daughter to leave the kingdom.

Fourthly, there is no reason to reject the King had no other daughters from other queens, given the proposition that the King would use to indulge in polygamy in the past. Hence, King Hariram might be a polygamist, given his declaration of having daughters in the statement purportedly made before his spouse. Further, he could have thought of rearing up Disru if there were no daughters.

Fifthly, there is no other evidence about King Hariram hating the growth of the female population in his kingdom so that he might have victimised his only daughter.

The King was an elephant hunter. So, on receipt of a message about the coalescing of a herd of wild elephants from his subject, the monarch left his pregnant queen in pursuit of hunting. Before he undertook the journey, the King reportedly chatted and hugged his queen. My mind's eye about the King's talk with his queen sounds as:

"We're having many female children, not the son. This time, we shall rear up only a son when born. In the event of the birth of a daughter, she should not remain alive" (*"Should the babe prove to be of the female sex, you had better get it, but if a male brings it up": I have quoted the italicised sentence from C.A. Soppitt's "A Historical and Descriptive Account of the Kachari Tribes in the North Cachar Hills", Assam Secretariat Press, 1885"*).

The contents in the paragraphs above mainly prompted the Dimasa Mother Association to celebrate Disru's birthday as Women's Day, which will go a long way in idolising her as an embodiment of freedom, tradition, beauty, integrity, strength and self-respect.

Alaidao Khersa as a Seer

Alaidao Khersa is abit similar fabulous character to Disru and Dimalik, who have suddenly shot up their popularity in modern socio-cultural milieu of the Dimasa tribe members. Dimalik reportedly cursed all Dimasa tribe members for being callous towards him, because his bravery did not match with anyone in the bygone era of the Dimasa kingdom. Still, they conspired against him. In contrast, Alaidao visited this planet as a community soothsayer.

All such historical prodigies as above got a privilege to become known in the modern world following the entry of Debolal Gorlosa into the BJP politics. He unveiled the tiger-rider statue of Alaidao aka Joypurdao Khersa.

Joypurdao Khersa was his original name, and Mikrodao Khersa and Malodi Khersa, according to a reliable source, parented him on the 22nd of September 1998 at a village named Dobongling nearby Gunjung. He also had another brother, and breathed his last in1832.

They said he left the village itself when he could not tolerate his maternal uncle who scolded him. Since then, he remained out of the trace or sight of anybody.

On all a sudden, one fine moonlight, he reportedly appeared coming down from the back of a tiger, saying:

"No fear, please! It's your Alaidao!"

Afterwards, he asked those who spotted him:

"To play with KHRAM MURI and SENG" (*These are the names of the traditional flutes of the tribe members*)

Then, the villagers followed him. Now he predicted, bellowing and shivering what stored for the Dimasa society in the "Kaliyuga".

Some accepted the veracity of his predictions in the tribal society.

Be that as it may, the Dimasas apparently based Alaidao's appearance before them on installing a Tiger-rider statue in Maibang Sub-Division area in the seer's memory.

Mention worthy, the village Gunjung where the people said Alaidao was born, has also preserved the sanctity of having produced several other prominent personalities of the tribe member since the time when it used to be the erstwhile North Cachar Hills' Sub-Divisional headquarters.

For instance, Nityalal Daulagupu, Jatan Kumar Thaosen, Hamdhan Mohan Haflongbar & Surath Chandra Daulagupu started their individual journey from this Dima tribe members hamlet above.

Even so, there is scope to boost up tourism potential in Gunjung and Dehangi areas. After the victory of Debolal Gorlosa from the Dehangi Constituency of the Dima Hasao Autonomous Council, the locality has seen light from the tunnel of darkness.

By integrating Gunjung with Dehangi, the Government could have upgraded the existing administrative establishments of these localities in the interest of development, which I must have raised on other occasions.

FOOTNOTE: All brief biographical accounts of Durga Malla, Ram Singh Thakuri & Chengjapao Doungel have got a place in the narrative because their statues have been standing mute, somewhere in Dima Hasao!

CHAPTER-III

Direction & Administration

Satire of positive development; How does the NCHAC get modelled; Cabinet Mission; Advisory, and Bordoloi Sub Committees; Recommendations; Actual Approval & inauguration; Body, strength and terms of the Council; District or Autonomous Council as a political entity or body; Dima Hasao Autonomous Council's Role; Executive Power; Dima Hasao autonomous council's managed major subjects; Dima Hasao Autonomous Council's Entrusted/Transferred State Subjects/Departments; Financial Power; Another aspect of Financial Ethics; Council's Sources of Revenue &Receipt; Judicial Power; Justice Delivery & Development Systems minus Panchayat Raj; Legislative Power; Office of the Chairman and Governor's role; Governor's intervention in the Council's matters; Additional role of Chairman, Dy. Chairman & Member of Autonomous Council; Council Session; Stipulations; Members of Autonomous Council & Blender; Aspect of discretions-I & II; Executive following bureaucracy; State bureaucracy accepting the DHAC as Administrative Authority; Ministerial posts creation in Transferred Subjects ; State employees' recruitment, promotion & transfer under Council; Public Accounts Committee; Encroachment of Council's administrative authority (Case-I); Transactional Ethics)Case-II); Child Care Leave Sanction (Case-III); Inconsistencies in Transferred Subjects (Case-IV); Plugging the loopholes

Satire of positive development

If we wish to dwell on the negative aspects of life, everybody has a lot to do, because negativity sprouts mainly from the growth of different desires. And the wants of man are the causes of chaos and conflicts in society. Hence, negativity only poisons the mind, resulting in anger and apprehension. Thus, I devote little time to such an issue.

Looking at the positive aspect of the political landscape of Dima Hasao, one would like to point out the installation of the statue of Mahatma Gandhi and Dr. Bhimrao Ramji' Ambedkar in the heart of Haflongtown. It reflects the rise of BJP's type of nationalism in modern times. The present generation also fixed the statues of Subash Chandra Bose and other local heroes of the erstwhile North Cachar Hills at Haflong, let alone in Delhi, besides the statue of Veer Sambudhan Phonglo in Guwahati.

The growth of career consciousness in the borough of Assam has increased to everybody's expectations; else the achievement of Diksha Langthasa as the first female Member from the Dimasa tribe in the Indian Police Service cannot tally with an inspiration for other female aspirants to conquer their chosen wonderful world from the district.

By the way, the selection of two female candidates from the Dima Hasao – namely, Sadhana Hojai and Sabita Langthasa - initially boosted the morale of many female aspirants for the Assam Civil Services. A former Government Girls' High School teacher cleared the Assam Police Service from the female Dimasa tribe member. She is Jayshree Khersa from Dikrik village. After her selection, only one female aspirant from Muolhoi perhaps got selected for the cadre service.

Both Sadana Hojai and Sabita Langthasa earned appreciation from the people when they served, holding different positions in this district. The former even represented Haflong, along with V.L.T. Bapui, who led a team to Delhi for the cause of the lingua franca– Haflong Hindi – in Dima Hasao, which the people can never forget to admire.

On the other hand, history will record it as a modern patriotism. The new concept of patriotism of the Bharatiya Janata Party helped achieve a stronghold everywhere as the strategy to remember India's heroes has grown.

In the past, the political activism of the Congress and other parties seeded unity in diversity. That's why most of the political stalwarts of the district exhibited their nobility by bringing different types of people together to rule the erstwhile North Cachar Hills. Their deed now ensures the unity of all people who fondly remember them. Their attitude of equality has implanted a lasting memory into the people.

For example, if our elders of the former North Cachar Hill were not secular and broad-minded, they would not have included an all-tribe members' delegation to submit the present sketch of North Cachar Hills Autonomous Council in a memorandum submitted to the Bordoloi Sub-Committee.

Let's know the classical autonomy.

How does the NCHAC get modelled?

The present Thirteenth Executive Committee to the Dima Hasao Autonomous Council consists of one Chief Executive Member and twelve other Executive Members. They are the elected representatives of the people.

In choosing all these Executive Members, every party winning the elections forms an Executive Committee for the Council to ensure fair representation of powerful tribes of the district. Therefore, the pictures subtly aim to accommodate the political aspirations of various groups of people.

All tribes become involved in running the administration of the Council, allotting different portfolios of the Transferred Subjects of the State to the elected Member of the Autonomous Council inducted to act as Executive Members into the Executive Committee headed by the Chief Executive Member.

The Chief Executive Member of the Council assigns portfolios to his colleagues by retaining some subjects for his own towards the efficient administration of the autonomous entity. His distribution of the portfolios becomes valid after the Governor of Assam's approval as per his recommendation.

The Dima Hasao Autonomous Council (North Cachar Hills Autonomous Council not officially changed yet) now unites more than forty State Government Departments, engaging them in preventing the agricultural and other economic problems of the hill people of the district under its administrative control.

As such, each of these departments plays a vital role in raising the economic condition of the poor people of the Dima Hasao district, on which I have dwelt in Chapter-VI.

Before that, let's peep into some lines on Cabinet Mission and others.

Cabinet Mission; Advisory, and Bordoloi Sub Committees

In 1965, the Cabinet Mission directed the Constituent Assembly on the 16th of May 1946 to form an Advisory Committee. Its role was to work out modalities towards administering the tribals' excluded and partially excluded areas.

Afterwards, the Government of India formed an Advisory Committee headed by Sardar Vallavbhai Patel as its Chairman, who then formed two Sub Committees consisting of two persons as Chairmen, A.V. Thakkar and Gopinath Bordoloi. The former Chairman of the Sub-Committee modelled the administration of the Excluded and Partly Excluded Areas outside the undivided State (now North-eastern States). At the same time, the latter submitted the report to the Government under the Chairmanship of the first Premier of the State (Gopinath Bordoloi) above regarding the hilly regions of Assam – (presently) Karbi Anglong, West Karbi Anglong and Dima Hasao.

Subsequently, the Northeast Sub Committee to the Constituent Assembly became known as the Bordoloi Sub Committee, in which Surath Chandra Daulagupu from Haflong, the district headquarters of the erstwhile North Cachar Hills, was also reportedly with the Members of the committee.

Recommendations

Following were the chief points of recommendation included in the report of the Bordoloi Sub-Committee submitted to the Advisory Committee headed by Sardar Vallavbhai Patel:

1. There shall be neither forced labour nor beggary in the tribal areas;

2. The right to practice individual customs and traditions shall remain preserved in the tribal areas;

Only the bonafide inhabitants shall participate.

1. in the affairs of the scheduled areas;
2. Elected Member of the Legislative Assembly shall have to approve implementing all clauses of the legislation passed by the Central and State Legislatures;
3. All administration of the hilly areas shall be in the hands of the local people, of whom shall be the officers of the locality;
4. There shall be a separate provincial cabinet (equivalent to the present Hill Areas Development Ministry) for administering the tribal areas of Assam.
5. There shall be two Members of the Legislative Assembly – one each from Mikir Hills (presently Karbi Anglong) and North Cachar Hills) (now Dima Hasao);
6. A Boundary Commission shall restrict the areas of the Council;
7. All Dimsas shall have to integrate under one political platform;
8. There shall be a separate secretariat for the management of tribal affairs;
9. The Council shall have the power to "make laws on subjects like an allotment, occupation or use of lands, the management of forests other than reserved ones, the use of canal and water courses for agriculture, regulation of the practice of jhum or other forms of shifting cultivation, the establishment of village or town committees or councils, the appointment or succession of chiefs or headmen, the inheritance of property, marriage and social customs" and so on.

10. "The District Council shall have not more than twenty-four members. Out of them, the people were to elect not more than three-fourths of them from their territorial constituencies based on adult suffrage ".

11. The District Councils shall have the power to run primary schools, dispensaries, markets, cattle ponds, ferries, fisheries, roads and waterways (sic)

12. There shall be a Council for each of the tribal groups present in the hill areas of Assam, which the Governor of the State concerned shall carry out the task;

13. The North Cachar Hills' demand for the franchise insisted on taxpaying capacity or academic qualification.

14. The Council shall have the power to collect taxes on the house, poll, land revenue, and village forest; the State and Central Governments shall financially assist the Council.

15. The autonomous Council shall have the power to constitute Village Councils or Courts for the trial of offences. However, any crimes punishable with death, transformation for life or imprisonment over five years, shall be beyond the autonomous body's jurisdiction. Furthermore, no provincial legislation shall apply to the independent entity concerning the entrusted subjects, over which the Council can exercise its control by issuing necessary orders.

16. The Council shall have a joint financial administration, as agreed upon.

17. The tribals shall have to get relaxation of qualifications in employment in Government jobs.

Actual Approval & inauguration

Afterwards, the Government of India created six autonomous districts, namely the Khasi and Jaintia Hills District (now Meghalaya and Tura), the Naga Hills District (presently Nagaland), the Lushai Hills District (Mizoram now), the North Cachar sub-division of Cachar District (now Dima Hasao) and the Mikir (presently West Karbi Anglong and Karbi Anglong) Hills District.

The Government's order also created a new Sub-division called United Mikir and North Cachar Hills, amalgamating the territorial areas of the erstwhile Mikir and North Cachar Hills. The autonomous entity was to exercise its role by considering the above stipulations.

Bishnuram Medhi, then Chief Minister of Assam, inaugurated the North Cachar Hills District Council on the 29th of April 1952.

The Government of India created the autonomous body by initially attaching 16(sixteen) members to it – giving the hill people the power to elect their twelve representatives, leaving four other Members of the District Council (MDC) to the Governor of Assam to nominate.

The Constituencies of the Council initially created attaching to the above autonomous body were: Gunjung, Garampani Christian Villages, Mahur, Maibang, Kalachand, Hajadisa, Langting, Lobong, Khunglul, Liasong and Harangajao.

Body, strength and terms of the Council

As per the provisions of the Sixth Schedule to the Constitution of India, the Deputy (now District) Commissioner acted as the Chairman of the District Council. However, in the United Mikir and North Cachar Hills districts, the Deputy Commissioner only looked after the general administration. Since it was a Sub Division carved out of the Cachar district, the Sub-Divisional Officer became the ex-officio Chairman of the North Cachar Hills District Council.

The term of office of the Chairman to guide the Council with the advice and guidance of experienced officers for the smooth running of the District Council was six years initially.

The same term applied to the Deputy Chairman.

Subsequently, they shortened the term to five years.

The elected Members of the Dima Hasao/ North Cachar Hills Autonomous Council elect their leader, who now becomes head of the Executive Committee to the political entity, known by CEM (Chief Executive Member). One fellow member gets elected from among them as the Chairman.

Next, the leader of the party, who has the majority support of the elected Member of the Autonomous Council, stakes claim before the Governor of Assam, who now conveys approval through his Commissioner to the Chief Secretary Assam, apart from authorising the District Commissioner to carry out the oath-taking ceremony of the Leader of the (majority) Legislative Party, allotting time to prove the claimant's majority on the floor of the house within the stipulated time.

Afterwards, the Chief Executive Member of the Council chooses all Executive Members from among the people's elected representatives.

The strength of the Executive Members is now twelve, headed by a chairman. In addition, the Deputy Chairman gets elected on the recommendation of the Chief Executive Member.

After the 125th Amendment of the Constitution, the number of Members of the proposed Dima Hasao Autonomous Territorial Council is to be 40 (forty) as per Memorandum of Settlement.

District or Autonomous Council as a political entity or body

Under the Sixth Schedule of the Constitution of India, the Dima Hasao district enjoys the provision for an Autonomous entity called the Dima Hasao/ North Cachar Hills Autonomous Council located at Haflong. The Constitution of India specifies the administration of the Council under Article 244(2). Hence, the Council is a State in miniature, having all the paraphernalia of the following powers to legislate and administer subjects like Land, Revenue, Primary Education, and Customary Laws.

Initially, the Council got on the saddle of autonomy with 12(twelve) elected & 4(four) nominated members and a secretary, with the provision of a Chief Executive Member and two Executive Members, vesting with its control over Revenue, Judicial & Legislative departments during the first Council, as envisaged under Paragraph 3 of the Sixth Schedule to the Constitution of India.

Over the years, the Council has gone through a process of tremendous expansion in both its structure and content. Today, it has 28 elected and two nominated members who represent almost all-powerful tribes and non-tribal communities who are permanent residents of the Dima Hasao district. Besides, all major tribes of the district have their own elected representatives.

The term of the Council is five years. Now, we turn to dwell on the role of the proposed Dima Hasao Autonomous Territorial Council.

Dima Hasao Autonomous Council's Role

The Dima Hasao Autonomous Council enjoys Executive, Judicial, Legislative and Financial powers under the Sixth Schedule to the Constitution of India. Let us illustrate how these powers get exercised as per my understanding of the functioning of the autonomous body because I am not a legal luminary or politician, but what I have observed about the functioning of the independent body since my schooldays, would like to share my thoughts with all esteemed readers in black and white by exercising the freedom of expression with due respect.

Executive Power

The Sixth Schedule empowers the Council to have an elected Executive Committee headed by the Chief Executive Member and twelve other executive members appointed by Assam's Governor.

All are people's elected representatives.

The Assam Hill Areas Development circular, issued by then Chief Secretary T.K. Kamilla, IAS, on the 31st Day of December 1996, defines the modalities of the administrative changes at Clause (E), in which it states the Autonomous Council shall have an IAS Principal Secretary who is to act as the Commissioner and Secretary to the Government of Assam does in a Government Department. In exercising its role as vested per standing agreement with the Government, it also states the State

Government is to "make available the services of two officers in the rank of the Secretary to the Government of Assam" (one of whom will be from a Technical Department) for appointment as Secretaries of the Council. Apart from these, the autonomous body is to get three Deputy Secretaries – one of whom will be from a Technical Department and the remaining ones from the Assam Civil Services – for appointment as Deputy Secretaries of the Council Secretariate.

Besides the twelve Executive Members, there are now two Principal Secretaries – one each from the Non-entrusted and Entrusted subjects. The former issues belong to the Council's managed ones and the latter, the State Departments.

In addition, six Secretaries – 1(one) Secretary, 2(two) Additional Secretaries and 3(three) Joint Secretaries – assist the Principal Secretary (N) in the sectoral services.

Three Deputy Secretaries from the State Civil Services Cadre give a hand to the Principal Secretary of the Entrusted Subjects of the State.

Out of 89(eighty-nine) Grades I and II posts of the Normal Sector Services, twenty-nine are in Grade I and sixty others in II categories.

Due to the perennial problem of disbursing the monthly salary of these two classified Dima Hasao/ North Cachar Hills Autonomous Council employees, the Government of Assam has recently resolved to bear their pay, thus mitigating the suffering of the fund crunch Council for these two categories. It seems that the blessings of the State Government have got bestowed upon the Council's Grades I & II employees as a part of the implementation of the Clause 3.4 of the Memorandum of Settlement signed between the Government and the cadres of the erstwhile proscribed Dima Halam Daoga headed by Joel Gorlosa and Dilip Nunisa. According to the Clause of the Accord, the State is to encadre these two grades of Council employees for filling up all vacancies under its control. However, the Council must manage from its revenue receipts, paying the monthly salary of the two other categories of Grades III & IV post-holders.

Further, per the standing agreement with the Government of Assam, the Council has concentrated on recruiting local youths by filling up the vacancies in Grades III and IV posts in all the Transferred Subjects. However, the concentration appeared visibly minimized, emphasizing the random engagement of the new hands in the Council's establishments.

As mentioned, until the Autonomous State Demand Committee and the Governments worked out a Memorandum of Understanding, the Karbi Anglong Autonomous Council used to manage the administration of the autonomous body with the State workforce. However, the Council started engaging its local hands after the agreement in 1996.

The non-receipt of their monthly pay made many employees feel aggrieved with the Executive Committee. Still, given the Chief Executive Member's recent assurance in a press conference, he astutely planned to address their problems once and for all.

The Government's decision above, when implemented, will perhaps help all the above officials get their salaries and other perks at par with those of the State Government Grade I & II officials. Till today, not a single team member of the Normal Sector has drawn their salary as per the recommendation of the Seventh Pay Commission.

Commenting on the issue, an opposition source criticised the ruling party for what they called ruling members surrendering the autonomy of the council to the State Government. According to them, it is the responsibility of the council to manage the salary of its employees, including high ranking ones, from its coffer.

The classification of central Dima Hasao Autonomous Council and State Department subjects transferred to the autonomous body follows.

Dima Hasao Autonomous Council's Managed Major Subjects

1. General Administration Department (GAD)
2. Taxation
3. Markets
4. Land and Revenue
5. Primary Education
6. Rural Development
7. Transport
8. Finance
9. Unclassified State Forest
10. Council Public Works Department

The Executive Committee exercises its role with a Principal Secretary (Normal) to head the Sector of the Council bureaucracy.

The State Election Commission is hitherto responsible for conducting the Dima Hasao Autonomous Council elections through the Election Officer of the district – District Commissioner.

Dima Hasao Autonomous Council's Entrusted/ Transferred State Subjects/Departments

In managing the State Transferred/Entrusted Subjects/ Departments under the Sub-Para of Paragraph 6 of the Sixth Schedule to the Constitution, the Government of Assam delegates power to exercise over the following Subjects of the State to the Dima Hasao Autonomous Council.

Initially, the Assam Legislative Assembly, at its meeting held on the 12th of April 1995, approved the Memorandum of Understanding, signed between the Chief Minister of Assam and the Autonomous State Demand Committee together with its sister organisations like North Cachar Hills Students' Federation, Karbi Students' Union and Dimasa Students' Union on the 1st of April 1995. The Memorandum of Settlement followed on the 8th of October 2012.

Mentionable, in approving the Memorandum of Understanding, the Assam Legislative Assembly resolved that the jurisdiction of the North Cachar Hills Autonomous Council and Karbi Anglong Autonomous Council for the exercise of the Executive powers will extend to the State Subjects/ Departments listed in the MOU. The Governments - State and Central- and Dima Halam Daoga signed a MOS (Memorandum of Settlement)

Sl. No.	Name of Transferred/ Entrusted State Subject/ Department	Details, if any
1	Agriculture	Including agricultural education and research, protection against pests and prevention of plant disease
2	Archaeology	Nil
3	Animal Husbandry and Veterinary	Including preservation, protection and improvement of stock and prevention of animal diseases; veterinary training and practice; and cattle.
4	Cultural Affairs	Nil
5	Co-operation	Nil

6	Education:
	College Education
	  a) Primary and Secondary
	  b) Higher Education
	  c) Adult Education
		General
		  a) Including Middle school
		  b) Including vocational training

7	District Museum	Nil
8	Excise	Nil
9	Forests	Nil
10	Fisheries	Nil
11	Flood Control	Protection of villages, paddy fields, markets, towns etc. (not of technical nature)
12	Finance	Including Sale Tax on the purchase of goods than Newspaper, Value Added Tax

13	Food & Civil Supplies	Nil
14	Handloom & Textiles	Nil
15	Health & Family Welfare,	Including Public Health and Sanitation, Hospitals and Dispensaries
16	Industries	Subject to the provisions of entries 7 and 52 of List I of the Seventh Schedule. Small, Cottage and rural industry, Trade and Commerce, and the production, supply and distribution of Foodstuffs, cattle fodder, raw cotton and raw jute
17	Irrigation	Including minor Irrigation, Canals, drainage and embankments
18	Intoxicating liquors, opium and derivatives	Subject to the provision of entry 84 of List I of the Seventh Schedule
19	Land Reforms	Nil
20	Lotteries	Subject to provisions of entry 40 of list I of the Seventh Schedule
21	Labour & employment	Nil
22	Libraries (Library services)	Museums and other similar institutions controlled or financed by the State, ancient and historical monuments and records other than those declared by or under law made by Parliament to be of national importance

23	Municipal Corporation, Improvement Trust, District Boards and other	Including Municipal Board, Town Committees
24	Public Works Department	Nil
25	Panchayat & Rural Development	Including District Rural Development Agency
26	Public Health Engineering	Water Supply, Water Storage. Water Power up to 5 Mega Watt, subject to the provision of entry 56 of List I of the Seventh Schedule
27	Publicity	Including Public Relations
28	Printing & Stationery	Nil
29	Registration of Births and Deaths.	Nil
30	Sericulture	Nil
31	Statistics	Nil
32	Soil Conservation	Nil
33	Sports & Youth Affairs	Nil
34	Social Welfare	Nil
35	Tribal Research Institute,	Controlled and financed by the State Government
36	Tourism	Nil
37	Theatres and dramatic performances,	Entertainment and amusement cinemas are subject to the provisions of entry 60 of the List.

38	Transport		Including roads, bridges, ferries and other means of communication not specified in List- I, Municipal tramways, ropeways, inland waterways, and traffic thereon subject to the provision of List I and List III about such channels; vehicles other than mechanically propelled vehicles
39	Urban Development		Town & Country Planning
40	Welfare of Hill Tribes		Nil
41	Weights & Measures,		subject to provisions of entry 50 of List I of the Seventh schedule

In the aftermath of the Memorandum of Settlement between the governments (Central and State) and the representatives of the outlawed Dima Halam Daoga, the Assam Government agreed to re-organise the Dima Hasao Autonomous Council as per the judicial process.

The Memorandum of Settlement also visualises renaming the North Cachar Hills Autonomous Council as Dima Hasao Autonomous Territorial Council under Clauses 2.2 of the accord. The BJP-ruled Council passed a resolution renaming the autonomous body as DIMA HASAO AUTONOMOUS COUNCIL, omitting the word "TERRITORIAL"

Financial Power

In exercising power under the Sixth Schedule to the Constitution, the Dima Hasao Autonomous Council can tax all goods and services entered and rendered, respectively, within its jurisdictional areas.

It enhances and curtails all kinds of tax and expenditure under its jurisdictional control.

It imposes a services tax from central and state governments' overall fund allocation under self-owned priority development (SOPD).

The Council used to re-appropriate the sanctioned funds by the Government from one work head to another. Likewise, it exercises power over the allocated fund under the similar salary heads of the same department.

Only works within the jurisdiction of the autonomous body get executed with its sanction or approval.

But then, the power of the Council to approve the grant of the staff's salary of the State Entrusted Subjects stands visibly abolished with the advent of online payment of wages of all. However, the preparation and submission of the annual allocation of the Salary Budget to the Government in the Finance Department rests with the District Heads of the Department, subjecting it to route through the Council.

As mentioned, until the Autonomous State Demand Committee party led the Executive Committee to the Dima Hasao/North Cachar Hills Autonomous Council, the Government employees used to get their salary after the approbation of the Chief Executive Member.

Another aspect of Financial Ethics

If the Chief Executive Member (CEM) of the Council wants the State funded works executed in its jurisdictional area without his involvement and the CHOD (Council Head of Department) has brought the funds to complete the particular projects, the CEM can give a pat on the back of the CHOD concerned. Why and how?

Well, the state-funded project– such as the External Aided Project funded by the ADBI – gets implemented from outside the allocation of the Annual Action Plan of the Dima Hasao Autonomous Council. Therefore, the initiative of the official under which the works get executed must draw an appreciation for rendering a favourable service to the people of the Council's area by causing an additional fund allotted by the State Head of Department (say Chief Engineer of the Public Works Department).

However, supposing the State allocating funds to the Council, which, in turn, wishes to implement a big project. In that case, there is no limit to any technical sanction within the territorial jurisdictional of the Dima Hasao Autonomous Council. In such a case, the Additional Chief Engineer acts as the Council Head of the Department, per the Memorandum of Understanding/ Settlement. Therefore, one must reiterate that all works executed by the department per Council's approval within its territorial jurisdiction bear the technical sanction accorded by the district Head of the Department.

Mentionable, the ruling regime extended the rank of Cabinet and State Minister privileges to the Chief Executive Member and Executive Member of the Dima Hasao Autonomous Council, respectively, beyond the State of Assam. Therefore, it led many to speculate about the Additional Director being granted the power to accord technical sanction matching with the Chief Engineer regarding the State works needing to be implemented in Dima Hasao.

However, no formal sanction exists for extending such a privilege to the official as above. For instance, due to the lack of communication, the PWD officials under the Council work out modalities of work to execute within the stipulated sanction.

Council's Sources of Revenue & Receipt

Everybody knows during the British regime, the erstwhile North Cachar Hills used to remain administered as an "Excluded Area". However, everything does not remain unchanged forever. As expected, the geographical area of the hilly region of Assam did not belong to the general administration; it remained distributed under a particular category.

In implementing the particular Provision under the Government of India Act, the local administrator could levy a tax upon those entering the locality to carry out business.

So, an interested person in doing trade in the erstwhile North Cachar Hills was to obtain permission from the local body, which, in turn, had to grant authorisation under the Provision of the Dao Tax.

F.M. Clifford, as an SDO of the British, enacted the law in 1918, preventing people outside the Assam hilly region from entering. Though the Tax was initially to apply to the temporary visitors, the British subsequently imposed it as a House Tax upon the locals as an outcome of a clash between the British and Sambudhan Phonglo's forces.

The Dao Tax seems similar to the Inner Line Permit. As long as the Provision is alive in the administration of the Dima Hasao Autonomous Council, there is no pose of terrible intrusion into the jurisdictional areas of the autonomous body.

A time will come when the local population with the sobriety of honesty and integrity will find the truth: neither the original local tribal nor non-tribals in the jurisdictional areas of the Dima Hasao Autonomous Council can ever be a threat.

However, there is a lack of sincerity about the purpose of the Council's existence; the Dao Tax will continue to attract as one of the worthy clauses ensuring safety and security to the tribals against the supposed intruders – But who are the actual persons needing permission to enter the jurisdictional areas of the Council? Let the term get understood well so that it provides its worthiness. It seems possible if we carry out some soul-searching exercises.

At the outset, the Dima Hasao Autonomous Council's status was similar to a decentralised autonomous organisation (DAO). It is an institutionalised powerhouse guaranteed by the Parliament and State Legislature to the district-level population to get them ruled themselves. So, it virtually stands as a State within the present State of Assam.

The primary objective should be to ensure future unity, peace, and paving for growth and development. There is no need to elucidate the process of gathering peels in the pond; on the contrary, our urgency is to nurture the safety and unity of all fishes in the water polluted by the greed for power and position towards personal success or accomplishment on the plank of rendering services to the people.

Some local parlance defines the Dao Tax as the Machete Tax. How?

Well, there is no applicable definition of the term Dao tax. But one presumes the region is hilly and full of thorns and shrubs; there was no scope for doing other business than clearing jungles, cutting grass, wood or bamboo and doing all such exercises required using machetes. So, the Dao Tax sourced from the reason. If it were today, some of us might swap the term for a new one because many need words in our rucksacks!

In the past, those who wished to carry out such activities were to pay taxes to the local authority—the previous system of imposing tax swaps for the prevailing Entry Tax. However, as per the rules, all goods or passengers' private vehicle entries into the Forests Check Gate are governed by rules, which the Executive Committee to the Dima Hasao Autonomous Council frame from time to time.

Four Forests' Check Gates in Dima Hasao cover the entire jurisdictional areas of the Dima Hasao Autonomous Council at four different places – Dittockcherra, Manderdisa, Diyungbra and Khandong or Garampani Check Gates. Two new Check Gates are to come up soon, somewhere in Jenam Valley areas.

The people entering the Council's territorial jurisdiction for green pastures, especially unskilled labour, must pay the Dao Tax. In the case of skilled labour entering the jurisdictional areas as government servants, they must pay their Professional Tax, realised from the monthly salary. Even the traders of Dima Hasao come under its Provision.

In paying the taxes for collecting quarry products, the contractors execute the work by producing Challan in Cash receipts from the Range Office of the Forests' Department managed by the Normal Sector of the Dima Hasao Autonomous Council.

The contractors who purchase the quarry products from the particular office establishment are to show the Money Receipt to the Guards of the Forests Department found standing on the

Entry Tax Gates installed near the potential areas of extracting the natural resources – sand, stone, wood, timber and so on.

Of course, the Dima Hasao Autonomous Council has also managed its Land Revenue and Settlement Department establishment. It carries out land Revenue Receipts and Registration and collects proceeds from the Mouzadars and contractors leased out to collect taxes from the people's houses. The department also deals with Income Tax, Professional Tax, apart from issuing Permanent Resident Certificates to the clients within the jurisdictional areas of the Dima Hasao Autonomous Council.

Further, the General Administration Department under the Council deals with the Service Stamps. Therefore, per the standing rules of the Dima Hasao Autonomous Council, clients applying for any Council's services should submit their applications by affixing a Service Stamp of Rupees ten denomination.

As part of enhancing revenue receipt of the Dima Hasao Autonomous Council, the present Executive Committee decided to establish some Petrol Pumps owned by the autonomous body, which the employees were to operate within its jurisdictional areas, for which almost all the Mechanics of the Transport Department of the Dima Hasao Autonomous Council operated the petrol depots for some months. On the other hand, the autonomous body might generate more revenue from the Solar Project, which is to come up in Diyungbra.

While such exercises as above are long-felt ones, apart from the need to introduce some Malls in Dima Hasao, what I sincerely feel satisfied is the authority of the Council well leased out the operation to the private parties.

Though I was not against the Council's decision, what haunted me as an uncanny fear is that if the retail outlet of Bharat Petroleum happened to operate like the Transport Department, it would be additional burdensome management.

The Dima Hasao Autonomous Council's significant sources of revenue come from the Cement factories, Forests, Coal extraction, and North-eastern Power Corporation Limited. Even the Sale Tax on the purchase of goods, except Newspapers & Value Added Tax, goes to the autonomous body's coffer.

Vehicle Registration Taxes realised by the State Transport Department of the Government of Assam, and the auction sale proceeds of all Government vehicles go to the Council's coffer as per the standing agreement with the Government.

Further, as per the Memorandum of understanding, the State Government empowers the Autonomous Council to finance the expenditure of the entrusted subjects without any difficulty, for the former "makes funds available as advance under the Head-K-Deposits Advances Part- III Advance not bearing interest Departmental Advance-Special Advance". The autonomous body seems duty-bound to submit separate details of fund requirements, based on which the Government releases twice every financial year – April and October.

To enhance the Revenue Receipts of the Dima Hasao Autonomous Council, the Executive Committee may approve establishing Petrol Pumps, Malls, Coffee Shops, Night stays, Cinema Halls, Amusement Parks, Public Transport and so on and get them operated by its employees within its jurisdictional areas. At the same time, it may lease out them to private parties to ensure efficiency and transparency.

The liquidation of taxes by the various users of the Council gets deposited into the District Fund/Personal Ledger Accounts of the Dima Hasao Autonomous Council.

The Principal Secretary of the Transferred Subjects is the custodian of the Council Purse, called Personal Ledger Accounts (PLA), where all Government and non-government transactions, including deposit transfers, occur.

Now-a-days, the SOPD (State Own Priority Development) fund from the State Government gets online transferred to the Council at appropriate times.

The Normal Sectors of Administration maintain additional accounts where the revenue receipts of the Dima Hasao Autonomous Council accumulate. Still, such receipts get transferred to the main PLA after deposits from the clients of the autonomous body become complete.

The Dima Hasao Autonomous Council, on receipt of funds released by the Government in the Hill Areas Development Department, allots funds to the respective Transferred Subjects under the administrative control of the autonomous body. The quantum of funds gets released based on the sectoral allocations carried out and submitted to the Government through the Council by the Council heads of department.

Having received the allocation from the autonomous body, the Council Heads of Departments now divide the fund from the Council among all their District level officials. In addition, the District or Divisional & Executive Engineering level officials divide the fund among the Range and Beat or field-level implementing agencies.

By the way, until recently, the Drawing and Disbursing officials of the Transferred Subjects of the Council used to submit their Monthly Accounts of expenditure to the Principal Accountant General, Guwahati. However, they are offering such Accounts that require counter signatures from the Treasuries and the Finance Department of the Dima Hasao Autonomous Council.

Therefore, from February 2023 onwards, all Drawing and Disbursing Officials started submitting their Monthly Accounts of expenditure to the Council, which, in turn, does the needful onward.

Undoubtedly, the decision of the Council to submit the Monthly Accounts of all its Transferred Subjects from its end ensures transparency. However, any anomalies in the Accounts of any Transferred Subjects may render the council officials hapless when they fail to reply to any queries at the Principal Accountant General's office while submitting the Accounts.

In such a situation, the Council's officials are to come back to their office and correspond with the department officials concerned to pay a visit to the Principal Accountant General to sort out all impending anomalies! Thus, the change portends a swap for the involvement of both parties until the Council decides to submit it from their end.

Judicial Power

Under the territorial jurisdiction of the Dima Hasao Autonomous Council, there are two types of Courts — one relates to the Administration of Justice Rules 1955, which tries to settle trivial cases up to the Council level court, while the District and Session Court present in the district entertains severe criminal cases.

In forming the Court, the Dima Hasao Autonomous Council exercises power under the Sixth Schedule to the Constitution of India. It constitutes Village/Traditional Courts and Council Courts of the trail of suits and cases between the parties who belong to the Scheduled Tribes. However, such courts do not include any instances that require judgment in the Magisterial or Session Court. The Council has its laws framed under the Administration of Justice Rules 1955, and the Court, popularly known as the District Council Court, where the Judge appointed by one of the tribe members who holds a Degree in Law, hears the cases.

Justice Delivery & Development Systems minus Panchayat Raj

The Sixth Schedule to the Constitution evolves a separate scheme for the administration of the tribal areas in the States of Assam, Meghalaya, Mizoram and Tripura through the Autonomous Councils. The political institutions enjoy legislative powers on the entrusted subjects of the States, apart from the privileges of setting up and administering their system of justice, taxing and maintaining administrative and welfare services.

The autonomous body has the power to frame laws and form courts because of the conspicuous presence of different customs and traditions, which the various groups of people follow, in their jurisdictional areas.

For instance, the Hon'ble Judge and Hon'ble Sub Judge of the Dima Hasao Autonomous Council Court exercise First-Class Magisterial powers respectively, conferred upon them as per Hill Areas Development Department, Assam's Order No.105/99/62 dated Dispur the 9th May 2003, under Chapter 3 of Code of Criminal Procedure 1973.

In Dima Hasao, the system of administration of justice remains divided into two distinct categories – District and Session Judge Court and District Council Court.

In 1955, the Dima Hasao Autonomous Council, which enjoys autonomy under the Sub-Paragraph 4 of the Sixth Schedule to the Constitution of India, framed its own rules for the Administration of Justice, popularly known as The North Cachar Hills Autonomous District Councils (Administration of Justice) Rules.

Initially, the erstwhile Subordinate District Council Court dispensed justice at the villages, retaining the lack of prejudice delivery system at the middle level. At the council level, the autonomous body established an Appellate Court at the top of its judicial system.

Subsequently, in 1997, the autonomous body renamed the above Courts as Subordinate Autonomous Council Court at the middle level and Autonomous Council Court being the Appellate authority respectively.

At the village level court, the higher Authority is the Mauzadar, who dispenses justice when the village headman fails to do it at the bottom.

In hearing both aggrieved and accused parties, including their witnesses, the village Appellate authority seeks the help of rural community headmen to settle the disputes. When the aggrieved fail to reach an agreement at the community level, the aggrieved parties knock at the door of the Council Court.

Under the above rules, the mauzadar or Khanong can accept cases in offences like hurt, rape, theft, illicit relations, adultery, assault, succession dispute, cattle ownership dispute, village boundary dispute, divorce, etc. They settle the dispute by imposing penalties, including compensation, which is prevalent in the respective traditions of the thirteen tribes. If this Court's judgement does not satisfy the aggrieved, they may appeal in the Council's Court.

Honestly, there are very few tribe members' cases which require settling at the District & Session Judge Court.

On the other hand, when the Autonomous State Demand Committee came to power after a landslide victory in the Council election following the signing of the Memorandum of Understanding with the Government, the party ruled Council led by Prokanta Warisa introduced the formation of Constituency Development Committee. Unofficially, the villagers used to form Village Development Committee. The committee led by a President and Secretary each, along with other members of the village concerned, used to suggest the Constituency Development Committee along with the Member of the North Cachar Hills Autonomous Council how and where the development departments should implement all schemes passed in the annual District Planning Board meeting.

Given the conspicuous presence of the village level Courts and Village Council to dispense justice and carry out development activities respectively, followed by the Hon'ble High Court's order on the non-implementation of the Panchayat Raj in the hilly region of Assam – Dima Hasao and Karbi Anglong, no scope to impose any fictitious Panchayat Raj exists if there is no political motive to ignite dissension in the hill society.

However, due to the presence of certain provisions for autonomy to the ethnic groups in the Constitution of India, there is a possibility to revive the evil spirit off and on. Hence, the Government of India would do well to deal with the issue in line with the requirement as mentioned in Chapter V by establishing a Sixth Schedule Cell in the Ministry of the Development of North Eastern Region in the interest of public service.

Legislative Power

The Dima Hasao Autonomous Council exercises its power over all Transferred and Normal Departments as enumerated under the Executive Powers of the autonomous body above. It has thirty members, twenty-eight of whom are the people's elected representatives. In contrast, the Governor of Assam nominates two Members of Autonomous Council as per recommendation of the Executive Committee to the Council. The two Members of the Autonomous Council represent two major non-tribal groups of Dima Hasao – viz. Bengalis and Gorkhas. The practice has been in vogue ever since the formation of the political body.

Mention worthy, the primary transfer of subjects of the State to the Dima Hasao Council occurred after the signing of a Memorandum of Understanding and Memorandum of Settlement signed by the Governments – Central and State – and the representatives of the Autonomous State Demand Committee together with its students' wings.

Frankly, the Memorandum of Understanding signed between the Governments – representing both and State – and the Autonomous State Demand Committee on April 1 1995, ensured the name change of the North Cachar Hills District Council to North Cachar Hills Autonomous Council. The change also brought about more powers, apart from providing the autonomous body more independence in exercising its role over the transferred departments of the State.

All participants in signing these two accords above accepted the need to strictly adhere to all established norms in maintaining the highest standard of integrity to thwart any misutilisation of public money meant for raising the economic condition of the people of the Dima Hasao. (In addition to being affected by the power of the Chairman)

Office of the Chairman and Governor's role

In its initial stage, the erstwhile North Cachar Hills District Council (now Dima Hasao) had the Sub-Divisional Officer (Civil) to administer it. As per rules, the Sub-Divisional Officer (Civil) acted as Ex-Officio Chairman of the Council for six years, per the Provision of Assam Autonomous Districts (Constitution of District Council) Rules, 1915.

Three persons held the office of Ex-officio Chairman of the Council – S.K. Bhuyan, R.S. Paramasivam and B. Dowrah. The Deputy Chairman was C. T. Thanga, an elected representative who won in the First Council election held in 1952 from the Kamphai Constituency of the North Cachar Hills District Council.

Since the Third General Council Election in 1968, the Dima Hasao/North Cachar Hills Autonomous Council (previously North Cachar Hills District Council) has had an elected Chairman from the Dimasa tribe member. The Chairman of the Council was Hamdhan Mohan Haflongbar, a nominated Member of the District Council, while P.K. Gorlosa was an elected Member of District Council (MDC) who represented Kalachand Constituency of the erstwhile North Cachar Hills

District Council as the third elected Chairman from the majority Dimasa. The first Deputy Chairman was C. T. Thanga from the Baite tribe member.

Though the Second Executive Committee to the erstwhile North Cachar Hills District Council headed by P. C. Langthasa elected Hamdhan Mohon Haflongbar as the first Chairman of the Council from the Dimasa tribe member on December 6, 1960, reports available state the Chairman belonged to the nominated Member of District Council. After the six-year term held by the ex-officio Chairman ended in 1958, the Member of the District Council elected Haflongbar as the first chairman and nominated member. Until then, the Deputy Chairman, M.C. Daulagupu, carried out the role of Chairman and remained in the former position (Dy. Chairman) till December 9, 1960.

As mentioned, when Sonaram Thaosen tabled a no-confidence against the Executive Committee headed by P.C. Langthasa, followed by the resignation of the acting Chairman as above, there needed to be someone to carry out the business of the House. Afterwards, the Governor of Assam intervened by appointing Shri Ingimbe Jeme and S.R. Thaosen as Chairman and Chief Executive Member, respectively. Notably, it was a caretaker Executive Committee consisting of Thaosen as Chief Executive Member and M. Daulagupu and Thangtinkhup Changsan as Executive Members.

Governor's intervention in the Council's matters

No intellectual agrees with the governor's role in the autonomous regions' administration, saying the gubernatorial position gets exercised under the advice of the Council of Ministers.

Further, the Sixth Schedule to the Constitution empowers the State to unilaterally resolve disputes between the two entities – the Council and State Legislature.

On the other hand, the existing clause undermines the objective of the autonomy grant envisaged in the Constitution, merely providing the scope for bettering the political ambition of the Council's leaders in the State Legislature.

Thus, it stands as a stumbling block for the Council leaders to broaden their mental horizons by being the people's representatives.

The Governor of Assam, when not satisfied with the functioning of the Executive Committee to the Dima Hasao Autonomous Council as per provision of the Assam Autonomous Districts (Constitution) Rules 1951, may take over the administration of the Executive Committee. When the Executive Committee's power remains suspended with such a takeover, the Governor of Assam appoints the District Commissioner to act as an Administrator.

Additional role of Chairman, Dy. Chairman & Member of Autonomous Council

In exercising the Legislative Power under the Sixth Schedule to the Constitution of India, all elected Members of the Autonomous Council select one from among them as Chairman, who heads the Legislature.

The Autonomous Council meets a year thrice – every four months. However, per the Council's Rules, the Chairman may summon the Session in emergencies.

Besides the Chairman, there is one Deputy Chairman.

As per Clause 3.1 of the Memorandum of Settlement, the Chairman and Deputy Chairman of the Dima Hasao Autonomous Council enjoy the status of Speaker or Deputy Speaker of the Assam Legislative Assembly, respectively, for protocol purposes.

The rules of the Council do not permit the Chairman or Deputy Chairman of the Dima Hasao Autonomous Council to simultaneously hold the office of the Chief Executive Member or Executive Member of the same Executive Committee.

As one could observe in the past, even a nominated council member could hold the position of Deputy Chairman. For instance, V. Varte, M.R. Joishi and T.P. Upadhaya held the position of Deputy Chairman of the autonomous body.

Council Session

The Chairman of the Dima Hasao Autonomous Council summons the joint Session of the Council, in which both elected and Nominated Members of the Dima Hasao Autonomous Council participate.

The decision of the Chair becomes known among all Members of the Autonomous Council (MAC) in the form of a notification, which gets circulated among them.

After knowing the Session's date, all MACs now get an opportunity to file their cases or questions concentrating on the functioning of all Subjects – including both Transferred and Normal sectors of the autonomous Council – attached to the independent body.

Further, all Members of the Autonomous Council may raise any issues that are relevant to the people of the jurisdictional areas of the Dima Hasao Autonomous Council.

Having received all questions submitted by the MACs, the office of the Chairman or the Legislative Department of the Dima Hasao Autonomous Council now sends such questions to all relevant Departments – including Transferred and Normal Sectors – where replies get prepared and sent to the Council.

After the receipt of feedback from the Departments concerned, the Secretary to the Legislative Department of the Council lets all MACs know the LIST OF BUSINESS, writing a letter wherewith it gets attached, besides detailing how the issues raised by the Hon'ble Members of Autonomous Council in the House are going to get answered before two days of the Session.

Of course, the prior delivery of messages about how their issues get dealt with in the House helps the elected Members of the Dima Hasao Autonomous Council know and hold a further discussion, if any, in the Assembly Session of the Executive Committee to the Dima Hasao Autonomous Council.

The Council Rules state the Chairman shall summon the District Council to meet three times in the financial year, which commences from the 1st day of April, and four months shall not elapse between its first sitting in the next session and the date appointed for its first last Session.

Stipulations

All portfolios of the elected Members of the Dima Hasao Autonomous Council become valid after the Governor of Assam approves their elections by the Executive Committee and duly supported and recommended by Assam's Hill Areas Development, Dispur.

As per the Council's standing rules, the Governor of Assam can nominate two members in consultation with the Chief Executive Member.

The North Cachar Hills Sub-Division's Sub-divisional officer (now Deputy Commissioner) acted as the Returning officer during District Council elections, in the past.

As per the Assam Autonomous Districts (Constitution) Rules, the duration of the Dima Hasao Autonomous Council, unless sooner dissolved, is five years from the date appointed for its first meeting.

Members of Autonomous Council & Blender

The Member of Dima Hasao Autonomous Council, who acts as Executive Member after the election by the people. And as recommended by the Chief Executive Member and per approval of the Governor of Assam, they exercise their role over the subjects which the Chief Executive Member allots them after the election.

The Chief Executive Member retains some important or chosen Subjects while assigning others to his Executive Members.

Though the exercise of powers of the Chief Executive Member is similar to that of the state Chief minister, the jurisdictional control of the former is narrower than that of the latter. However, while exercising all powers over all Transferred Subjects as per the standing protocol, the position of the Chief Executive Member is no less formidably responsible and sensitive for a seasoned politician.

The Dima Hasao Autonomous Council functions similarly to the Assam State Legislative Assembly, and the Executive

Members act as the Ministers of the State on behalf of the people who elect them in the Council elections, which occur every five years.

To dwell on the power of the elected representatives of the Autonomous Council, they enjoy vast power within its jurisdictional areas on how to exercise control over the forests, fisheries, land, entertainment, public health, social security and other transferred subjects of the State. Moreover, their laws become implementable after the Governor gives the necessary consent.

Even though I am not a constitutional expert or legal luminary, I beg permission to exercise the right to speak about how my conscience dictates to me the role of the elected representatives of the people within the Dima Hasao/North Cachar Hills Autonomous Council's jurisdictional area. To this end, the Council may raise objections against the legislation passed by the State legislature or Parliament. In that case, the Governor or President, if desired, may chalk out modus Vivendi in implementing the bill or law passed by the State legislature/ Parliament as per the suggestion or representation by the concerned Council.

Aspect of discretions-I

Let us begin to dwell on the issue by citing an example. The scope for implementing the Citizenship Amendment Bill passed by the Parliament without the consent of the Dima Hasao Autonomous Council seems nil within the Sixth Schedule areas if one were to believe the existing autonomy to the autonomous entity indicates a State within a State. It may restrict the grant of settlement to the people, whether tribals or non-tribals, from outside its jurisdictional area. Thus, the North Cachar Hills/ Dima Hasao Autonomous Council may not allow any rights to purchase land to all groups of people, including those granted Indian Citizenship from Bangladesh, Pakistan and Afghanistan during the rule of the Bharatiya Janata Party. It may also impose restrictions on carrying any trades.

Thus, the scheduled areas have ample powers to safeguard the rights of the people. The Autonomous Council decides if somebody has the right to reside in the autonomous region to pursue the clauses of the Citizenship Amendment Bill passed by the Parliament as above.

At the same time, most of the ruling parties of the States concerned indirectly rule the Executive Committees to the Autonomous Councils; the autonomous bodies do not usually antagonise their State Legislatures. On the contrary, they typically implement all state governments' decisions without any demeanour. However, the Councils have the right to object if the laws passed by the State Legislatures/Parliament are distasteful to the people of the jurisdictional areas of the autonomous body.

The autonomous Council enjoys the State's power within a state under the Sixth Schedule to the Constitution, on which we may cite an example where the independent body does not exercise its role and how.

For instance, the Higher Education Department does not come under the Council, yet the autonomous body has to streamline its functioning. Reason: All higher education students belong to the children of the residents of the independent body's territorial areas. So, if the Govt fails to preserve the students' rights amidst the autonomous body's presence, the Council must have earned the right to intervene.

Aspect of discretions-II

The Autonomous Council has the power to exercise the posting of officials. If the political body does not intend to allow the joining of an official deputed by the Government of Assam, it may refuse the union of such an official.

On the other hand, if an official posted by the Government of Assam fails to meet the expectations or requirements of the autonomous body, it may relieve such officials from their assignments.

In short, every authority the autonomous council exercises as per the standing agreement with the Government under the Sixth Schedule of the Constitution must have reflected sufficient justification for its successful disposal in case of any legal dispute.

Following the failure of the Council in justifying its refusal to accept the joining of some grade III technical category of staff recruited and placed by a Head of Department at the autonomous body's disposal in one of the Transferred Subjects in the nineties, three numbers of staff got to work under its jurisdictional establishment.

Frankly, the exercise of power by the Autonomous body does not usually bring about any dispute between the two entities – Council and State – if these administrative agencies become ruled by the same party, Government at Haflong and Dispur.

At the same time, the Dima Hasao Autonomous Council can exercise its power over the posting of officials by the State if it is repugnant to the ethical code of conduct of business between the two entities.

For instance, the State Government places the service of an official belonging to the cadre of Assam Civil Services. Besides, it deputes such a public servant outside the jurisdictional area of the autonomous body to carry out additional assignments in the same capacity; the Dima Hasao/ North Cachar Hills Autonomous Council can refuse to accept the joining.

Since this involves disbursing pay and perks to the official from the Council's coffer and the joining or posting fails to ensure rendering required services to the people of its jurisdictional control, the Executive Committee may disallow accepting the official's union.

However, if the delegation of the official is to carry out the additional assignment outside their place of posting, and the additional charge is higher than the present position, the Council allowed the posting and delegation in the past.

Executive following bureaucracy

When I said there is a need to appoint devoted and honest Members of the Autonomous Council to act as Executive Members, I meant they should have a sense of being and belonging to this region.

As such, the persons who hold the office of the Executive Member handling all major Subjects dealt with by the Dima Hasao / North Cachar Hills Autonomous Council can do justice in the Dima Hasao. Because such Departments execute several noble schemes every year, proper implementation of all adopted schemes ensures alleviating the economic condition of many people at a time.

Given the circumstance, if the head of the Department is the one whose integrity is beyond doubt, they can ensure cent per cent implementation of such schemes.

They do not allow any unequal distribution of funds allotted to their particular Department. They insist on an equal division of funds for development between the divisional and sub-divisional establishments.

The unequal allotment of funds facilitates misappropriation.

For instance, a Transferred Subject receives an allocation of rupees seven crores. There are two divisional and one headquarters in Dima Hasao of the Department.

Supposing the annual allocation of the Department is seven crores. As the practice goes, the District Head of the Department divides the fund into three establishments – two divisional establishments and one headquarters establishment.

If the District Head of the Department bifurcates the fund received from the North Cachar Hills Autonomous Council's Finance Department between the two establishments – two crores for Haflong Division, seven crores and seven lakhs for Maibang and Headquarter establishments respectively.

As mentioned, the headquarters establishment belongs to the District Head of Department. The fund allocated under this establishment gets utilized by the Accounts Beat or Range Office attached to the District Head of Department.

As shown in the words above, the discriminatory distribution of funds encourages the deprivation of the Haflong establishment. It unnecessarily favours the establishment of Maibang, paving the way for the growth of evil misappropriation.

However, if the Executive Member is honest and has the sense of being and belonging to the hill region and notices the anomaly in the allotment of funds carried out by the District Head of Department after the receipt of funds released by the

Finance Department of the Council, they can intervene the matter! They can disallow the disparity in allocation.

Why should the Executive Member interfere in it? Because the elected representative prides on their sense of being and belonging to the locality, feeling the development is necessary for both Haflong and Maibang, they can exercise their power by insisting on an equal fund allocation.

At the same time, if the Executive Member insists on indulging disparity in the allocation of funds between the two divisional and headquarters establishments, the District Head of the Department may well bring the matter to the notice of the Principal Secretary of the Council in the interest of preserving work ethics of the Department concerned and act accordingly.

Usually, the Executive Member concerned goes by the suggestion of the Council's Head of Department, which streamlines the smooth conduct of transactional business between the people's representative and bureaucracy

State bureaucracy accepting the DHAC as Administrative Authority

Immediately after the receipt of the transfer and posting order from the Personnel Department, Dispur, the State Government official- including the one to act as the prospective Council Head of Department, holding the designation of Additional Director or Additional Chief Engineer or any other type of designation belonging to the Class I and II Cadres of the post, applies to the authority of the Council, requesting to approve their joining.

The Chief Executive Member is the final authority to accept the joining of an official, routing through the Secretary In charge of the Department and or Principal Secretary, apart from the approval or recommendation of the Executive Member of the Department.

Any violation of the procedure invited penalty – Show Cause Notice — in the past.

Having received a formal acceptance from the Council, a State Government official must carry out handing and taking over charges. Given their posting and joining, they accept the autonomous body as their administrative authority. However, they are Government officials in Dima Hasao; they can only leave their headquarters with the prior approval of the Principal Secretary and Executive Member concerned.

As per the standing agreement between the State Government and Autonomous Council, the latter is to place the services of all District Heads of Departments belonging to the Government under the disposal of the former. Before the Assam Government places the service of an official under the disposal of the Council, it is to consult the autonomous body as per the standing protocol.

As the practice goes, all correspondence to the Government about establishing the Transferred Subjects should route through the North Cachar Hills Autonomous Council. No recommendation or personal opinion on any structural changes can go directly to the Government of Assam from the district Head of Department without the knowledge of the authority of the Council.

In case the District Head of a Department has some suggestions or intricacies to iron out and require moving their higher authority, they can do so by first letting their administrative head know. Any advice or correspondence from the departmental officials to the Government without the consent of the autonomous Council violates the standing code of conduct of transactional business between the two – Councils and the District Head of the Department.

For instance, the District Head of the Department of the Council feels it necessary to establish a new Beat Office to ensure administrative efficiency. They can submit such a proposal to the Council, which, in turn, approves it on condition that the proposal submitted by the District Head of the Department does not involve allocating additional expenditure on its management.

In case any proposal for creating a new establishment, including post creation, abolition or upgradation, involving the addition or the subtraction of annual expenditure to the yearly outlay of the Department concerned comes up from the District Head of Department, the Principal Secretary of the Council now demands of the physical presence of the departmental official at the Council Secretariate, where they sit and discuss together. If satisfied, the authority of the autonomous body afterwards forwards such proposals, attaching the Council's endorsement to the Hill Areas Commissioner, Government of Assam, Dispur for onward necessary action.

Ministerial posts creation in Transferred Subjects

As per the standing protocol between the State Government and North Cachar Hills Autonomous Council, the latter exercising as the Borrowing Authority, can submit a proposal for creating new posts in any of the Transferred Subjects of the autonomous body.

The need for new creation should arise from the mind of the Head of the Department of the Allotted Subjects under the jurisdiction of the council. The issue becomes justified if it carries a valid explanation.

Under the administrative control of the Council, the District Head of Department submits such a proposal to their Administrative Authority, which, in turn, endorses it with supporting justification before they forward it to the Government in the Hill Areas Development, Dispur.

Every new creation obtains the approval of the Finance Department of the Government of Assam.

In the past, the State Head of Department, representing the Director level of Senior Officials, could only submit the proposal received from the district-level entity of the State to the Secretary of the particular department concerned for obtaining the Cabinet sanction.

Further, the State Head of Department had to move the proposal if it related to the creation of the Grades- I and II posts after receiving a formal application from the District Head of Department. Unlike the Grades III & IV posts, the Administrative Authority of the Transferred Departments would apply based on the recommendation of the District Head of the Department.

However, such power got delegated to the Administrative Authority (Dima Hasao Autonomous Council) soon after the Governments – Central and State – and the leaders of the Autonomous State Demand Committee together with its sister organisations like Dimasa Students Union in 1995 signed the Memorandum of Understanding.

Under the circumstance, for instance, even the Principal Secretary to the Dima Hasao Autonomous Council is to act as the Head of Department in all matters — tendering approval online to the Principal Accountant General, Guwahati – including sanctioning the Temporary or Non-Refundable withdrawal of General Provident Fund Advance of the employees of the Transferred Subjects.

Even in the case of the submission of a proposal for creating Grades I, II, III or IV posts to the Hill Areas Development Department about the jurisdictional areas of the Autonomous Council, the administrative authority of the Allotted Subjects, one feels safe to presume, is to do the needful.

State employees' recruitment, promotion & transfer under Council

As per the standing agreement with the Government of Assam, the authority of the North Cachar Hills Autonomous Council conducts promotion, transfer, and recruitment and accepts the joining or rejects the resignation of all grades III & IV staff of the Transferred Subjects under its jurisdictional control. Because the autonomous body functions in Dima Hasao, as does the Janata Bhawan at Dispur, the bureaucracy of the self-ruling entity is to similarly conduct the business of all the Allotted Subjects of the State under the administrative control of the political body.

As for recruitment, the Council Secretariate calls for reports on the position of vacancies from the District Heads of the Allotted Subjects. Some of them submit themselves the report before the Council writes for it.

On receipt of the vacancy status of the Grades-III & IV posts, the Transferred Department of the Council obtains the approval of the Executive Committee. Afterwards, the Principal Secretary conveys the decision of the Executive Committee along with instructions to recruit the Council Heads of Department, who, in turn, execute the assignment. Before submitting the proposal to the autonomous body, the Council Heads of Department of the Transferred Subjects obtain the relevant data from their Divisional Officers or Executive Engineers. Having obtained the feedback from the Divisional level, the Council Heads of Department now forward the relevant data received to the autonomous body.

Though the Council assigns the District Heads of the Department of the Entrusted Subjects to hold the recruitment of staff from time to time, there is no permanent Recruitment Board analogous to the Staff Selection Commission in Dima Hasao, subtly paving the way for raising irregular expenditure over the whole exercise.

For instance, some Council Heads of Department sometimes recruit Grade III and IV staff under the jurisdictional areas of the Council twice or thrice a year due to the lack of any established stricture within which an entity can conduct the recruitment. As a result, one cannot comprehend how the issue, when snowballed into a storm in future, will get tided over.

In the case of the Bodoland Territorial Council, they have established a Recruitment Board and carry out the exercise, subject to the availability of vacancies in the above categories of posts.

Likewise, the authority of the Dima Hasao/ North Cachar Hills Autonomous Council accepts the resignation of the Grades-III & IV staff on receipt of recommendation from the Heads of Department, which act upon such a proposal in the form of a petition received from the staff concerned by their Divisional Officers or Executive Engineers.

Similarly, as the Council transfers funds from one scheme to another within the same Major Head of Account, it orders the Council Heads of Department to execute a State Government employee's transfer from one establishment to another, though there is an intricacy in the transfer of the staff of the above categories between the divisional and headquarter levels of establishment.

For example, there is no promotional provision visible for the Head Assistant of the Division Office of the establishment of the Transferred Subject to get upgraded to Superintendent and posted at the establishment of the Council Heads of the establishment. In contrast, the Superintendent of the Council Heads of Establishment can become the Registrar of the Directorate at the State Level.

Regarding the promotion of these two categories of post holders, the Council Heads of Department of the Allotted Subjects look well advised to prepare the Seniority List of Staff within the territorial jurisdiction of the Council. Based on the order of seniority and merit, as per the Roster Point of Reservation, which seems essential to work out in line with the Government of India's Reservation Rules, the Recruitment Board, when set up by the Dima Hasao Autonomous Council as per Clause 3.5 of the Memorandum of Settlement, will have to chalk out a Reservation Policy pertaining to the employees of its Transferred Subjects.

After promoting the above categories of staff, the Council or the District Head of Department marks a copy of the promotion order issued under the jurisdictional areas of the Council to their State Head of Department for ensuring regularising the order of seniority of staff belonging to the above two categories. It will go a long way in ensuring transparency between the State and Council.

Public Accounts Committee

As the practice goes, the State Government forms a Committee on Public Accounts, Assam Legislative Assembly, consisting of several elected Members of Legislative Assembly representing both ruling and opposition parties, including its chairman and some officials of the State Government. They conduct a study tour of the Sixth Schedule Areas of the State – Dima Hasao, Karbi Anglong East and Karbi Anglong West.

Yet, such a committee gets occasionally formed when the area starts seething with dissent over any allegedly unequal grant of privileges to the citizens.

The Committee's main aim is to study the pulse of the people. Hence, its members are to visit places where the Government spends public money implementing schemes.

It interacts with the villagers or beneficiaries, trying to unearth the actual utilisation of Government allocated funds, studying which it also gets first-hand knowledge about the disorder or dissatisfaction, if any, of the electorates.

In case of any anomalies in implementing the Government adopted schemes, the Public Accounts Committee reports to the Government, which empowers to suggest remedial measures.

For instance, if the officials responsible for implementing schemes fail to meet up the expectation of the beneficiaries in its opinion, the Committee may recommend their replacement. But, on the other hand, it detects the shortcomings rooted in the political level of the Councils concerned. In that case, the

Committee's suggestion may also bring about the reshuffling of the Executive Committee to the Autonomous Councils.

Though the formation of the Public Accounts Committee ensures transparency in the Government expenditure in the Sixth Schedule areas, a unit of the Principal Accountant General as a watchdog of the public finance, if established, will go a long way in streamlining the Government spending in the particular areas.

Mentionable, the Principal Accountant General advised the Council to form a Public Accounts Committee representing both ruling and opposition Members at the council level during his last visit to Haflong. As per his suggestion, the Executive Committee to the Dima Hasao Autonomous Council was to elect a Chairman and Members in line with the formation of the Public Accounts Committee by the State Legislative Assembly for the Assam's Hill Areas from among the elected Members of the Autonomous Council.

Encroachment of Council's administrative authority (Case-I)

Supposing a teaching staff with requisite qualification and experience engaged by the autonomous council requires moving from pillars to posts to regularising their service following the submission of a fictitious report by the principal to the Higher Education Department. One can ask a question to gauge the severity of the communication gap: Why does the College under the Council's jurisdictional areas not like to seek the autonomous body's opinion even if it is essential? Such an impasse happens to crop up when the college officials boast of being higher ranked than some Council officials. The former needs to devote more time deal with such issue. If the college authority is to send any report against the council's engaged teacher to the Government, they are to route such cases through the engagement authority. The office of the College Principal cannot ethically exercise such an option unilaterally.

The college authority is not the final authority. Because if the Council notices their authority has remained encroached, they may raise objections and the State Government in the Hills Areas Development, in the case of Assam, requires sorting out any misunderstanding between the two entities – autonomous body and State Government.

Likewise, some departments' staff under the administrative control of the Council get sometimes their Modified Careers Assured Schemes sanctioned by their directorates. Again, however, they required getting the issue dealt with by the Council because it was best known.

In such a situation, the feeling of the people is that a leader holding the charge of the Chief Executive Member of the Council should cite some examples as others did on the first engagement of the teaching staff of the Haflong Government College.

Elected representatives aware of the autonomous Council's role help iron out many administrative creases. The bureaucracy always feels duty-bound to remain answerable to Dispur. In such cases, the role of the elected representative calls for giving justice to the deprived lot hailing from the Council's jurisdictional areas. The state officials always tend to encroach upon the jurisdiction of the autonomous body.

Transactional ethics
(Case-II)

Ethics and reasons apply well to the transactional businesses between the Council and non-entrusted Subjects. With this, the power of the Council seems more utilised, as above.

On the other hand, the Council cannot exercise over the Higher Education Department. However, supposing a degree college exists in its jurisdictional area, the Autonomous body can exercise its ethical control over the educational institution.

For instance, the Government needs to appoint some teachers in the college timely, because the students' studies suffer. In that case, the Council can recruit qualified teachers locally on a contract basis, fill up the sanctioned strength of posts as per recruitment rules and forward copies of engagement letters to the Government for Approval.

At the same time, if some officials of the Higher Education Department obstruct approving the selection of the contractual faculties of the colleges, the councils may write to the Government to honour the former's decision as a Borrowing Authority. By insisting on regularising their services towards granting justice to the local candidates, the selection of candidates by the Councils itself reflects the fulfilment of the aspiration of its people, for which the autonomous body exists.

Moreover, supposing the contractual teachers appointed by the Council are above-board residents of its jurisdictional area. In that case, the officials of the Higher Education Department cannot auspiciously question the authority of the Council in the interest of fostering the relationship between the two entities.

Secondly, assuming the Higher Education Department orders the transfer of an affiliated college of one university to another within the jurisdiction of the Council based on the opinion of the Principal or Head of the particular college or Education Department. In that case, the autonomous council can intervene in the transfer order. Citing the reason for a unilateral recommendation by the head of the Education Department of the particular institution, jurisdictional areas, the authority with the mandate of the people has the right to speak of their interest.

Broadly speaking, the more power the authority utilises, the more it feels satisfied. The majority tribe of the Dima Hasao wants to integrate with all its tribe members who have settled outside it under a political platform.

Similarly, the Nagas of Nagaland and Karbis of Karbi Anglong and West Karbi Anglong crave the same privileges. Likewise, other ethnic groups of the whole North Eastern region have fostered the spirit of unity. The issue of unification and integration of the ethnic groups in the entire North-eastern Region of India is a complex one. If you solve the problem of one entity, others crop up in no time.

Child Care Leave Sanction
(Case-III)

Assuming that a lady executive's service gets placed under the disposal of the Dima Hasao/North Cachar Hills Autonomous Council, with the recruiting authority attaching her to the office of the Council Head of the department under which she got a permanent job. Having been recruited as an executive, she now tied her nuptial knots with Prince Charming. The cohabitation led to the birth of a child after about two years of the couple's matrimonial alliance. Hence, she decides to avail of the privilege granted for Child Care as per the Leave Rules of the Government of Assam.

In such a case, she is to apply for such a Child Care Leave to the Secretary to the Government of Assam through the proper channel – presuming the Council Head of Department establishment where she has got her posting under the administrative control of the autonomous body as above and the Principal Secretary to the autonomous body.

The official cannot submit any Leave application to her Sanctioning Authority at Dispur directly through the Council Head of the establishment and the State Head of the Department.

Her application should route through the Council Head of Department and Principal Secretary, Dima Hasao/North Cachar Hills Autonomous Council to the Sanctioning Authority because her service gets placed under the disposal of the autonomous body, the official now draws a monthly salary from the budget allocation of the council. Given the premise, the autonomous body has every right to exercise its power over whether the officer deserves the concession of her prayer. Without the recommendation of the council as the head of the particular department, the Service Lending Authority (State Government) cannot ethically sanction any of such leave.

Any sanction of leave by Dispur without the prior recommendation or approval of the Council based on the Council Head of Department's recommendation infringes upon the established code of conduct of transactional business between the North Cachar Hills Autonomous Council and the State Government as per the standing agreement between the two.

Inconsistencies in Transferred Subjects (Case-IV)

During the tenure of the District Head of Departments, some officials of the State Government did not scrupulously exercise their power vested by the Autonomous Council as per the standing agreement between the two entities - State and Council.

For instance, they entrust the settlement of contribution towards the Group Insurance Scheme by the Grades III & IV staff to the State Heads of Department.

Secondly, they forward the proposal for the Voluntary Pension Scheme opted by the staff to the State Heads of Department;

Thirdly, some State Heads of Department insisted on not allowing the District Head of Department to approve the technical sanction of any schemes if they are not a permanent incumbent.

These issues above have not formally concurred on granting the Technical Sanctions from the State Government nor the North Cachar Hills/ Dima Hasao Autonomous Territorial Council, Haflong.

The State Head of the Department of the Council's Transferred Subjects has drawn controversy over the authority to grant technical sanction of schemes.

Plugging the loopholes

Mentionable, all the Divisional level Officials of the State Subjects under the administrative control of the Dima Hasao Autonomous Council belong to the Assam Civil Services, and the District Head of Department of the Council's jurisdictional area is a member of the same category of senior post.

The anomaly results from the need for a clear-cut standing order from the authority of the Dima Hasao Autonomous Territorial Council. All grants should go by the person who holds even the temporary charge of the District Head of the Department should get executed by the Chair, not the seniority of the position.

CHAPTER-IV

Etymological Alignment

Colourful tribe members, their stocks and identities; Stocks' likeness, lenience and language & analogy between Dimasa and Tripuri; A Good Samaritan; Dimasa monarchs & their rapport; Transactional relationship; Transactional relationship; How do we have the Dimasas, the descendants of Bhim in Mahabharata; Generosity & Secular propensity; Titbit on man and matters

Colourful tribe members, their stocks and identities

In Assam Janata Bhavan, there is the Hill Areas Development Department. All files relating to the administration of the hilly areas of Assam, namely Dima Hasao, Karbi Anglong and West Karbi Anglong, go through the entity of the Government of Assam.

Its inhabitants are colourful. As per official records, thirteen tribes are the inhabitants of Dima Hasao: the Dimasas, Jemes, Kukis, Hmars, Baites, Karbis, Jaintias, Hrangkhols, Vaipheis, Rongmais, Thadous, Mizos and Khelmas. Apart from these tribe members, non-tribal settlers like Bengali, Gorkhas, Manipuris – Bishnu Priyas and Meites; and Biharis, Punjabis, Assamese and others, including a few people from Southern India.

The non-tribal settlements, like Bengali and Gorkhas settlements, originated from the days of the Dimasa regime after the British entered the hilly region of Assam.

The need for vegetables and milk in their daily food led the British to allot grazing and cattle rearing to the Gorkhas in the erstwhile North Cachar Hills. Many of them also worked as labourers of the North Eastern Railway, which brought them to work in constructing the railway track passing through the above district of Assam.

Some of them also built temples in different places and spread spirituality. So, it is safe to say the Railway construction works, along with the rearing cattle and spreading the message of Hinduism, caused the birth of the Gorkhas' settlements in the erstwhile North Cachar Hills (presently Dima Hasao). Regarding the Bengali settlers, you'll get to know in other pages dwelling on rapports of the Dimasa monarchs with the Bhadralok.

The Gorkhas have several stocks on which one can comment because many details are already available. However, some tribes have no such niceties. Hence, let me try to incorporate a few lines about the Dimasa and Jeme tribe members (sic)

Stocks' likeness, lenience and language & analogy between Dimasa and Tripuri

We now turn on stocks' likeness, lenience and language of the tribe members.

Let me dwell on one of them as an example – the majority tribe member (Dimasas) of the Dima Hasao, because the relationship between two men starts from the exchange of words, which we call language, and everything flourishes through it.

The Dimasa tribe members seem broadly divided into four stocks - the Hashaosha, Hawarsha, Dembrasha and Dijuwasha. Those who hail from the Dima Hasao belong to Hashaosha; the Hawarshas are from the Cachar, Karimganj and Hailakandi areas; the Dembrashas relate to the settlers of Lanka, Hojai and Nogaon areas. The Dimasa, having the origin of Nagaland and Karbi Anglong, belong to the Dijuwasha.

In the Dima Hasao, the majority belong to the Hashaosha. Though Wargongsas are also from the same clan and the population density is small, they seem chiefly scattered stocks in the district. Likewise, there are the Hamrisas whose presence one can spot in the Thaijuwari area. In the same way, we find the Semsas group from the tribe members in the hilly region whose roots are in the Semkhor area.

Some prominent persons from these groups are worth knowing.

For instance, Veer Sambudhan Phonglo, one of the freedom fighters from the tribe during British rule, married Nosodi, one of the residents of Semkhor. She belonged to the Semsas. Similarly, Palon Chandra Langthasa, former Chief Executive Member, hailed from the Semsas group, to which Sonaram Thaosen, Ex-Minister Assam, also belonged.

Among many alive and rendering services, Kulendra Daulagupu, the former Executive Member of the North Cachar Hills Autonomous Council, belongs to the Wargongsa group. Dilip Nunisa, the former DHD supremo, hails from the Dembrasha clan of the Dimasa.

However, the first IAS officer from the Dimasa tribe member, Bikram Thaosen, who is no longer among us, belonged to the Hashaosha, to which Jatan Kumar Thaosen, the former Member of the Assam Public Service Commission, also belonged.

Each clan of the Dimasa slightly differs from others in their language or accent. "The Dimasa tribe members do not resemble the present Hindu Assamese people of the Brahmaputra Valley, from a cultural and anthropological standpoint. Some used to practise the Shakta religion of Bengal, and some followed the animistic faith, in which they treated the cow (Mushu) as impure (gushu)", said Dhruba Hojai. Some still follow the tradition. However, they are from the same tribe members, said Debojeet Thaosen, the erstwhile Chief Executive Member of the North Cachar Hills Autonomous Council.

By the way, the people of Semkhor are culturally akin to the Jeme tribe. As such, they can speak the Jeme dialect with equal fluency. Likewise, Zemes could speak the Dimasa language during that time.

According to Dr Dhruba Hojai, who belongs to the Dimasa and is no longer alive, forty of these patriarchal clans were present in the Zeme community and still exist to some extent.

Further, the original language of the Tripura tribe has some similarities with the Dimasa tribe members of the Dima Hasao (sic).

As for the collocation of the Dimasa words with the Kok-borok (KB) language of the Tripura State, it seems to have happened ever since the reign of Monarch Kumar Dakshin, who ruled the southern part of the Dimasa Kingdom in the last part of the 14th century. King Kumar Dakshin was the 2nd son of the Dimasa King Trilochan, the tribesman monarch. The latter ruled the Dimasa kingdom during the 14th and 15 centuries.

Replying to a query, one of the stakeholders of tribal society from the State of Tripura, Bikash Roy Debbarman, who is himself Minister in the present BJP party Government in the State, said, "Kok-Borok and Grau-Dima (GD) belong to a common ancestry. Almost 80 % of Kok-borok root words are either the same or have a specific pattern of sound shifting in Dimasa dialect.

According to Debbarman, "Any word that ends with 'au' sound in Grau-Dima (Dimasa language) becomes words ending with 'ok', 'ng', 'ao' and 'ak' in Kok-borok (KB). Here are the examples: "Gashao (rotten-GD)) – kosok (KB); Gathang/ Guthang (GD) (red) – kuthang (KB); gajao (GD) (red) - kuchak (KB)"

Further, when the question of the development of the Dimasa language comes up, one must know its origin. As per reliable sources, the language has become popular after the entry of Dimasa monarchs into the erstwhile district of North Cachar Hills (now Dima Hasao).

Previously, the Dimasa intellectuals like Joy Bhadra Hagjer and Sonaram Thaosen were the prominent persons who founded the Bodo Sahitya Sabha, and both were proficient in the Bodo language. For instance, the latter was the first president of the Sabha during the period 1952-1966; the latter was General Secretary.

Some of the prominent tribe members, like Dr Dhruba Hojai, admitted the two intellectuals above were of the view the Dimasas would be stronger if they could get identified as Bodos, for the people recognised them as the Bodo during the reign of the Dimasa monarch in some parts of the Brahmaputra valley. Under this circumstance, they formed the literary organisation hoping to assimilate the two tribes – Dimasa and Bodo – into one nation. However, the geographical gap and their failure to attend to every need while shaping their vision into reality occasionally between the two localities impeded accomplishing the task above.

Further, while pursuing their idea into reality, the two visionary leaders departed. Meanwhile, Satish Chandra Basumatary became the first President of the Bodo tribe in 1966. Still, he was the successor of Joy Bhadra Hagjer, the first president of the Bodo Sahitya Sabha in 1952, and the latter served about seventeen years as President.

Having demit the presidentship of Bodo Sahitya Sabha, Joy Bhadra, and Sonaram started concentrating on developing the Dimasa language. At this juncture, the Bodo language developed to such an extent that it got incorporated into the Eighth Schedule of the Constitution of India. So now, there is scope for doing post-doctoral courses in the Gauhati and Bodoland Universities, unlike the Dimasa, which lagged due to the lack of support from its intelligentsia.

As mentioned, the Dimasa once ruled the State of Tripura. Hence, some Tripuris, who speak the Kock-Borok dialect as their mother tongue, could talk to Dimasa as fluently as the above two Dimasa visionaries. The two visionary leaders above also knew the Bodo language, so they held the positions of President and General Secretary of the Bodo Sabha.

Be that as it may, the Dimasa language has started seeing the light from the tunnel's darkness. The Tezpur Central University has already reached the final leg, preserving and developing the script of the dialect. So, one must keenly observe how the contents of the MoS will fulfil its objective as per the standing clause of the Memorandum of Settlement inked between the Governments – Union and State – and the Dimasa National Liberation Army.

When the question of analogy crops up, it is not only the language, but the annual harvest festival of the Dimasas is also the same as that of the Tripuris. Their semblance is visible when one compares their festival, Bisu and Busu. Some Dimasa intellectuals point out that the original name of their Busu was Bisu, and the Tripuris celebrate their festival by the name. Admittedly, the present-day Dimasa tribe members call the festival Busu Dima.

Be that as it may be, the Bisu or Busu is the post-harvest festival of the people who celebrate it in almost all States of India in different names. The Dimasa might not come out open sticking out how they feel about the Tripuris, but one can keenly observe how the educated and mature former show the latter.

However, the difference between them has little relevance here. So, one likes to say there is some similarity in broadmindedness, which helps one draw the above proposition. Of course, everybody is not similar, but an analogy is possible from the political and intellectual relationship between two individuals.

On the other hand, when an individual's action turns memorable, it finds a place in history. Here's an example how Umananda Longmailai Barman saved the Dimasa tribe members' identity:

A Good Samaritan!

Some said the similarity between the two tribe members – Jeme and Dimasa – led to the growth of inter-caste marriage, posing a subtle threat to the identity of the Dimasa tribe members. Hence, once social reformer Umananda Longmailai Barman saved the tribe members from the intercaste union, popularly known as Gushu-Gathar. Thus, his noble exercise helped the tribe members escape the extinction of their identity (sic).

Citing an example of his relation to one Haikembe Zeme (Lungkhip) of Mabao village in the Hadingma Constituency to the North Cachar Hills Autonomous Council, Dr Hojai said Zeme originated from Hojai. The relations between the two were those of uncle and first paternal nephew.

Dimasa monarchs & their rapport

The relationship of the Dimasa Kings with Bengali was always cordial, which one can gauge from the speech of one Chief Guest in a literary meet called Nikhil Bharat Banga Sahitya Samelan,

Haflong Branch. He said that kings Suradarpa, Krishnachandra and Gobindachandra translated a part of the poem and prayer song they composed in Bangla.

According to him, the King emphasised the need for following 'Danda Nidhi' or Kachari Niyam written in Bangla and Sanskrit by Suradarpa, later modified by Krishnachandra and Gobindachandra are the last Dimasa kings.

Mentionable, Maibang was the main centre of learning during the reign of King Tamradhvaj. And it was Sonaram Thaosen, who related to the erstwhile Prime Minister of the Dimasa Kingdom, who first began popularising the tribe's language in the Dima Hasao. Kulodhar Ranjan Hojai used to take equal interest in the language, and both once undertook a study tour to Tripura and Bodoland Territorial Council before the tribe members adopted the Roman Script.

Together with the sameness in their stocks, there are some tales of friendship among other tribe members who seem immortal.

Further, the establishment of villages of different tribe members took place near each other, highlighting the interdependent nature of the tribes people of various types.

Transactional relationship

One would like to corroborate the transactional relationship of the Dimasa King with Bengalis. A history researcher from the tribe member said that during the reign of the Dimasa King, the currencies of the kingdom floated in Bangladesh plenty, which proved the cordial business relations with Bangladesh before the British dethroned the tribe's dominion.

Further, one is to reiterate that several of the founder members of the erstwhile North Cachar Hills studied in Bangladesh. On the other hand, some prominent elders of the district underwent some Gurukul teachings; one was Naiso Daulagupu, who reportedly had a Guru when he was in a Gurukul Bangladesh.

Mentionable, the people of Haflong Constituency to the erstwhile North Cachar Hills District Council, elected a Member from the Bengali community. He was Harimoy Das Barman, on whose name a brief biographical story I have already inserted in my last published title.

By the way, his uncle, Gynandra Das, was also responsible for constructing the Lord Jagannath temple at Haflongmarket, in the heart of Haflongtown.

Thus, the Bengalis have been equally in charge of spreading the message of Hinduism and Buddhism, like some Gorkhas of the erstwhile North Cachar Hills (now Dima Hasao).

By the way, the Buddhist Gorkhas of the locality are slightly different from their counterparts belonging to Hinduism.

How do we have the Dimasas, the descendants of Bhim in Mahabharata?

The Dimasas, one of the oldest tribe members of the North Eastern region of India, are the descendants of Bhim and hold a majority in Dima Hasao, whose name we find in the Epic, *The Mahabharata*. In a write-up to the social media, Dr Dhruba Hojai, former Director of Health Services, Government of Assam, said the son of Bhim and Hirimdi helped Pandavas win once the battle of Kurukshetra.

During Mahabharata, the actual name of the present Dimapur was Hidimbapur, also known as Dimbapur, which subsequently got the name of Dimapur, and the Hidimbapur (Dimapur) was under the reign of one King Hidimba, who had a sister named Hirimdi. Bhim of Pandavas tied nuptial knots with Hirimdi. He married the princess after obtaining permission from Pandavas' common wife, Draupadi.

She reportedly granted permission to Bhim, stating that he would not live with Hirimdi after the birth of a child. So, the marriage by Bhim after obtaining Draupadi's consent seemed righteous. Afterwards, Bhim left Hirimdi following the birth of his son Ghatotkacha. Bhim's son was a great warrior who had the potential to defeat Kauravas on the Kurukshetra battlefield.

As Ghatotkacha appeared invincible, Duryodhana ordered Karna to kill Bhim's son by using the powerful weapon of Dev Raj Indra reserved to kill Arjun. Thus, Hirimdi's son lost his life in the battle of Kurukshetra. But he paved the way for ensuring the Pandavas' victory on the battlefield.

Generosity & Secular propensity

Everybody knows the Dimasas were one of the oldest tribe members of the North-eastern region. They ruled some parts of the countryside, besides fleeing from Assam to Dimapur. Afterwards, they shifted to Maibang. However, the escapee character of the tribe kings does not alone attribute to fear or rue; it sprouts from an urge for freeing from subjugation. Nevertheless, they faced suppression from the Muslim, Ahom, and British rulers.

The longing for freedom and their repeated take-off indicated a non-confrontationist attitude of the Dimasa Kings

– Does the same relaxed attitude of the tribe members who settled beside the river have enough potential to suit the word "Dimasa" (Di – water/river; masa – settler/dweller= Settler/dweller of the big river)?

But, as the water of the river is serene and peaceful, the tribe elders were peace-loving, apart from being kind, not suspicious, or hard-hearted, which is noticeable from the exhibition of their hospitability when they truly represented the presence of all tribe members of the hilly region before the Bordoloi Sub-Committee, which received a representation before the grant of the District Council.

Titbit on man and matters

The relation between man and matter! Some say the date of birth of the stakeholders of their particular locality matters much. To which category does the Thursday-born man belong? It is a pertinent question. So, my friends would like it when asked and answered the literary titbits simultaneously.

Some people born on the date 13th May belong to the prominent literary group but appear outwardly a bit lazy. But, at the same time, some are sound executives or politicians. Even if they do not get an opportunity to serve better, they try to excel in whatever they do. Both prominent politicians of Dima Hasao – Nandita Gorlosa and Debolal Gorlosa– belong to the same date.

Of course, getting an opportunity is not reach of everybody; I always turn a bit philosophical and shift my thoughts towards satisfying myself, citing an example for me:

"Even if somebody does not belong to the group above, there are writers. So, let us dwell on writing in the Dimasa language, which brought few laurels during his lifetime; Sonaram Thaosen has been getting it now. But he seeded the spirit of literature in the tribal dialect during his lifetime in the erstwhile North Cachar Hills. At the same time, nobody can reject the contribution of Jatindra Lal Thaosen and associates who first formed the Dimasa Sahitya Sabha. These Thaosens also carried out several literary translations.

Apart from these, Phanindra Johari wrote a dictionary in the language from the tribe member. It was for the first time in Dima Hasao. Of course, other writers in the speech were there in the Cachar district.

When the question of Hmar comes up, much of the contribution credit must go to V.L.T. Bapui. Their monetary investment towards developing their respective languages brought little return, but they rendered a yeoman service to their communities.

Let me cite an instance of Bhanu Bhakta's contribution. Even if he did not get what he deserved during his lifetime, he needed to catch up on rendering services to his community. His literary activities helped many people understand what the epics – The Ramayana – contained in it. In an easy language in those days, he made a tremendous contribution.

Every writer above contributed a lot towards their languages.

Likewise, the accessible translated version of the epic above by the Nepali poet helped the community shape their customs, traditions, and beliefs. They interpret most of the contents of the epic in their transactional business. Hence, even in the twenty-first century, some people in the community are honest beyond expectation. Because they have firmly fixed their innocent and orthodox beliefs in deep inner consciousness, it guides them to be practically genuine in their transactional business.

The benefit of opting for innocence always ensures peace and progression in every field; modern social life is complex, and the primarily innocent get used or created for the benefit of the intelligent. But the success of the wise at the cost of the guiltless does not last long! Hence, often, the clever seem to suffer from different kinds of problems because they seed difficulty in them as they try to outsmart others. So, every whit of courage applied by the intelligent for harming the ignorant or weak seems unpardonable in the language of the vast existence reflected in literature or books written by great writers, for which many regard litterateurs as the torchlight of society. Literature sources from languages; man's speech originates from their heart, and every heart relates to it differently.

It is the voice of existence and gets disseminated among the people through the communication or writing of a man in various types, subtly interpreting the language of reality.

So, the Nepali Language was already in existence but had no shape of its richness. Bhanu Bhakta facilitated its development by translating Ramayana from Sanskrit.

Nobody perhaps thought it necessary, nor could everybody translate the epic into Nepali from Sanskrit. Nor did the poet perhaps believe he would ever get a pat on his back for solving it after him.

Contextually, like the Dimasa writers who have translated some works of epic into their language, other tribes may well follow it so that it helps all groups know the spirit of India's unity in diversity.

Given the presumption, a man interested in literature seems gifted with the different aspects of imagination – one that an individual does not expect anything in return if they feel inspired to do something worth lessening the toiling masses.

Lastly, there is no success without hard work, which does not go unnoticed. What man did does not matter; how they inspired other new generation writers does it. It reflects the history of man in their literature, dwelling on the discovery of every society.

CHAPTER-V

Republic & Ethos

How does the division of people get fostered; Tear-jerking regional force growing up; Sixth Schedule unrelated schemes not harmful in Dima Hasao; Panchayat Raj haunting in Dima Hasao; SSPC, hunger strike, Autonomous State issue: More power uprising and After; Panchayat Raj and Autonomous Council's Difference; GI Tag syndrome of land encroachment: Separate Electoral Roll for NCHAC; Whither any encroachment of tribals land; Election trends; Electorates' arbitration; Electorates in exercising their choices -I;

How does the division of people get fostered?

Having learned about growth and development, we now dwell on Dima Hasao's ethos. First, let us be clear: India is a unique abode of multi-ethnic and cultural settlers. But what is somewhat familiar is that an average observer like me sees an individual quickly attracted to others from the same ethnic and cultural backgrounds. When they go to a new place, they see if the people from their locality are present. Because the presence of familiar persons helps them interact, the attitude is visible in almost ninety per cent of the country's citizens.

However, the above outlook is more robust in the North easterners. It has penetrated to such an extent that it does not inwardly reject the idea of calling for a separate locality belonging to various groups. But, of course, some of our political enthusiasts feel comfortable fueling divisive growth to fire ensuring their position.

Today, society has become the breeder of suspicion and hatred; even a tiny issue tends to snowball into a significant political controversy. For, even the wrongdoer blatantly gets backed by the community people, one finds the region seems divided into two groups – liberal and obscurantist.

What I find unbiased is that people in the region get united to speak, not to scrutinise, against any issue. For instance, some political enthusiasts fuse over minor issues, which the people do not examine; even if they are politically motivated and harmful, they support them as though somebody's intention was always favourable.

So, any issues raised by political enthusiasts turn out to be the final proposition in the countryside, and many times, some trifling cases get over-sensitised.

From the layman's perspective, one sits as an opponent who trades on suspicion and hatred for political gain, and another belongs to what goes on under the ruling dispensation.

We have rooted in the above ethos. Thus, there is a need to foster a strong leadership that deals with the wrong without fear and favour in the Dima Hasao. But, unfortunately, as the body politics of the whole region subtly seethes with dissent from inequality, greed and arrogance, the hilly area of Assam, as one of the parts of North-eastern India, tends to get swept away by the evil of perennial debate from time to time.

It is essential to look at the following political heartbreak of the North-eastern region.

Tear-jerking regional force growing up

In politics, the desire to have power eclipses some people's vision, which leads to the butchering of the people off and on. The enthusiasm to wrest it is high and does not guarantee everlasting peace, fulfilling the immortal craving for influence. It is a strange phenomenon in the North-eastern region where every entity's eyes are getting major.

Of course, some have valid reasons for getting swamped by immigrants. But on the other hand, the race for power encourages division brought about by inevitable competition. Some participants in such power games even go to the extent of allowing the settlement of the migrants, inwardly longing to realise the façade of accomplishment.

Besides, the faulty provision, which allows the distant clan members to settle into the permanent residents' locality without restriction, poses potential threats to the latter group. How?

Supposing the intelligence of the distant stokes' kin happens to defeat that of the permanent residents one and construing it as a privilege granted to an individual after an outcome between two. Similarly, an individual who is the leader of a particular social unit wins the election.

The participants in the power marathon about some groups lose their relevance by not following individual growth and development. Thus, when the support brings about an inevitable breach of trust between the two, it becomes evident that an individual supports their group candidate. When victory gets celebrated by the non-deserving candidate, it harvests the seeds of heartburn, portending the danger of permanent discord in society.

After that, it mars an age-old relationship that exists between or among the permanent groups of inhabitants in their short-sighted game for a better tomorrow. But peace ensured the idea of supporting the cause of the people who are the permanent residents of the particular region instead of indulging in sheltering the distant clan members or immigrants, hoping a better political future for their social units. Further, it helps in working out modalities for streamlining all elements posing imminent threats to the survival of the permanent residents of the locality concerned, right from the birth of intelligent competitors in the distant stokes, which take away the vitals of the permanent residents.

In such a situation, the presence of a secular leader or candidate in whose leadership the people repose is a must to work out policies and plans — some of which are also inclusive in the narrative — that ensure safety and security to all permanent settlers of the hilly region.

Frankly, the region remains out of the sight of peace in the area where the competition for a better tomorrow a community has yet to accept all the stakeholders of the society. Subtly, it asserts that any changes foretelling no better prospect for a community should only get the support of some conscientious stakeholders of individual social units.

Sixth Schedule unrelated schemes not harmful in Dima Hasao

As per the Sixth Schedule to the Constitution of India, the State Finance Commission assigns the revenue of the Dima Hasao Autonomous Council in exercise of the financial power guaranteed to the autonomous body. The Government of India initially envisaged a two-tier system of administration, having a strong Central government at the centre and states as its components. But the 73rd Amendment Act, 1992 formalised the addition of one more tier to the existing two, subsequently recognising a three-tier system of governance, consisting of a village or district, State and Central level each. We know the grass-root level of administration by the terms "Panchayat Raj", which is synonymous with the 3F type of administration – money, power and rulers (aka funds, functions and functionaries).

Now the three-tier system of management stands partially modified with the grant of the Autonomous Council (also known as North Cachar Hills/ Dima Hasao Autonomous Territorial Council) at the district or local or village level of administration in the Sixth Schedule areas of Assam.

Under the circumstance, the Sixth Schedule Protection Committee advocating direct central funding needs to know the devolution of funds by the State Finance Commission supplements the proposed Dima Hasao Autonomous Territorial Council's resources, and not to supplant the autonomous entity. Hence, the report of the Standing Cabinet Committee headed by Anand Sharma highlights the opposition of the State Government to the direct Central Funding.

Within the ambit of its existing autonomy package, the rulers of the autonomous body need to make a determined and sustained effort to augment the Council revenue, apart from sticking out their administrative skill in managing the day-to-day financial requirements of the Dima Hasao Autonomous Council.

Of course, there is mess between the two entities – State and the Sixth Schedule Protection Committee supporters speaking in favour of more financial power to the Autonomous Council. The actual demand of the SSPC is to take back the 125 th Amendment if it does not align with necessary provision for a direct funding to the Dima Hasao Autonomous Council from the Central Finance Commission.

The dilutionary projection of the implementation of certain Clauses by some officials of the Panchayat Raj institutions in contravention of the Memorandum of Settlement seems to create a golden opportunity for the SSPC to harden its stand.

For instance, the officials occasionally use certain phrases in the execution of schemes by the Panchayat and Rural Development. In contrast, some tribal leaders bristle at some phraseologies like "Panchayat", "Sarpanch", "Gram Panchayat", "Gram Panchayat Secretary" and "Gram Sabha" used by the departmental officials in formal communications to their counterparts of the Dima Hasao within the jurisdictional boundary of the Dima Hasao/ North Cachar Hills Autonomous Council where such words are uncommon or foreign to the people of the countryside.

So, the paraphrasing subtly widens the growth of suspicion, working out dissent towards separation between the State and hill areas of Assam. They alleged the Government conspired aligning with the Panchayat Raj institutions.

Given the circumstance, some went to the extent of opposing the Directorate of Panchayat and Rural Development to directly correspond with the Council, irrationally dictating to route their correspondences through the Hill Areas Development.

On the other hand, the Government, from time to time, requires exercising its role conferred to examine and amend some Clauses as envisaged in the DHD Accord towards fulfilling its commitment made.

In the fewest possible words, it is due to the lack of scrupulous paraphrasing of above terms by some Department officials involved in exercising their role to implement certain Clauses of the Sixth Schedule that harvested the seed of concerns among the three entities – State, Dima Hasao Autonomous Council and Sixth Schedule Protection Committee.

Agreeing on it or not, in implementing relevant clauses, conspicuous by their presence in the 3F type of administration under the Panchayat Raj Act in the Sixth Schedule Areas, the Government requires involving in extending some schemes to the sixth schedule areas.

For example, during the Sixth State Finance Commission, the Haflong Town Committee got upgraded to Haflong Municipal Board. Apart from that, the presence of such clauses in the above Act perhaps facilitated enhancing the status of the Chief Executive Member and other Executive Members beyond the jurisdictional areas of the Council for protocol purposes. As per Clause 3.1 of the Memorandum of Settlement, signed between the DHD and Government, the rank of the two guaranteed for protocol purpose was within the jurisdiction of the Dima Hasao Autonomous Council.

By the way, there was also a recommendation in the Sixth Finance Commission in which the Town Committee (equivalent to ULB) should have a democratically elected body to "benefit from the recommendations for grants of the Central Finance Commission and the State Finance Commission". As a result of this recommendation, the Haflong Municipal Board must have got the posting of an Assam Civil Services Cadre officer. However, the official did not reportedly get his joining.

Undeniably, as per the recommendation of the Sixth Finance Commission at Sl. No.110(v), the Principal Secretary to the Dima Hasao Autonomous Council started receiving the Direct Transfer of annual allocation from the Finance Department of the Government of Assam.

Thus, though it may not be rational to say all clauses implemented within or outside the ambit of Panchayat Raj administration are repugnant to the people of the Sixth Schedule areas if there is no threat to the existing autonomy guaranteed to the Dima Hasao Autonomous Council under the Sixth Schedule to the Constitution of India, some leaders of the Sixth Schedule Protection Committee bristled at the official phraseologies.

Panchayat Raj haunting in Dima Hasao.

The Panchayat Raj system seems applicable in India, where there is no provision for the implementation of the Sixth Schedule to the Constitution. The centralisation of power deprived some sections of society of development. However, it is optional in the Autonomous Council areas.

For instance, the Government of India constituted the North Cachar Hills and Karbi Anglong Autonomous District Councils under Art 244(2) of the Sixth Schedule of the Constitution. The Constitution of the autonomous bodies became necessary after the submission of a report by the Gopinath Bordoloi Sub-committee. The Government entrusted it to study the economic condition of the Tribal communities of North Eastern India in the aftermath of the formation of the Constituent Assembly. As such, several tribe members formed a political entity – Autonomous Council/Territory –to ensure the economic development of their respective regions after the Constituent Assembly approved the relevant recommendation by the above Committee.

So, in some parts of India, the people have already been enjoying the power to rule their locality under the above Constitutional Provision. The autonomy package to the erstwhile North Cachar Hills Autonomous Council under this schedule includes the grant of a political entity. It can dominate some state subjects, which the Government transfers to the political entity.

The sixth schedule came into force under the Government of India Act 1935. The Act classified Tribal areas of the undivided Assam. The State comprised Arunachal Pradesh, Meghalaya, Nagaland, Manipur, Mizoram, Tripura, and Assam. In addition, the Government classified the Northeastern region into three parts: Excluded, partially Excluded and Frontier areas.

The erstwhile North Cachar Hills and Karbi Anglong came under Excluded and partially Excluded areas, respectively. So, it is because these areas' administrations were not under the jurisdiction of the Provincial Government; they were under the direct control of the Government of Assam. Nevertheless, the practice is still in vogue, treating them as Assam's hilly regions – namely, Karbi Anglong, Karbi Anglong (West) and Dima Hasao.

Under the existing constitutional set-up, the Council's territorial areas' power seems rooted in the Village Council/ Constituency Development Committee or village-level traditional system for development activities.

However, there were speculations about introducing the Panchayat Raj system in the Autonomous hill districts – Karbi Anglong, Karbi Anglong (East) and Dima Hasao – in Assam to ensure better development. The Government allegedly contemplated that the autonomous regions of Assam's hilly areas remained backwards due to the lack of sincerity on the part of the people's elected representatives of their respective Council areas.

Introducing Panchayat Raj means replacing the traditional system. But, according to a political leader from Dima Hasao, Tripura's fate will occur upon the people of Assam's hilly region if the Government introduces the Panchayat Raj.

Commenting on the Panchayat Raj issue, Joel Gorlosa, who once fought for more powers to the North Cachar Hills Autonomous Council, opposed any move to introduce it while insisting on preserving the Sixth Schedule to the Constitution of India. Though he did not contest in the just-held Council election, many genuine issues aired need a judicious hearing because cross sections of the greater Dima Hasao society still support him. He spent fourteen years in jail for the cause of the hilly area of Assam. Even if some in Dima Hasao now take such issues to simple political rhetoric, the Government in Delhi and Dispur would do well to examine them from a proper perspective. All moves should ensure everlasting peace in the region.

Another leader's view on the issue is that if the Government wants to introduce the Panchayat Raj, the people should first get their privileges granted under 244(A) or Full Statehood as per the existing special Provision in the Constitution. The constitutional Provision has existed since 1969 and deals with Karbi Anglong and Dima Hasao.

Thus, the above fear in the minds of the hill people led to raising a hue and crying against it. Some persons who taught and raised the issue believed the Government was attempting to dilute the Council's power.

An organisation called Sixth Schedule Protection Committee (SSPC), which came out of the disgruntled elements of the former ASDC, Congress and BJP in Dima Hasao, has already submitted a memorandum to the Assam's Chief Minister, Dr. Hemanta Biswa Sharma through the Sub Divisional Officer (Civil), Maibang, highlighting the demands on: -

1. Withdrawal of Order No. DH/RD/MGNREGA/ GPDR-1183/2019-20/64 dated: 25-09-2019, introducing features of the Panchayat Raj Institutions in Sixth Schedule areas, which is inconsistent with the constitutional provisions(sic);

2. Protection of Sixth Schedule Autonomy Against the 125th Constitution Amendment Bill,2019. The SSPC strongly opposed the proposed amendment bill that jeopardises the autonomy and rights guaranteed under the Sixth Schedule(sic).

The tribal intelligentsia implored the concerned authorities to invite and involve the representatives of the SSPC to review the observation of the Annand Sharma Committee justifiably before the Lok and Rajya Sabhas pass the 125th Constitution

Amendment Bill 2019, reminding of the proverbs, "Prevention is better than cure" and "A stitch in time saves nine"! It foresees an uncertain future as the tribal leaders find some of the recommendations are contrary to what the stakeholders have proposed, subtly emphasising the need to work out a solution to the political aspirations of the hill people. (sic)

Be that as it may, there is an order dated 12th September 2022 passed by the Hon'ble High Court in a Case No. WP©/3854/2021, filed by Kome Kemprai and two hundred twelve others. He was the son of Late Bojendra Kemprai, a resident of the village Tularam, in the district of Dima Hasao, Assam, Haflong. It states:

1. No such record on issue of Notification for implementation of Panchayat Raj System in Dima Hasao District is available in the department (*representing Panchayat & Rural Development of the Government of Assam*);

2. The office of the Project Director, DRD (*District Rural Development*), Dima Hasao is available in the district of Dima Hasao. The main function is development of rural area and rural poor people;

3. No such record for amendment of sixth schedule to the Constitution of India for extension of Panchayat Raj System in the sixth schedule area of North Cachar Hills Autonomous Council of Dima Hasao district is available. (sic)

Nevertheless, some well-wishers of the SSPC pointed out Meghalaya and Mizoram are also under the Sixth Schedule Areas but are fine. According to them, introducing the three tiers of the Panchayat Raj in 1978 led to the Balkanisation of some tribal groups. For instance, it reduced them to the status of a minority, confining them to the Tripura Tribal Autonomous District Council areas.

So, they are reiterating the demand for a Separate State known as Tipraland for the tribals who once ruled the entire State of Tripura.

Afterwards, some leaders of the ruling party, Bharatiya Janata Party, clarified the issue, denying the allegation against the party, saying there is no such proposal for replacing the traditional rule.

Hence, any efforts towards introducing the Panchayat Raj system would seem irrelevant in the Sixth Schedule areas if it were not to dilute the existing powers of the Council. The people covered under the Provision of the Constitution have already been enjoying power transferred to them as per the standing agreement between the Government and the people. Of course, there is slim chance for anybody to balkanise the tribal society in Dima Hasao where the leadership seems well-read. However, it will be a big achievement for everybody if both SSPC and ruling regime work in tandem with each other.

SSPC, hunger strike, Autonomous State issue

Till today, there is no individual democratic representation in either house of parliament between Haflong and New Delhi. Of course, the people of the hilly region of Assam have only one Member of Parliament to represent both Karbi Anglong and Dima Hasao. The lone representation does not fulfil the aspiration of the people of the erstwhile North Cachar Hills, which is an abode of the various groups.

Though the BJP Government of Assam led by Dr. Himanta Biswa Sharma, Chief Minister sympathetically looked into the aspiration of the people of this countryside in the past, it would have shown a good gesture to them if he worked out a nomination of their representative to Rajya Sabha. Or let the contest of the Lok Sabha MP candidate from Diphu Constituency be worked out on agreed terms between Karbi and Dimasa.

One does not know if it is right to ask: why does the Karbi candidate only get to contest from the Diphu Parliamentary Constituency? Are not the Dimasas in majority, Dima Hasao, and can not contest from this constituency? Because the seat seems reserved for the tribals, and the majority Karbis have hitherto got privileged from the reservation, there is a need to take cognizance of the issue and chalk out mechanism to mandatorily elect a Dimasa candidate from this Parliamentary constituency. The proposal should get implemented in the right perspective if the Government can not sanction a Parliamentary Constituency for the people of the Dima Hasao – an abode of officially recognised thirteen tribal groups and non-tribals, not specifically meaning for any particular tribe members better fitting to rule of the hilly region of Assam – Karbi Anglong and Dima Hasao. Mr. J.I Kathar echoed the view in a press meet.

Undeniably, Dima Hasao has the higher representation of various groups of people than Karbi Anglong, but it may not be in terms of their population, although. Next, the Dimasas are one of the oldest tribe members of the North Eastern region, and have the record of being secular and liberal in their give and take approaches towards all smaller brethrens in Dima Hasao. Hence, one feels it right to say it is not unwise to get the Dimasa tribe member candidate elected from the Diphu Parliamentary Constituency every alternate term of five years till the Dima Hasao gets a Parliamentary Constituency. And as the leaders of the Brahmaputra Valley, including the present ruling dispensation, the Assamese Danguria would do well to look into the sensitive issue of the various settlers of Dima Hasao where, agreeing on it or not, the seed of division gets always fertilised from the source of Karbi Anglong. As a result, the main issue gets diverted towards trifling it, though it is bitter to accept the truth.

Amidst the demand for an MP and two more Members of Legislative Assembly, which the Government did not concede in the recently concluded delimitation, a nomination to Rajya Sabha, if worked out by the leaders of the Brahmaputra Valley, would doze off the fire of aspiration of ethnic politics till the Government implemented the proposal above. When the question of preserving the right and aspirations of the people of Dima Hasao and Karbi Anglong comes up, the blessings of the Brahmaputra Valley are absolutely necessary. Besides, the symbol of strength of all groups in Dima Hasao in Rajya Sabha could have by now pursued solution to such relevant issues as the 125th Amendment Bill and Panchayat Raj.

However, the issue of Panchayat Raj and the demand for an Autonomous State raised by the Sixth Schedule Protection Committee (SSPC), in the long run, seems to substitute for the erstwhile Autonomous State Demand Committee movement, in which the people had to suffer from many prominent persons' death and the destructions of public properties. The ASDC's movement gained momentum after the celebration of the Dimasa Students' Union conference at Maibang. It is premature to say if the SSPC concluded seven-day hunger strike on the 18th of July 2024 will finally shape the future movement of the outfit.

Agreeing on it or not, the birth of the ASDC movement led to the birth of many fissiparous elements in the entire northeastern region, under the leadership of Dr. Jayanta Rongpi. Nevertheless, I don't ever demonise the SSPC because it has got the moral support of both politically conscious tribals and non-tribals. Hence, I liked the District Administration receiving a memorandum consisting of the main demands of the party. In hindsight, my suggestion for an election/nomination of the Dimasa candidate of the present Dima Hasao to Lok Shaba or Rajya Sabha is not without any humane reason above.

But it remains unjustified in supporting J.I. Kathar, a member of the All-Hill People Leaders Conference who said in a press meet during their hunger strike by the representative of SSPC, that the influx of non-tribals posed a threat to the tribals if he meant for Dima Hasao.

In the case of the large chunk of the non-tribals doing business in Dima Hasao, which perhaps sources from the local tribals' licences! Regarding restricting the leased-out stalls, the stakeholders of Dima Hasao should decide, instead of fueling an uncanny apprehension of being swamped by them going by J.I Kathar's suggestion. Further, there is no threat from the white colour jobs seeker non-tribals in the council conducted recruitment of staff pertaining to the Grades III & IV posts of the Transferred Subjects' office establishments for more than a decade, everybody knows it is below one per cent in these categories. Of course, my assertion does not reject the recruitment of teachers and other grade-III categories of post carried out by the State Level Recruitment Board in the educational & other institutions. Hence, I don't think the non-tribals pose a big threat to their tribal brethrens. Further, not a single non-tribal has ever got privileged without the tribals' sanction. On the contrary, my submission would be not to lose the legacy of the past. Moreover, a permanent non-tribal does not ever imagine taking out any bread from their esteemed tribal brethrens.

Personally, one would like to go by the stand of Joel Gorlosa, who publicly admitted it not wise to privilege anybody, whether tribal or non-tribal, who is not a permanent resident of the Dima Hasao. Contextually, without a Permanent Resident Certificate and North Cachar Hills Autonomous Council Voter List each in the jurisdictional areas of the Dima Hasao Autonomous Council, nobody should avail of any facilities granted under the Sixth Schedule to the Constitution of India.

On the other hand, it is heartening to note that the North Cachar Hills Autonomous Council/ Dima Hasao Autonomous Territorial Council has already set up an Election Cell at its secretariate. Now that it has already come into existence, the Election Cell should get scrupulously activated in ensuring every grant of privileges to the people. The officials dealing with the subject should have the sense of being and belonging to the Dima Hasao. It will go a long way in addressing any inequality within the jurisdictional areas of the Council, apart from obviating the problem of influx in future the countryside. So, the political enthusiasts require thinking of improving education together with an economic independence of the permanent residents, not in terms of politics or the particular social units

By the way, given the subsequent statements of Joel Gorlosa and Daniel Langthasa, Adviser and Convenor respectively of the SSPC not going by what J.I Kathar said, which one could understand when they appealed to all sections of the greater Dima Hasao society, including the non-tribal settlers of the Dima

Hasao who have settled since 1950 or so, to join their hands with the outfit for realising the objective of an Autonomous State.

Contextually, there arises a representation from the majority tribe member in Lok Shaba or Rajya Shaba, subtly shimmering a better acceptance of all ethnic groups of Dima Hasao. Because the smaller tribe members and non-tribals have hitherto accepted the Dimasa tribe members' leadership, perhaps due to the conspicuous absence of any historical blunder by the oldest tribe members of the Northeast.

Likewise, my support to a Dimasa tribe man as Member of Parliament does not speak any evils of other tribe members of the Dima Hasao.

Though the non-Dimasa tribe members or non-Karbi members are hard-working, hospitable and honest in the countryside, they have not yet stuck out having free from the clutch of their particular clansmenship in politics.

For example, the North Cachar Hills Autonomous Council/ Dima Hasao Autonomous Territorial Council allots Executive Members from all major smaller tribes. Despite being conspicuous by their presence in every ruling dispensation, their lending a helping hand to other tribe and non-tribe members does not ever stick out the acceptance of their individual leadership by all tribe members.

Intriguingly, when the Indigenous People Forum (IPF) sponsored an agitation against what they called the deprivation of all non-Dimasa tribe members in the past, not a single minor tribe group came out in appreciation of whatever the major one hitherto offered to all ethnic groups in Dima Hasao, thereby exhibiting the symptom of their conditional support to the outfit. It apparently undermined the objective of the party pledging the voice of all smaller groups of non-Dimasa tribe members of the hilly region. Assuming that only an intellectual leadership brings about changes in any society, on which both arguments for and against the movement get traded to examine their merit, the leadership of the IPF could not justify their stand, subtly facilitating the majority leadership to contain the influence of their opponent in the past.

Hence, my suggestion reflects the unbiased recommendation above for the Dimasa Tribe member. At the same time, it would be wise for us to honour the views of all stakeholders in the interest of ensuring peace in future the hilly region.

To know the past history of separation, we need to have a look at a few issues which ignite unrest in Dima Hasao.

More power uprising & After

The misunderstanding between the leaders of the erstwhile North Cachar Hills along with those of Karbi Anglong and Dispur over sharing privileges during the Assam Gana Parishad (AGP) ruling of the State Assam led to the demand for more autonomy package in the Assam's hilly region.

In the hilly borough of Assam, the movement for an Autonomous State spearheaded by the Autonomous State Demand Committee, Dimasa Students' Union, North Cachar Hills Students' Federation, and others ignited the growth of regionalism, laying stress on preserving culture, community and land for the first time in the Dima Hasao's history. Its impact was the increased intensity of the subtle division of people.

If division happens to originate from any other ulterior motives, the logical idea of it tends to root in the feeling of insecurity or deprivation. So, the planners would forever do well to work out modalities to contain the sense of universal egoism, leading to an impasse in which the State, country, or district loses many precious lives. Any standoff in Dima Hasao is not an exception; every problem sources from economic deprivation.

Anyway, the ASDC movement initially aimed to achieve an autonomy ensuring a direct Central Funding of the hilly regions of Assam – North Cachar Hills and Karbi Anglong. The Sixth Schedule Protection Committee's demand is also getting the same tune of the ASDC.

However, the Anand Sharma Committee recommendation in Clause 2 Para 3.1.11 states as under:

"The Committee feels that direct funding of ADCs by the Centre will not only be against the existing Constitutional scheme but also would unnecessarily affect the relations of ADCs vis-à-vis State governments adversely. The very purpose of amending Article 280 of the Constitution is to make an institutional provision for augmenting the resources of ADCs through the State Finance Commission. The said provision is on the lines of Article 243(I) and 243(Y) meant for Panchayats and Municipalities and 73rd and 74th Constitution Amendment Acts"

Commenting on the Clause above, the Sixth Schedule Protection Committee in a memorandum to the Chief Minister of Assam said any amendment of the "Article 280 of the Indian Constitution on the lines of the Articles 243(I) and 243(Y) will adversely affect the sacred tribal institution and spirit of the Sixth Schedule to the Constitution of India".

The 125th Amendment Bill of the Sixth Schedule to the Constitution of India proposed by the Government aimed at fulfilling the need to implement certain clauses of the Memorandum of Settlement, which the tribal militants signed with the Government – Central and State – in 2012. The Sixth Schedule Protection Committee (SSPC) demanded of the Government to let the people know how the it planned to amend the Sixth Schedule. And how was the response of the Council to the proposed amendment? Afterwards, the Dima Hasao Autonomous Council held an interactive session of all stakeholders. On the occasion, the Chairman of the Council, Mohet Hojai discussed in detail with them, apart from seeking their opinions to carry out necessary additions and deletions in the Council's replies prepared to submit for onward action, at the District Library Auditorium, Haflong on the 14th of July 2024.

Further, a delegation of the ten Autonomous Councils led by the Chief of the Tipra Moth Party (aka Tipraha Inndigenous Progressive Regional Alliance), Pradyot Bikram Manikya Deb Barman, met the union Home Minister, Amit Saha, to whom they submitted a memorandum each, highlighting their grievances. The Home Ministry formed a committee headed by Nityanand Rai, Minister of State for Home Affairs, to study their problems and submit a report within one month.

Frankly, the Union Government would do well to include one Dimasa tribe member from Dima Hasao in the three-member team headed by the Union Minister. Of course, only a Karbi tribe member, namely, Elwin Teron from Karbi Anglong, has been representing the hilly region of Assam.

The main points of demand of the Sixth Schedule Protection Committee (SSPC) are: -

i)   All funds released from the Centre should get deposited into the District Fund/Personal Ledger Accounts of the proposed Dima Hasao Autonomous Territorial

Council. The SSPC argues the Council should not allow anybody to encroach upon its financial autonomy guaranteed under the Sixth Schedule. As such, there should be no involvement of the State Finance Commission in utilising its earnings – revenue receipts and expenditures.

ii) The Dima Hasao Autonomous Council should get the privilege to avail of the similar relaxation the Autonomous Council of Meghalaya enjoys. The Meghalaya autonomous council does not require electing members of the Village Council. The SSPC, without opposing other councils' right to exercise the choice, is of the view that electing the village council amounts to politicising the sanctity of traditions and customs hitherto preserved by the tribal villagers.

Further, whether they are the Dimasas or other tribe members, who are already covered under the schemes adopted by the Panchayat Raj institution in Plains, their lots have not improved much more than those of the people of the Sixth Schedule Areas, remarked Samarjit Haflongbar, former CEM, who also wants the Government to include one senior member, whether from opposition or Sixth Schedule Protection Committee, Dima Hasao.

iii) The SSPC does not agree on the Assam Government's objection in which the latter cannot adopt and implement any big projects if the land right gets bestowed upon the Autonomous Council. It points out the North Cachar Hills Autonomous Council's no obstruction in the conversion of Broad-gauge track of the N.F. Railway and the construction of the National

Highway No.27, which are the two big projects of the Government and their implementation has been going on without any obstruction from the Council. Hence, the land right should rest with the proposed Dima Hasao Autonomous Territorial Council, which could hardly be the cause of any obstruction in allotting land to carry out similar prominent projects.

iv) The Governor of Assam, on the advice of the Chief Executive Member of the Dima Hasao Autonomous Territorial Council, should nominate four Members. Any nomination without the people elected Executive Committee's recommendation undermines the objective of the establishment of the autonomous body.

v) There should be an independent entity to deal with all matters relating to the election of the autonomous council under the sixth schedule – conducting election to the Member of the Autonomous Council, deletions and inclusion of the voters' names. Its independence seems guaranteed without losing an autonomous character, similar to the Election Commission.

vi) If the Government can establish a mini Secretariate at Silchar and upper Assam, which is similar to an Autonomous State, and the Dima Hasao holds the status already since the signing of a Memorandum of Understanding between the Autonomous State Demand Committee along with its sister organisations and Government, there should be no opposition to the direct funding to the Dima Hasao Autonomous Territorial Council (DHATC).

vii) Scrap the reservation to nominate two female members, out of the four Government nominations to the proposed DHATC. Because twelve seats, out of forty, already exist in the one-third reservation proposed for them in the 125th Amendment bill.

The feeling of the tribals of Assam and Tripura is the same. However, the stand of the Assam Government is different because it is well aware of the problem of the tribals, unlike the Government of Tripura run by the non-tribals.

Be that as it may, the autonomy package along with the movement for an Autonomous State always provide many political aspirants with their leadership qualities, as it did in the past, after the ASDC's movement was over. In the interest of ensuring peace and tranquility in the hilly region of Assam, the State may well work out an absorption plan for the new political brains, apart from convincing the SSPC by making its real intention clear.

By the way, the reference of the Anand Sharma Committee report above is contextual only. The main point of the ASDC's movement is after the party came to power, some of its supporters left their government jobs, which they offered to their spouses, because they had an understanding with the Council leaders who needed the support of able people to work in the party.

Secondly, the people who offered help to the movement leaders had an equal potential to lead their respective groups of people of the Dima Hasao. So, when they got no political privileges to enjoy in return for their help to the party's leadership, they poisoned the people's minds by seeding hatred or demanding division or separation.

Thirdly, the leaders of the above outfits should have realized the gravity of the situation when they encouraged the formation of different groups of people in Dima Hasao. Some even went to the extent of assuring in meetings about granting autonomous regional councils. The concept of autonomy ensured the unity of the people and helped the parties' leaders garner the masses' support on the ethnic line. There was a time when the parties' leaders enjoyed the status of a Saviour of the ethnic groups.

What is heartening to note is the division did not ensure disunity in the hilly region of Assam, given the presence of the Dima Hasao Autonomous Council, which is an abode of representations of all major groups of people – the Dimasa, Jeme, Kuki, Hmar, Baite, Karbi, Jaintia and Hrangkhol.

Thus, the spirit of patriotism is alive.

We now turn to dwell on the 125th Amendment, 2019

The 125th Amendment Bill, 2019

When the Government – Central and State – signed a Memorandum of Settlement, granting more autonomous powers to the proposed Dima Hasao Autonomous Territorial Council, with the tribal militants, namely, Dimasa National Liberation Army and Dimasa Peoples' Supreme Council, whose movement for the above issue led to the birth of the agreement, it brought about an inevitable implementation of certain clauses as committed in the agreement.

While fulfilling the commitment, certain concerns and misgivings on the 125th constitutional Amendment Bill cropped up, requiring addressing. So, they held an All-Party Meeting on the 28th of August 2024, which the Chairman of the Dima Hasao Autonomous Council, Mohet Hojai, presided, apart from Sri Debolal Gorlosa, Chief Executive Member, who addressed the meet, Sri Elwin Teron, former Executive Member of the KAAC, represented as an advisor to the Chief Executive Member, Karbi Anglong Autonomous Council. Several political parties, including Bharatiya Janata Party, (BJP) Indian National Congress (INC), All India Trinamul Congress (AITC), Autonomous State Demand Committee (ASDC), Aam Admi Party (AAP), All Party Hill Leaders Conference (APHLC), Sixth Schedule Protection Committee (SSPC) took part in the meet on the 28th of August 2024.

Before we understand the stand of the Dima Hasao Autonomous Council ruled by the BJP, let us know why and how the Government of India intends to amend the Constitution of India. Accordingly, the Constitution (One Hundred and Twenty-fifth Amendment) Bill, 2019, inter alia, provides for the following, namely: -

(a) To amend article 280 of the Constitution enabling the Finance Commission to recommend measures needed to augment the Consolidated Fund of the States to supplement resources of the Sixth Schedule Autonomous Councils, Village Councils and Municipal Councils;

(b) To rename the existing autonomous District Councils;

(c) To increase the number of seats in the District Councils;

(d) To provide for reservation of at least two seats for women in the District Councils;

(e) To transfer additional subjects to Karbi Anglong and Dima Hasao Autonomous Territorial Councils;

(f) To constitute the State Finance Commissions in the States having the Sixth Schedule areas;

(g) To conduct elections to all Autonomous Councils by the State Election Commission;

(h) To provide for disqualification of elected members on account of defection.

Earlier, the Dima Hasao Autonomous Council held an interactive session of all conscientious citizens, including some prominent citizens, participated in it at the District Library Auditorium. The council's agreed terms on the existing clauses under the Sixth Schedule to the Constitution got known after the interactive session was over, which we may stick out in the given tabular form as under:-

Clauses No of Memorandum of Settlement signed on April 27, 2023	Existing clauses under the Sixth Schedule to the Constitution of India	Dima Hasao Autonomous Council's agreed terms after a public interactive session and an All-Party Meeting
2.2	**2. Constitution of District Councils and Regional Council** Paragraph 2 has been amended in its application to the State of Assam by the Sixth Schedule to the Constitution (Amendment) Act, 1995(42 of 1995), s.2, so as to insert the following proviso after paragraph (3), namely: "Provided that the District Council constituted for the North Cachar Hills Autonomous Council constituted for the Karbi Anglong District shall be called as Karbi Anglong Autonomous Council"	In the Sixth Schedule to the Constitution, (a) In paragraph 2 (i) In sub-paragraph (3), for the first proviso shall be substituted, namely: - (b) The District Council constituted for the Dima Hasao District shall be called the Dima Hasao Autonomous Territorial Council;

2.4 - POLITICAL	**2. Constitution of District Councils and Regional Councils –** [(1) There shall be a District Council for each autonomous district consisting of not more than thirty members, of whom not more than four persons shall be nominated by the Governor and rest shall be elected on the basis of adult suffrage] There is no provision of reservation for woman member to be nominated by the Governor.	In the Sixth Schedule to the Constitution, (a) In Paragraph 2 (i) In Sub-paragraph (1), after the proviso, the following provisos shall be inserted, namely: - Provided also that the Dima Hasao Autonomous Territorial Council shall consist of not more than forty members, of whom four members including at least two women members shall be nominated by the Governor and rest of the members shall be elected on the basis of adult suffrage.
2.5	(6) The Governor shall make rules for the first constitution of District Councils and Regional Councils in consultation with the existing tribal councils representative or other representative tribal organisation within the autonomous districts or regions concerned, ad such rules shall be provided for - (C) the qualifications for voting at such elections and the preparation of electoral rolls therefore.	8)The superintendence, direction and control of the preparation of election rolls for, and the conduct of, all elections to the District Councils, Regional Council shall be vested in a State Election Commission appointed by the Governor of the State. Provided that nothing in this sub-paragraph shall apply to a Village Council and Municipal Council in the State of Meghalaya until approved by the Governor of the State.

6-Institutional Change	[Article 244(2) and 275(1)] **Provisions as to the Administration of Tribal Areas in [the States of Assam, Meghalaya, Tripura and Mizoram] 2. Constitution of District and Regional Councils: –** (7) The District or the Regional Council may after its first constitution make rules [with like approval) regulating – (a) the formation of subordinate local Councils or Boards and their procedure and the conduct of their business.	Bill No. VIII of 2019 The Constitution (One Hundred and Twenty-fifth Amendment Bill,2019 "2A.(I) Within a period of one year from the date of commencement of the Constitution (One Hundred and Twenty-fifth Amendment Act,2019, each District Council shall establish Village Councils for a village or a group of villages in the rural areas and the Municipal Councils for an urban area or an agglomeration of such areas of the District".
6.8	Provision not available	In Article 280 of the Constitution, in Clause (3), after sub-clause (c), the following Amendment sub-clause shall be inserted, namely: - "(ca) the measure needed to augment the consolidated Fund of a State to supplement the resources of the District Councils including Village Councils and Municipal Councils in the tribal areas within the State referred to in clause (2) of Article 244 on the basis of the recommendation made by the Finance Commission of the said States"

Having cast a look at the Constitutional Amendment Bill, let us now examine the difference between Autonomous Council and Panchayat:

Panchayat Raj and Autonomous Council's Difference

As per the Panchayat Raj Act, governance is rooted in a three-tier administration structure for rural development, beginning with districts, zones, and villages. The aim of the Act was to organise village Panchayats by devolution of powers, enabling them to function as units of self-government.

Under the Sixth Schedule to the Constitution, a state government, the Council, formed by the Member of the Autonomous Council (MAC) to implement plans and policies, including schemes adopted. They (MACs) are thus the representatives of the people who elect the former.

The MACs, as elected representatives of the people, exercise their role of representing the people who choose them to exercise the governmental authority, adopt and implement (plans and policies, including schemes) the role in the different capacities of appointed officials.

Contextually, if my conscience does not misguide me in the Sixth Schedule areas, the elected Member with the majority support of the people rules the Council, an institution analogous to Zilla Parishad. The Village/Constituency Development Committee/Council Members who participate in electing MACs represent the will or choice of the people, subtly defining the fulfilment of the administration term equivalent to the Panchayat Raj as above.

To distinguish between the two entities—Panchayat Raj and Autonomous Council—the Government—representing both State and Central—adopts schemes, frames policies, and makes plans. In the Panchayat Raj system, it is the Zilla Parishad (District Development Council) or Gaon/Gram Panchayat whose duty is to implement them through their functionaries.

The head of the Gaon/Gram Panchayat is Sarpanch, who has minimal power to exercise in economic and social welfare, unlike an elected Member of Autonomous Council who acts as an Executive Member, enjoys the privilege of a Minister of a State. One cannot imagine any dilution of such a vast power given by the State. Still, there can be the possibility of misinformation or the misuse of it by the elected MAC as they are allowed to undermine their position when in power backed by the voters, for which I have cited several Cases as examples of how the power of the Council gets encroached in the book.

So, in the case of the Sixth Schedule type of administration, the State (speaking of the Central and State Governments) adopts schemes, frames policies, and plans through its official functionaries. The Government's responsibility to implement all adopted plans and policies rests with the people's representatives.

In exercising the role of the Autonomous Council, the elected Members of the Autonomous Council (MACs) not only act in the capacity of Executive Members (EMs) and Chief Executive Members (CEMs) through their bureaucracies but also represent the support or will of the Constituency/Village Development Committee/Court/Council.

Further, in the scheduled area, participation in the formation or representation of the Central and State Governments lies in electing a Member of Parliament (MP) and a Member of the

Legislative Assembly (MLA) from the territorial jurisdiction of the Autonomous Council. All the elected representatives of the people or voters are directly or indirectly participants in the formation of the Village Committee/Court/Council.

Though some have raised a hue and cry over the issue as above in Dima Hasao, there has been no formal communication from the Government stating any need to infringe upon the Council's autonomy by implementing the Panchayat Extension to Scheduled Areas (PESA) Act, 1996.

Moreover, even the former Chief Minister of Assam, Sarbananda Sonowal once said there would be no introduction of any Panchayat Raj in the Dima Hasao district.

On the other hand, one must honestly admit there is no harm if the Government implements some development schemes, which it carries out within the jurisdictional boundary of the Panchayat Raj institution, in Dima Hasao.

By the way, the PESA Act aims to grant privileges by devolving political power, by which the tribal people can participate in electing their representatives to act for their development. In exercising the role as stated, the elected representatives are to preserve and safeguard the customs and traditions conducive to their requirements, thus preventing the higher authority from unilaterally infringing upon the rights of the village people, which is guaranteed.

Such rights as above were hitherto not available for the tribe members outside of the States of Meghalaya, Mizoram and Nagaland and the hilly region of Assam in the North-eastern region, where no provisions for any Panchayat Raj exist, nor does it seem essential, given the presence of Autonomous Councils for fulfilling the political aspirations of the tribals under the sixth schedule of the constitution. The power guaranteed under the above Act to the Panchayat already exists in the Sixth Schedule areas. So, the chance is minimal to dilute the Autonomous Council's autonomy for accommodating clauses envisaging the development of the tribal region.

When the party-led Executive Committee to the Dima Hasao Autonomous Council decided to implement the Gram Panchayat Development Project in the District, the opposition leaders accused the ruling party of having reduced the status of all 28 constituencies to that of a SARPANCH, which is equivalent to GB or Mukhiya(sic).

The contention is that the Member of Autonomous Council of the Dima Hasao Autonomous Council enjoys the rank of Member of the Legislative Assembly, and the position of the Chief Executive Member of the Council is analogous to the Cabinet Minister of the State.

The opposition was recently referring to the content of the Memorandum of Understanding, whose signatories were the Union Government, State Government and Autonomous State Demand Committee, Karbi Students' Union, Dimasa Students' Union and North Cachar Hills Students' Federation at New Delhi on the 1ˢᵗ April 1995 in the presence of the Union Minister, S.B Chavan.

According to the school of thought, the Dima Hasao Autonomous Council should not have accepted the GPDP, which the Government implements under the Eleventh Schedule of the Constitution of India. The apprehension is that if the Dima Hasao Autonomous Council implements such schemes pertained to the Eleventh Schedule, the Government might clandestinely impose the Panchayat Raj System, making the role of the North

Cachar Hills/ Dima Hasao Autonomous Council under the Sixth Schedule of the Constitution redundant. Therefore, the intelligentsia shrewdly corroborated with the Government of Assam's proposition to rename its Hill Areas Department as the Sixth Schedule Areas Development Department. However, the BJP Government rolled back following the stiff opposition by the people of the hilly regions – Dima Hasao and Karbi Anglong and West Karbi Anglong.

I want to commit to my memory of a political leader from Karbi Anglong commenting on the aftermath of an agreement with the Karbi underground outfit. He said, "What is pertinent to remember is that governments worldwide, under any political dispensation, are reluctant to part with power unless they are under some compulsion. The BJP is under no compulsion to devolve powers to the hill people of Assam. The BJP would aim to make political gains for the present and the future. It might need a more dedicated force to ensure victory in the coming Karbi Anglong Autonomous Council election. This move is also part of the long-term plans of the BJP for a permanent foothold in Assam. The BJP was lucky enough to scrape through the Assam Assembly election.

This forthcoming agreement could be part of the larger strategy of constructing new political equations in Assam that would be more durable than the present ones. But, unfortunately, this style of creating new vote banks seems borrowed from Congress".

GI Tag syndrome of land encroachment

Though Meghalaya is a full-fledged State of the Indian Union, it still functions under the Sixth Schedule. The existing provision has enough potential to smoothen the functioning of the Autonomous Council. Likewise, some residents of the Council jurisdictional area in Dima Hasao feel such provision fosters the growth of healthy relationship between the Council and State, which exercises its control guaranteed within the ambit of autonomy sanctioned to the autonomous Council under the Sixth Schedule, which ensures power similar to a State.

Under these circumstances, should the Government wipe out all clauses obstructing the smooth functioning of the transactional relationship between the North Cachar Hills Autonomous Council/Dima Hasao Autonomous Council and the State Government? It subtly envisages a new creation, for which the Government may have hitherto restricted such a grant to the people of the hilly region of Assam.

However, the exercise of power unnecessarily creates fear, which the two entities could sit together well and work out modalities that kill the snake without breaking the stick.

The people of the Assam's hilly region – Dima Hasao and Karbi Anglong -feel the Government introduced the Article 244A to grant a special autonomous status to them. Enacted in 1969, this Article aimed to address the unique socio-cultural and administrative needs of the hill people, allowing creating an Autonomous State within Assam. This provision was to provide these regions with greater control over their administrative affairs, including Legislative Powers on matters specified in the State and Concurrent Lists (sic)

How does one detect the anomaly? To go by the standard conscience, when the Government of India wants to take up schemes for developing the hilly region, it must allot more funds direct to the Dima Hasao Autonomous Council. In contrast, the

Government sometimes chalks out some schemes – including the acquisition of eight villages in Umrongso areas where a plan reportedly exists to establish a Cement Plant. How can that convince the people of Dima Hasao that the Government has done an excellent job? Because there is a political institution with autonomous power to rule, the plan could have been processed to execute with the involvement of the North Cachar Hills Autonomous Council/Dima Hasao Autonomous Territorial Council backed by the village headmen in the territorial area of the autonomous body. I, for one, say, "Absolutely Right"! Where do the Government officials know which schemes are suitable for implementation by sitting at Delhi and Dispur? All answers perch on the supposition that the Government collects information about the feasibility of implementing schemes based on the online geographical indication (GI), popularly known as the GI tag.

In the aftermath of the selection of some schemes and the allotment of works to contractors from outside of the hilly region without allowing the share of participation of the authority of the North Cachar Hills Autonomous Council/ Dima Hasao Autonomous Council, the decent efforts towards development made by the Central and State Governments ignite the feeling of the encroachment upon its jurisdiction. So, those who hitherto felt proud of being citizens of India, born and brought up in Dima Hasao, governed under the Sixth Schedule to the country's Constitution, think of a systematic deprivation of their power granted to the Dima Hasao Autonomous Council. So, they insist on:

1. Implementing Article 244A by honouring the commitment made to the tribal communities and

> providing them with the promised autonomy thereof(sic);
>
> 2. Strengthening Article 275 by ensuring robust financial support directly to the Councils, enabling them to undertake development initiatives effectively (sic).

For a generation advocating not implementing any schemes chalked out under the Panchayat Raj Act, any efforts of the Government without the autonomous Council's go-ahead do not stick out as a good gesture. Reason?

As per the standing agreement between the two identical entities—the Government and the Council—they represent Lending and Borrowing Authorities. According to the Memorandum of Settlement signed between the Autonomous State Demand Committee and the Government, the Autonomous Council can control all issues covering Transferred Subjects as a Borrowing Authority within its territorial jurisdiction. In that case, the Government is to tender its consent to the decision of the autonomous body as a Lending Authority.

According to a reliable source, some contractors outside the jurisdictional area of the Council who wanted to execute some schemes under Government sanction could not even do so.

Some knowledgeable sources term selecting a site unilaterally for executing schemes without the involvement of the Council amounts to the encroachment of the people's land in violation of the existing clause of the Sixth Schedule.

The issue of land rights coupled with the role of the Autonomous Councils is very sensitive to the tribals of the Assam's hilly region. If I am not wrong, even the British acknowledged and recognized it, though they politically divided the tribals and non-tribals and dominated them. Likewise, the founding fathers of the Indian Constitution maintained the status quo relating to the issues(sic).

In the villages, the land is a common commodity and belongs to the whole village/ villagers, and the tribe members do not usually make land leases/patta (except may be in some urban or municipal areas), because the whole land belongs to the villagers. The tribe members take pride in knowing that the land, since time immemorial, belongs to them, their ancestors and their descendants, and their very existence rests upon the land, streams, hills and valleys (sic).

Perhaps no apprehension as above would surface if the Government worked out modalities to implement the Clause 3 (c) Para 3.8.16 of the Anand Sharma Standing Committee Report, which states:

"The Ministry of Home Affairs has averred that the 125th Amendment has been incorporated to implement the Memorandum of Settlements (MOSs) with United People's Democratic Solidarity (UPDS) and Dima Halam Daoga (DHD). The Committee presumes that MOSs have the concurrence of State Government of Assam. But now the State Government of Assam has expressed some reservations about inter-alia 'land' transferred to Autonomous Councils of Dima Hasao and Karbi Anglong Districts' Autonomous Councils before the Committee. Moreover, some other stakeholders like Autonomous Councils and Members of Parliament from the State also have a contrarian view than the State Government on the subject"

Agreeing it or not, such a communication gap brews serious complications in fostering a healthy relationship between the Government and autonomous entities. Given the intensity of the demand, the Centre might grant the land rights to the

Autonomous Council of Tripura. With the authority to exercise power over the land resting with the Government of the State not dominated by them, the tribal leaderships of Tripura seem more justified in raking up the issue on the plea for being insensitive. In the case of the hilly region of Assam, it is unpredictable. The problem in other States like Meghalaya and Mizoram is abit different. For instance, the Government of these States are always sensitive toward the issue. These entities require justifying ironing out the administrative crease in the interest of ensuring a lasting peace in the hilly region.

Separate Electoral Roll for NCHAC

There is a demand for preparing a separate Electoral Roll to elect the Member of Autonomous Council. It seems to have based on the instruction of the Hon'ble High Court, for which the Sixth Schedule Protection Committee once reminded the Assam Government of implementing the contents of the judicial institution order in Case No. PIU/13/2019 dated 23-05-2022. It directs the North Cachar Hills Autonomous Council to frame necessary rules for conducting elections autonomously within eight months from the date of issuance. (sic)

Though the issue raised occasionally is genuine and deserves consideration per the existing clauses of the Sixth Schedule to the Constitution of India, we should understand the intricacies involved in executing the assignment.

For instance, if the Dima Hasao Autonomous Council is to carry out the exercise, it requires setting up a separate Election Cell, where it should recruit new staff, excluding the head of the Department, given that the Council has several secretaries whose services the autonomous body can utilize for managing it. According to a reliable source, the Executive Committee has already resolved to establish an Election Cell at the Council Secretariate, Haflong. The Election Branch of the autonomous council conceded the demand of the Sixth Schedule Protection Committee.

Agreeing on it or not, any new recruitment, whether in Grade I or Grade III & IV categories, involves extra financial burden for the already fund-crunched Council. The Council can now maintain voter lists of its own, but it can share with the District Election Office, Dima Hasao, to conduct elections. If necessity arises, the Council can well entrust the entire task to the Election Office. It is justifiable as per the Clause 2.5 of the Memorandum of Settlement signed between the Governments – State and Central – and the Dima Halam Daoga (DHD).

Though the Council is now to carry out the assignment, it must maintain a close liaison with the State Election Commission. It must have obtained the basis of the election data (supposing Voter Lists) provided by the District Election Office, which has hitherto conducted all elections – Parliamentary, Assembly and Autonomous Council.

Though the autonomous body depends on the Voters' List provided by the District Election Office, Haflong, the most significant achievement in ensuring transparency is nobody can become the voter of the Council without the consent of the autonomous body.

Commenting on the issue, Dr Dhruba Hojai, the former Director of Health Services, Assam, said: "The Assam Panchayat Act does not apply to any Sixth Schedule Areas of India as per Rules laid down by the Constitution of India. Hence, the just concluded election can be said to be illegal in the eyes of the Law. Thus, the term "Autonomous" cannot apply to the present Council conducted by the Assam Panchayat Act from the voter's List prepared by agencies other than the Council. The Constitution of the Sixth Schedule to the Constitution of India had given enough powers to the Council to make its Laws to rule the 30+ Departments given to it in 1995. The Council now needs to be more robust & not powerless to rule the Departments.

The MDCs of the first Council should have sat over a Session of the Council under the Chairperson who had the powers to make decisions to form the separate Electoral Rolls of the Council and the Customary Laws on the Constitution of the Sixth Schedule to the Constitution of India valid by accent of His Excellency, the Governor of Assam without involvement of the Council of Ministers, Government of Assam within one year which did not happen due to ignorance".

Contrarily, the Executive Committee of the North Cachar Hills Autonomous Council will perhaps have to hold consultations with all stakeholders and frame necessary legislation on how to execute this gigantic exercise. The date or year of imposition of such law based on the Voters' List provided by the Election Department of the Government of Assam may have to obtain the approval of the State Government.

Secondly, the North Cachar Hills Autonomous Council/ Dima Hasao Autonomous Council may work out the preparation of a Separate Voters' List for electing its members every five years. Once the Election Cell or Office completes the task, any inclusion of new names after the attainment of eighteen years of the electorates should route through the Autonomous Council duly approved by the Executive Committee. The method, when adopted, will go a long way to ensure transparency in electing the Member of the Autonomous Council.

Thirdly, the Council may recommend the names of new voters to the Election Office once a year if they agree on preparing and maintaining the List at the office itself. However, no intermittent submission should exist under any circumstance. Frequent recommendations for the inclusion of names encourage the birth of elements inimical to the local people's interest.

The process of validating the Permanent Resident Certificate undertaken by the Autonomous Council has been going well.

A separate Electoral Roll, coupled with an insistence on attaching the Permanent Resident Certificate issued by the authority of the North Cachar Hills Autonomous Council in the Normal Sector, where the need to grant any privileges to the local arises, will surely go a long way in ensuring the constitutional safeguards to them within the autonomous entity's jurisdictional areas, under the Sixth Schedule to the Constitution of India.

Agreeing on it or not, the widespread growth of education does not match the ever-growing population. So, the legislation, when framed and properly implemented, will successfully discourage the entry of migrants into the hilly region of Assam in search of green pastures.

Whither any encroachment of tribals land?

During the Thirteenth Council election campaigns, some prominent persons with political and non-political affiliations raised objections over what they called the encroachment of land rights of the tribals in Dima Hasao, apprehending the imposition of Panchayat Raj; rumours were going around that the Government has been trying to impose it.

However, no formal communication is available in any responsible media house about the planned introduction of the system in the hilly region of Assam, where it has no scope - one must reiterate it.

But trust some political enthusiasts to fuse over the trivial issue.

As per the sixth schedule to the Constitution of India, nobody can encroach upon the land right guaranteed to the tribals without the consent of the North Cachar Hills Autonomous Council/ Dima Hasao Autonomous Council.

If my knowledge does not play away, the North Cachar Hills Autonomous Council/Dima Hasao Autonomous Council wants to facilitate establishing Three to Five Stars Hotels in Dima Hasao following the decision of the Executive Committee to give a new thrust on tourism development.

Different from other parts of the State, Dima Hasao has limited rich people, and they can hardly afford any such investment.

On the other hand, many prominent personalities of the hilly region have made Guwahati their new abode ever since the birth of the insurgency problem.

The solution to the political problem of the hilly area of Assam long back has yet to ensure people's return home.

Agreeing on it or not, the temporary stay of the prominent persons of the locality reflects a setback for development. Everybody staying outside their home district is a choice they can exercise according to their conscience. However, their regular presence in Dima Hasao offers a good omen for the people of this locality.

So, there is no alternative to expecting outsiders' investment. They can invest in building such hotels as above to provide the required accommodation to the tourists. Thus, those who wish to invest in the sector will require relevant provisions ensuring easy access to purchasing land to establish luxurious hotels.

The authority to grant land to any party rests with the Autonomous Council. Everybody can now see that the autonomous body led by the Chief Executive Member seems more concerned than anybody else about how to work out modalities to preserve the interests of the people of the Dima Hasao.

Nevertheless, should such a problem persist, the stakeholders would do well to produce the local people with sound financial positions to carry out the task so that they can build such palatial structures on their land; else, it is no use making mountains out of molehills, the tourists should get the required facilities if we are to lure them in this locality for their long-term benefits.

Election trends

One of the striking features of the council areas in the Assembly elections is that only the support of all groups of people ensures victory for the man who participates in the election to the Member of the Legislative Assembly. Their votes get them recognised as the leader of the mass base.

In electing their representative, the electorates ensure that their leader is outwardly an apostle of secularism. I said publicly because a man may or may not be the same in private life.

Let's be philosophical in dealing with the case. Nobody is an inward saint; nobody strictly fulfils the eligibility criteria for becoming a saint, which is what I meant for that. But, further, there is no shortage of assertion, nor any material evidence fulfils the requirement of the feeling of humanity.

For instance, if you grant something to one entity, another feels deprived. Nobody looks into their heart to see if they are fit for the grant because everybody is superior to their conscience. Today, our race to possess something is in quantity rather than quality, subtly seeding the growth of vices stronger than virtue. Why has it happened so?

Electorates' arbitration

The people of Haflongtown examine the candidate's subtle transactional relationship with various groups of people. Then, they celebrate the victory in the election for a candidate, which sticks out as the proud peacock feathering.

In short, the judgment on selecting their representative counts upon the person having an outward exhibition of secular colour in their day-to-day dealing with the public.

However, in exercising their choice over the election of the Member of Dima Hasao Autonomous Council, the voters apply a slightly different strategy from their Member of the Legislative Assembly.

Take the case of the Haflong Constituency, where the voters are of multi-ethnic breeds and supposedly have different options to exercise in selecting one of the many secular candidates from the other political parties. In that case, the candidate's method of dealing with the different groups of people under different circumstances, coupled with their smartness, is considered in the election.

Of course, some candidates tried to garner community support on communal consideration. But their people rejected them, perhaps feeling the snake does not deplete its poison intact even if it gets milk-fed regularly. But, on the contrary, it spreads the tentacle of toxins, among others.

In the past, the most prominent faces who got elected from the Haflong Constituency of the erstwhile North Cachar Hills Autonomous Council election were Rup Kumar Daulagupu and Nindu Langthasa. Unfortunately, the latter is no longer among us. However, his son, Daniel Langthasa, got elected from the Haflong Constituency of the North Cachar Hills Autonomous Council.

As mentioned, Daniel Langthasa's activities were regularly getting flooded with likes from the people of Haflongtown Constituency of the Dima Hasao Autonomous Council, who elected him five years back to represent them.

In most Assembly elections, the voting pattern has remained virtually the same for many years in almost all cosmopolitan areas of the Dima Hasao – Umrongso, Maibang, Harangajao and Mahur. Though the blueprint is not exact in the Diyungmukh regions, it does not differ very much. Especially in areas bordering the hilly region of Assam, the colony's culture has influenced the people – an admixture of different groups of people living together with a secular attitude in electing their representatives.

Everybody may have different views, but selecting a candidate in the election becomes stern when the community-wise distribution pattern of the local population is heterogeneous. I remember once my friend said:

"If you want to get elected from a locality, you should be able to get proven as a brand tomato, which gets mixed up with most vegetables. Then, it is possible to win the election with a friendlier or secular attitude. You may have the power of money or muscle, but the ballot is secret. The people will take cash or mince no word about their choice but exercise it accordingly.

At the same time, there are some people who the prospective candidates can influence with money or muscle power. But the percentage of such a group is microscopic."

Electorates in exercising their choices -I

Out of the thirteen tribes who are the residents of the Dima Hasao, the voters are metropolitan, and some constituencies of the North Cachar Hills Autonomous Council belong to the candidates of particular groups. Still, no other tribe members have ever remained repeatedly elected except those from the majority tribe members.

To begin with an instance, the Jatinga Constituency! It gets reserved for the Khasi-Jaintia candidate every term. Every political party contesting in the council election mutually allots one seat for each of the several smaller tribal groups to represent them individually in the above autonomous Council. It elects a new body called the Executive Committee after every five-year term. The ethnic group above gets one seat from the Constituency, where the population of the tribe members holds a majority.

Of course, the Constituency consists of tribal and non-tribal members of different segments as voters. Excepting the non-tribals, who cannot field any candidate, all tribal groups can well field a candidate from each of their respective groups as per the existing clause of the Sixth Schedule to the Constitution of India. And the majority tribe, namely, Khasi-Jaintia, gets a seat from this constituency.

All candidates hitherto registered as voters from the different segments of the tribal and non-tribal groups under the Jating constituency cast their votes for the Khasi-Jaintia candidate.

Nevertheless, Chungsang Haolai from the Kuki tribe broke the mould by registering his victory in the 2013 council election in this Constituency. Because the former ruling Congress party, riddled with corruption, sponsored a Khasi-Jaintia candidate, but the voters elected Chungsang, who was amiable, from the Kuki tribe!

Similarly, the Dimasa candidate gets elected every year from the Haflong Constituency because the tribe members are in the majority, and the voters of the locality seem to endear the tribe candidate. There are various groups of tribal and non-tribals enrolled as voters to choose the candidate for the seat.

Anybody registered Dima Hasao Autonomous Council Constituency voter can contest the autonomous body's election from its Haflong Constituency. Barring once in the 2013 election, Shri L. Hlima Keivom belongs to the Hmar tribe, and Harimoy Das Barman, a non-tribal, all candidates elected from the seat were from the majority tribe.

Some said L. Hlima Keivom won the council election from the prestigious Haflong Constituency when the majority of Dimasa fielded several popular candidates, putting the voters both tribals and non-tribals in a quandary who should get their votes. In the case of Harimoy Das Barman, he was the ablest candidate in those days.

Likewise, the electorate of the Garampani, Mahur, Jatinga, Diyungmukh, Langting, Maibang East & Maibang West and Harangajao Constituencies of the North Cachar Hills Autonomous Council belong to both tribal and non-tribal groups. But only the popular candidates having secular outlooks from the major ethnic groups by which the seats specifically remain reserved get elected.

There is one striking assumption among some leaders of the smaller groups of people in the Dima Hasao. For instance, they find the non-tribals always standing by the will of the majority of Dimasa. If such a hypothesis bears any syllogism, one guesses it is due to the lack of probable evidence sticking out any remarkable help rendered to the non-tribal groups by such a leader in power past. Because they exhibited concentrating their help more on their community people, the non-tribal groups perhaps remain indifferent towards such attitudes and issues.

Honestly, one cannot imagine such things, for when the tribal groups raised any issue aiming at ensuring peace, unity and prosperity of all citizens of Dima Hasao, the non-tribal groups instantly supported them.

Due to the growth of political consciousness among the people following the spread of education, the electorate of the Council's Constituencies has started asserting their right to field their chosen candidates in the autonomous body election. In the past, the leadership of the political parties would decide where they should sponsor which candidates. Now, the issue of selection has become burdensome.

For example, though the Harangajao Constituency enrolled different groups of people as voters, and the Dimasa tribe members were in the majority, they voted Thonghen Thadou to power in the third District Council election held in 1962. In contrast, the electorate of the Hatikhali Constituency was demanding the fielding of a locally chosen candidate in the Thirteen Council Election despite the Constituency remaining essentially represented by the majority tribe, namely, Dimasa.

In short, claims and counterclaims between two persons bring about a slugfest in the human relationship. The migration of voters or people from one place or Constituency to another tends to foster the growth of changes in any traditional management system. Hence, the authority of the North Cachar Hills Autonomous Council could work out relevant mechanisms towards negotiating such changes before they snowball into a major headache. A political entity sticks out to be stronger and taller when it notices such a change that it dwells exhaustively towards arresting any fissiparous elements into the prison of its authority.

CHAPTER-VI

Managerial Acuity

Pastille of Unity; Reflection work execution; District HOD of Transferred Subjects' role; District HOD's provided Services; Encountering Approaches; Grievance redressal mechanism with clients; An adverse effect of changing farming; Government entities' objectives; Government entities' objectives; Affect & remedy on eulogy; Development entity's significant parody; Fund transfer and ethical proposition; Eagle-eyed view; Stumbling Blocks in Council administering ; Stumbling Blocks in Council administering; Honouring emotion; Visible Remedies Sought; Peace ensures the ray of light; Rancorous tale.

Pastille of Unity

Though the signing of agreements with the militant groups, followed by the change of Government at Dispur and Haflong, restored peace in Dima Hasao, the division of people has not disappeared. On the contrary, they have given a new meaning to splitting up, allowing it to grow from the educational institution. Where will they get land to accommodate the political aspirations of all groups of people if the trend continues unabated? So, it is high time all groups realised the need to work out modalities to preserve unity in diversity accordingly.

For instance, community or ethnic freshers meet the educational institutions allow holding. However, the provision has ensured the seeding of division for the sake of identity. Thus, one can only guess the beauty of unity has hitherto got no chance to grow in people's minds inwardly right from a college education.

On the contrary, it seeds the idea of division by saying that difference ensures unity in diversity. They have created a subtle provision in which every student group becomes clear that they need to celebrate their individual freshers' meet because everyone is not one, nor can they achieve it – as if somebody were ensuring each group's survival with the practice.

Intriguingly, nobody has the correct answer if the difference between two individuals does not ever pave the way for uniting them. To get a response to the question, they should work out modalities towards wiping out any provision or scope for the seeding division. From the educational institution itself, the people should discourage the seeding of division, and the teachers should explain why it is essential to reject the practice after receiving the necessary instruction from the competent authority.

But then, their division perceptibly fulfils the aim of their leaders for dividing the people into ethnic lines on the plank of rendering services to their particular groups or representing them. Though the people's economic condition may not ensure development, the political enthusiasts prospered.

Thus, there is no such dream of unity. On the contrary, the systematic division ensures a perennial seething in dissent of the locality concerned – one group instantly dislikes others inwardly, if not outwardly. Moreover, the division has the potential to become a vote-capturing machine. The more an individual speaks against others, the more they become capable and trustworthy in the eyes of their people! But the impact of an individual hurling diatribe upon another is dangerous.

Hence, it is high time we broke off the seal that still obfuscates an answer to the question of how the political enthusiasts' leadership has ensured the economic development of the people. About seventy per cent of the Dima Hasao constitute the tribal population, and the farming community's economy is also agricultural and rural. The tribe members' villages are nearby forests. Their production depends on the potential woods where they carry out shifting cultivation for their livelihood. They need bamboo, firewood, vegetables, brooms, and so on. So, the main concern should be finding a solution to the problem of jhuming.

Let there be answers to these questions for optimum growth and development – What is the percentage of success against the relentless jhuming (shifting cultivation) of the jhum frontier, extraction of timbers, bamboo, and quarry products by external interest or agency? Has it not resulted in the depletion of forest resources and land degradation? Has not the increased biotic pressure from the growing population, the lack of awareness, and poverty put the forests' ecosystem and resources under extreme stress? What are the wildfire-controlling measures? How successful is the work implementing agency? Does the investment ever match with returns? If not, where lays the actual problem? Is there no gap between the demand and supply of forest resources? Does not the extent of resource depletion followed by land degradation call for immediate restorative activities? What are the manageable environmental and ecological measures available? If unavailable, does the Dima Hasao need more natural calamities like those that wreaked havoc with their lives and properties?

As for tourism development, what has impeded declaring the Hajong Tortoise Lake as a Bio-Diversity Heritage Site? Has the appropriate authority moved the Assam State Bio-Diversity Board to get it said? Why does it not deserve to be a Bio-Diversity Heritage Site? If not, the Dima Hasao Autonomous Council can perhaps intervene well.

The official records say Dima Hasao is an abode of various wildlife species: tiger, elephant, leopard, wild cats, crab-eating mongoose, monitor lizard, hill tortoise, monkey, gibbon, porcupine, hares, wild goat and various kinds of reptiles. However, has the protection agency ever conducted any census operation of the wildlife? If so, why has it yet to be made public to lure tourists or alert the villagers to be cautious?

However, the outward good governance followed by the suppression of militancy in the hilly area of Assam has stuck out the birth of peace, in which it pledges to foster fellow feelings in Dima Hasao.

Frankly, peace in a locality is possible only when there is honesty in the judicious utilisation of public funds. But, on the other hand, if there is integrity in public life, gun culture does not get practised, ensuring the mighty have the right to take advantage of some clauses in the Written Constitution.

Mentionable, if the growth of political consciousness, competition and greed becomes controlled, any place regales the story of fortitude.

Reflection in work execution.

The political enthusiasts of this countryside may know how to repeat and interpret history better than the people of any other parts of the country. But unfortunately, the search for identity in the aftermath of knowledge automation has concentrated on subtle disunity better than unity.

On the other hand, even if there is better sharing of power and privileges, the elasticity of demand or greed for accumulating wealth and property has guaranteed a façade of disunity. So, the problem is perennial. The more people get politically, economically, and socially advanced with the growth of educational facilities at their doorsteps, the more they become divided.

The community-wise meets of freshers ensure that the innocent soul or spirit of knowledge learns how to remain different or foreign to each other.

Though the groupies do not openly raise the rebellion against one another, they subtly long to remain foreign to each other, as if the growing feeling of staying unique and different ensured Heavenly bliss for everyone.

While one does not oppose anybody's political aspiration or interpretation of the history of the North Eastern Region, one should say that if peace is to remain alive in the countryside, each of the seven sister States and Delhi should work out a strict modality in which power of the people goes to the hand of the correct entity in every election and that each of the various groups' aspiration does not become the cause of the beginning and end of the civilisation.

Suppose one wants to understand the political psychology of Assam's hilly region. In that case, one should find necessary clues from reading the history of conflicts and how the political game gets organised in the most politically and administratively sensitive states–Meghalaya, Nagaland, Mizoram, Arunachal Pradesh, Manipur and Bodoland Territorial Council.

Though there is a call for a sporadic unity of the three hilly districts of Assam – comprised of Dima Hasao, Karbi Anglong and West Karbi Anglong – the true spirit of politics gets delicately seeded from the six places above. I have not heard much about any ruling party leaders of the Dima Hasao and Karbi Anglong reflecting their vision in their lectures, similar to the administration of other states of the Indian union. However, several of them have even travelled abroad on study tours.

District HOD of Transferred Subjects' role

The Head of the Transferred Department in the hilly zone of Assam's State, namely, the Dima Hasao, is to assist the Dima Hasao Autonomous Council, which acts as the administrative authority per the Memorandum of Understanding or Settlement signed between the Governments and Council.

The aid to the Council by the District Heads of Department pertains to the structural allocation of funds. In addition, they monitor the submission of Monthly Accounts and the implementation of the schematic activities of their respective departments.

The District Head of the Department helps the Council frame policies, wherever necessary, towards ensuring accountability in implementing the departmental schemes and objectives in line with the latest guidelines of the Government of Assam.

Next, they assist in preparing Annual Budgets, which they approve in the Planning Board meeting they hold annually. Finally, after the finalisation of the Annual Action Plan, the Council sends it to the State Legislature through the Hill Areas Development Ministry of the Government of Assam for approval.

The State Government does not usually modify schemes worked out and submitted as the Annual Action Plan to the State Legislature by the Dima Hasao Autonomous Council.

In implementing their respective roles as the District Head of Department (DHOD) of the Transferred Subjects of the Government of Assam to the Dima Hasao Autonomous Council, the Government officials cause the implementation of their respective Departments' schemes finalised by the Planning Board annually.

In exercising their role as the DHODs, the Government Officials in the rank of an Additional Director or Additional Chief Engineer help in planning and executing the schemes adopted by the Government from time to time through their implementing agencies. Besides, DHODs issue the technical sanction of projects, dispose of the Right to Information Cases relating to their departments and recruit Grades III and IV staff in the territorial council areas of their establishments per recommendation by the Dima Hasao Autonomous Council.

District HOD's provided Services

We may reckon the services of the Transferred departments with the appointment of local staff in Grades III and IV as per the Government's standing instructions to implement all the departmental schemes passed by the District Planning Board. They stand as a vanguard of development, especially in the matter of all those schemes which are viable to give a piggyback drive upon the families of all farmers of shifting cultivation.

All State Subjects under the administrative control of the Dima Hasao Autonomous Council treat the hill people as their principal clients. Therefore, they motivate them to adopt the scientifically adopted method of agriculture practices, considering that all adopted schemes aim to facilitate the poor hill people's concerns in the district. Undoubtedly, introducing all projects by the State Subjects indeed ensures their adoption as private fiefdoms for the poor farmers.

Besides playing a vital role in improving the economic condition of the poor people of the Dima Hasao District, some state development entities have introduced the Cash Crop Development Scheme there. It consists of rubber, tea, cardamom, agar, sandal, gamari, salt, betel, broom, bamboo and guava plantations as a substitute for producing food for the farmers' livelihood. Apart from cattle rearing, including Mithun rearing, some departments also encourage piggery, duckery and bee farming.

For years, the Transferred Departments have been encouraging entrepreneurship, besides changing their development strategies, keeping in mind the ever-growing educated unemployment population.

Mention worthy, the farmers of Dima Hasao practise "jhum kheti", which is equivalent to "Shifting cultivation". Though the changing farming came into existence due to the tribal members' need in the past to search potential food areas from one place to another, and the practice turned their habit, the Government's efforts have been to wipe out the course. Because the farming puts the environment in danger, government development agencies adopted schemes like afforestation. Apart from converting the abandoned land after the shifting cultivation, the Government also encourages the farmers to adopt wet cultivation. It ensures financial grants towards executing schemes like Gully Control Work, Contour Bunding, Land Terracing, and Construction of Irrigation Channels. The afforestation mainly aims to help farming families escape the danger of soil erosion due to the "burn and slash" method they adopted to ensure their livelihood. On the other hand, it provides the availability of fuel, fodder and timber apart from stabilising the degrading of the environmental forests.

Encountering Approaches

Development entities have emphasised rooting out their age-old habit by introducing Protective Afforestation and Nature Conservation Schemes, in which they plant ornamental plants, helping the farming families get seedlings, including manures, from the Agriculture Department at free or reasonable prices.

Over the last several years, the development departments have swapped the State Plan and Hill Areas Development Plan for State-Owned Priority Development (SOPD), envisaging a sustainable goal towards ensuring a pleasant ecology and environment.

Besides, they have adopted convergence schemes, carrying out ginger, turmeric, papaya, lemon, and dagger plants (*Agave Americana*) on the existing Afforestation Plantation. The convergence aims to provide financial returns to the poor villagers during the off-season plantation. Moreover, there is an emphasis on implementing double cropping. The Government has even encouraged Groom Cultivation to ensure the tribals' economic development in Dima Hasao.

Grievance redressal mechanism with clients

Implementing the Right to Information Act 2005 has exponentially increased the volume of work. One after another, queries from the public come. To streamline the byzantine tasks, which require taking great care of even the most minor issues, some senior officials of the Allotted Subjects of the State act as Public Information Officers per the Act.

By sharing all official information with the RTI applicants within the stipulated period, as envisaged in the contour of the standing procedure of the Government, the development entities ensure an esprit-de-crop with the former. Apart from that, it restricts an ill-conceived notion of any officials towards rendering prompt public services with short reports, which brings on facing the hostility of information seekers.

Agreeing on it or not, the RTI applicants get information about the performance of the development departments of the Government of Assam under the Council's administrative control. On the other hand, each application ensures an increase in the autonomous body's coffer because the applicant has to buy the Council Services Stamp in the ten rupees denomination.

An adverse effect of changing farming

In shifting cultivation, the farming tribe members gratuitously cut down the forests, which they dry in sunlight for about one month. Afterwards, they burn the dried bushes to ashes, uproot the stumps and sow the rice seeds. Besides, they produce vegetables in the fields for their livelihood.

However, the changing farming results in the loss of top soils and causes ever-increasing landslides in precipitation. Apart from that, it poses a regular threat of soil erosion and widespread drought besides conceiving the danger of reduction of groundwater plate.

In the fewest possible words, all the development entities of the State Government of Assam are present with an overt and covert mission to wean the shifting farming away from the soil of Dima Hasao.

Government entities' objectives

Contextually, all schematic activities stand directed towards realising an undying objective – conserving natural resources like air, water, and soil. Therefore, each Entrusted Subject of the Council acts as an entity of development in the hill district. They are ensuring an ecological balance by adopting various schemes as approved by the Government to be suitable for alleviating the situation from time to time.

Undeniably, conserving the ecology and environment depends on long-term and expensive commitments. However, as long as the commitment remains alive, it induces the development entities to implement all schemes in the interest of public service effectively. Further, the Government has a similar objective towards achieving optimum success and efficiency.

Accordingly, no apprehension of expensive management should crop up in need for formulating appropriate policies towards efficient institutional management.

Affect & remedy on eulogy.

The technical workforce has gained undue currency in holding higher positions. But, on the other hand, the non-technical crew seems ignored, with no sight of its visible presence. As a result, the non-technical work efficiency sticks out in its feeble parody of the institutional management of several entrusted departments.

On the other hand, there has been a persistent communication gap between the beneficiaries of schemes and officials of the Jenam Valley precisely because of geographical reasons.

Hence, setting up some office establishments would help the development entity cater to the need for a deeper understanding of landslides, including the topography. Furthermore, because the hazard of soil erosion perennially turns an ugly head in the area during precipitation, the presence of the department officials would help better encounter the annual inhibitions.

Development entity's significant parody

The action of road, railway and airway communications measures every locality's development. Contextually, the Public Works Department is one of the significant development Departments of the Government of Assam, which functions under the administrative control of the Dima Hasao Autonomous Council.

It has been divided into four administrative units – Haflong, Umrongso, Mahur and Maibang Divisions, including Building one separately in the district headquarters – and maintains a 2074 km road length in Dima Hasao. The department has floated a tender for constructing Diyungbra to Jatinga and Dehangi to Gunjung Roads with two lanes. The project is to cost 250 crores under the Axom MALA Project.

All major development entities under the administrative control of the Dima Hasao Autonomous Council function like the Public Works Department with different organisational units

In the past, it was the Central Public Works Department.

The Additional Chief Engineer of the Department can grant technical sanction about the State sponsored works that do not exceed five crores. If the State wants to construct a road in the district from its funds, the Additional Chief Engineer can only approve technical sanctions within the limited sanction as aforementioned.

By the way, the Public Works Department established its Additional Chief Engineer office in 2000 at Haflong. The Chief Engineer office of the department at Diphu used to approve schemes executed in the Dima Hasao until 1994. However, following the signing of a Memorandum of Understanding between the Government representatives and the Autonomous State Demand Committee in 1994, the department abolished the Chief Engineer office, forming two administrative units of the department – an Additional Chief Engineer office for each of the two plus one hill districts of Assam – Dima Hasao, Karbi Anglong, Karbi Anglong(West) – became created and attached to Dima Hasao Autonomous Council and Karbi Anglong Hasao Autonomous Council as per clause of the agreement.

Mentionable, until the Government of Assam in the Public Works Department issued a notification bringing the Haflong Territorial Building Division under the jurisdiction of Haflong (Roads & Buildings) Circle under the Public Works (Roads) Department, it was under the jurisdiction of Diphu Building Circle. Rajesh Kemprai issued the order as Special Commissioner and Special Secretary, Government of Assam, Public Works Roads Department, Dispur, on the 26th of July 2022.

The Chief Engineer Office in the State capital, Dispur, floats tenders and allows works to the lowest bidder. There is no problem between the State and Council because if the Chief Executive Member or Executive Member does not feel dissatisfied—unhappiness crops up due to misunderstanding, which we will get clear in other chapter.

Nevertheless, the execution of works brings about dissatisfaction between the Council and the District Zonal Head of Department. In that case, it may limit the transfer of the DHOD or relieve the official's service from the Council's disposal.

Fund transfer and ethical proposition

Serving in Government establishments means receiving salary and perks from the public exchequer in return for monthly services rendered to the public as their servant. How? Well, they feed the Government employees. How? We will later dwell on the issue sequentially.

First, we must know what executing public works with Government money means. It is equivalent to carrying out activities after receiving a ceiling from the Government and utilising the fund in public service.

In our democratic system, everybody knows the people elect the persons of their choice in the election and send their elected representatives to work for them. The winner of the election now acts as a public servant.

As already stated, the public servant gets paid from government funds. All the Government money accumulates from the taxes the officials realised from the public in exchange for services rendered by them on the payment of monthly salary.

The public is the taxpayers, who belong to different earners. They are to pay the taxes fixed by the Government based on their monthly or annual income. We may include Government and Non-Government employees and money earners in the tax-realising group of the Government. Thus, an individual gets classified as a taxpayer based on their earnings.

As for those who say, "We spend the Government money as a government servant", "one must understand it is part of the money we accumulate from paying taxes in Government funds.

Contextually, the Government money is also our money, which requires good spending, not just saying:

"I am spending Government money". Or the money does not belong to my rucksack because it may not be an individual's natural wealth, property or cash but belongs to the citizens. One will dwell on the following points on such issues minutely.

In this connection, I feel convinced that it is not logical to say the Government's money does not belong to its citizens in a democratic country like India. Those who do not treat the Government as their own can never be responsible citizens in a democracy. Therefore, there can be no indifference towards utilising public and or Government money by making different excuses.

Honestly, man's ignorance leads them to ignore such a vital issue.

Further, we need to understand how the money or funds received from the public exchequer get utilised in Dima Hasao. Having dwelt on their role, let us illustrate how the transactional business between the District Head of the Department and their Divisional Officers or Executive Engineers sticks out to have better maintained.

As per modus operandi, the district head of the department should answer to the executive member of the particular transferred subject concerned in all matters about their department.

Likewise, the Divisional level officials designated as Divisional or District Officers or Executive Engineers should be accountable to their District Head of Department;

Similarly, the range-level officials are responsible to their divisional or district executive engineer-level officials in implementing annual action plans, which the executive committee passes in the district planning board annually.

Of course, when satisfied with the recommendation of the Hill Areas Development Ministry of the Government of Assam, the State Cabinet approves the Annual Action/ Operation Plans.

As for the allocation of funds, the Hill Areas Development releases funds on the passing of the Budget from the Finance Department.

In submitting proposals to the Government routed through the Hill Areas Development Ministry towards releasing funds for executing schemes within its territorial jurisdiction, the Dima Hasao Autonomous Council attaches Utilization Certificates, Non-Duplicity Certificates of plans (projects), Works Completion Certificates/Reports, Technical Sanctions of Schemes and Administrative Approval with their letters.

By the way, the authority of the Dima Hasao Autonomous Council accords Administrative Approval of all schemes selected for execution in its territorial jurisdiction before it gets fund allocation from the Government of Assam. The District Heads of Departments submit such proposals to the Autonomous entity.

Mention worthy; the autonomous body only gets new funds allotted to it from the Government when embodying the above documentary evidences.

The Autonomous Council obtains all relevant documents as above and submits them as an administrative authority of all Transferred Subjects to the Hill Areas Development Ministry to the Government of Assam.

Eagle-eyed view

The State Government transferred thirty plus State Subjects to the North Cachar Hills and Karbi Anglong Autonomous Councils based on Clause 3 (ii) of a Memorandum of Understanding between the Governments and the Autonomous

State Demand Committee along with its sister organisations in 1995. With the transfer of those departments, all executive powers remain delegated to the autonomous bodies. However, no amendment to the Acts under which the Government entrusted those subjects to the political bodies seems essential. But there has yet to be a clearance from the Government in some cases. As a result, some departments reportedly still need to be fully functional under the administrative control of the Dima Hasao Autonomous Council.

Some political enthusiasts are slowly and steadily professing to fight for more autonomy, ranging from an Autonomous State to a full-fledged separate state, for the hill districts of Assam - Dima Hasao, Karbi Anglong and West Karbi Anglong. The political show will continue till the Government of India institutes a high-powered committee to revisit the Sixth Schedule to the Constitution of India, taking initiatives to address the autonomy issue in the particular schedule once and for all. The committee should also consist of educationists and enlightened tribal leaders from North-eastern India who can take all the stakeholders into confidence. Some political enthusiasts show off themselves as rebel groups and feel they have made mistakes by giving up arms, subtly reviving the bogey of Autonomous State politics.

Mentionable, the creation of the autonomous Council with legislative, executive, judicial and financial powers was an excellent concept of autonomy. It emerged from those who initially submitted a memorandum to the Gopinath Bordoloi Sub Committee for its creation. Honestly, the grant has also ensured the representation of all groups of people in some parts of the region, including the Dima Hasao Autonomous Council, which is the oldest autonomous body.

For instance, tribal groups like the Dimasas, Jeme-Nagas, Hmars, Kukis, Biates, Karbis and Hrangkhols, have their Executive Members on the Dima Hasao Autonomous Council. Apart from these tribe members, two major permanently settled non-tribal groups – Bengali and Gorkha – have earned each nomination.

What and how they – electorates and their representatives– have been rendering services to the satisfaction of their respective communities within the ambit of the grant is there to measure among themselves the yardstick of success in particular constituencies. Whenever they notice any shortcomings, they should equally shoulder the responsibility to deal with them as an individual share of contributions to their specific social units.

However, to speak reasonably, the Dima Hasao has achieved much more development in the last five to seven years than ever before, though it is not to say that there was so much fund allocation in those days as it exists now, and that not a single past achievement in uplifting the economic condition of the people ever existed since the creation of the Council.

Nevertheless, supposing the people of Dima Hasao are to live fulfilled in the Sixth Schedule to the Constitution of India within the jurisdictional area of the unnamed Dima Hasao Autonomous Territorial Council. In that case, they must have their direct voice heard and convinced in Parliament. Hence, it seems impossible for one Member of Parliament to represent three districts – Dima Hasao, East Karbi Anglong and West Karbi Anglong.

If I am right, the insides of the committee's Memorandum, submitted before the Bordoloi Sub Committee, laid stress on protecting, preserving, promoting and integrating all Dimasa people living outside the jurisdictional boundary of the erstwhile District Council.

So, the Government – Central and State – have recently fulfilled some of the points of the same previous demand after so many years in an agreement with the Dimasa National Liberation Army.

The autonomy issue mainly aims to acquire power with which the political leaders can make necessary changes in the electoral process in line with the power of the Tripura Tribals Autonomous Council without diluting the Government's hold over these councils. Besides, the political vision aimed at including all the Dimasa and Karbi tribe members of the plain areas, who are in the majority in these hill areas of Assam as above, under the jurisdiction of their respective councils (sic)

The ruling party may only find it irrational on any significant devolution of power when it consolidates more power in the Centre, State and Councils, especially after the Bharatiya Janata Party took the reins. It might want to make its permanent bastion. The number of assembly and parliament representatives from these hill districts might need to be more significant. Still, two ministers are in the Cabinet of Dr Himanta Biswa Sharma – one from Karbi Anglong and another from Dima Hasao. With the representation in its Assam ministry, the BJP already sticks out to have appeased the hill people because the entire hilly area of Assam is firmly in its fold (sic)

Stumbling Blocks in Council administering

There is inequality in the allotment of funds between the Territorial and Autonomous Councils in the State.

For instance, the Bodoland Territorial Council always gets more financial allocations through the State Finance Commissions than the Dima Hasao Autonomous Council.

Intriguingly, the name of the Dima Hasao's Council is "DIMA HASAO AUTONOMOUS TERRITORIAL COUNCIL, but they have named it by omitting the word "Territorial", setting aside the word they wish to add, perhaps after the full implementation of the Memorandum of Settlement signed between the Government and Dimasa National Liberation Army.

Honouring emotion!

The issues of nationality, nationalism, or culture are emotive in North-eastern India. Tactically, the Bharatiya Janata Party lays importance on such matters to become a household name. How far the party will succeed in garnering the people's support in some Congress bastions, one will know when the time comes.

Till the fruit bears from the tree planted, one sees the present Government of the Dima Hasao Council has raised such an issue that even the hardcore opponent of the party feels it has executed an exercise that hitherto remained ignored. What is that?

Well, I refer to the people of the hilly region of Assam – Dima Hasao – who got the district on the 2nd of February 1970, having a total geographical area of 4,888 sq. km in the State of Assam. However, they never thought there was a need to celebrate having earned the district.

Of course, they celebrate Council Foundation Day on the 29th of April yearly.

So, this year, they have started celebrating the District Celebration Day for the first time during the Bharatiya Janata Party-ruled Executive Committee to the Dima Hasao Autonomous Council.

Visible Remedies Sought

Some proponents of more power to the Council support periodical examination of the autonomous district councils' administration by a Commission instituted by the Government of India. It implies the Commission suggesting the devolution of more power to the independent bodies if they act according to the clauses of the Constitution. Hence, they point out the existence of some provisions in the Constitution requiring the Union Government to assess the functioning of the States of Nagaland, Jammu, and Kashmir under the Special Treatment plan.

Likewise, if the Government agrees, it may well work out modalities in which the Council can function without the aid and advice of the State and that no Act of Parliament or State Legislature shall apply to the Councils in respect of religious or social practices of the administration of civil and criminal justice and ownership and transfer of land and resources unless passed by the Executive Committee to the Autonomous Council.

At the same time, Dima Hasao always looks for visionary leaders. So, the determination to rise from past failure should now be like "Phoenix rising from the ashes".

Previously, the fund allocation needed adequate comparison to the present.

Let the revenue earned by the Autonomous Council meet half of the expenditures towards annual development work so that the Government's allocation can fulfil the overall requirement of funds.

The initial requirement is to work out some strategies in which they can regularly pay the employees' salaries of the Dima Hasao Autonomous Council and the Haflong Municipal Board. In addition, it requires political will and honesty in governance.

The last seven years have shown the face of development under the territorial jurisdiction of the autonomous body. In the past, people would see every whit of action in the urban areas, unlike the present Executive Committee to the Council, which has concentrated on developing the rural regions. While emphasising rural development, it has already exhibited the autonomous body's keen interest in Sports. It will indeed go a long way in uniting the people, some of who even represented the Dima Hasao in international Football, Cricket &Table Tennis – Gokul Chandra Hojai, Narendra Kemprai and Hyder Ali Rymbai. A new sports stadium is to come up in the Dima Hasao, including a Cricket Stadium in Umrongso.

Meanwhile, the Dima Hasao Autonomous Council has also stressed its keenness to ensure employment for the youths of the rural areas. It has established a Skill Development Centre to hone unskilled labourers' skills. If it succeeds in accomplishing the task, the SDC will solve the problem of the people dependent upon the workforce from outside the Council's jurisdictional area by electrifying their rural huts and providing similar services. The SDC produces electricians, barbers, plumbers, masons, and other unskilled workers.

Considering the physical progress achieved by it, the people of the rural areas shower more praise on the Dima Hasao

Autonomous Council because they feel privileged in better housing, water supply and road conditions.

Moreover, this Government has ensured the development of the culture and practices of the tribe members, who have already been stuck out from the inauguration of some parks while trying to lure tourists from outside the locality.

Undoubtedly, the construction of the Entrance Gates of the Dima Hasao Autonomous Council at Haflong and of the ancient capital of the Dimasa Kingdom at Maibang around these localities, followed by the erection of the statues of some cultural and war heroes, mushroom pillars, and naming roads after prominent persons, subtly identified the presence of the majority tribal members' locality.

Peace ensures the ray of light

Along with the above putting in place, the BJP party-ruled Dima Hasao Autonomous Council could have well installed the statues of Joy Bhadra, Nityalal Daulagupu, Hamdhan Mohon Haflongbar and Desondao Hojai if they still needed to talk about others who participated in setting up the Council. The four had significant contributions! Any importance given to the local founders would gladden the people's hearts of the locality. Even when the non-BJP party Government was in power, it would do the same if it had a similar party manifesto of protecting citizens' rights, culture and heritage.

Agreeing on it or not, both ruling and opposition parties have been learning from each other. In the North-eastern region, the success of the BJP is the restoration of law and order. Peace has ensured whatever development the Government has planned to execute in the States of their ruling.

Unfortunately, the non-BJP Government did not look into the issue from the proper perspective. Somewhere, it gave little importance to ensuring tranquillity; somewhere, the ruling party gave lukewarm support to the point of peace. As a result, the hooligans ruled the roost in almost all States led by the Non-BJP Government.

Frankly, peace in the BJP-ruled States has ensured the availability of fuel for the party to light the lamp. As such, the ray of light indicated the restoration of justice amidst the need for equality and opportunities without disturbing the interest of the tribals. After all, there is no difference between tribals and non-tribals; both are competent enough. Gone are the days of intelligent tribals feeling side-lined by the intelligence of the non-tribals, where they have provisionally lived at the grant of some privileges or of mercy, and conscientious resources sprouted from the broadminded tribal intelligentsia.

Rancorous Tale

By the way, I have a story based on the content of which some may know how the tribal rulers got booted out of power in the State of Tripura. I do not commit to the story's truth, but it is interesting to enjoy. Here is the detail:

Once, two executives lived – one elected and another a government official – in a State. The Elected Representative asked the Government Official (GO), who was high ranking, to carry out specific works, which the latter smelt like a rat.

Seeing a professional hazard, the GO did not carry out the order of the ER. Instead, again, the ER asked the Government official to carry out the former's ruling, which amounted to a sheer violation of the official code of conduct of business between the Government and the public.

As a result, the ER could only get work done within the Government's established norms through government officials. What the ER thought was that he could do any illegal work through the GO because the latter belonged to his clansman and was elected Representative.

However, the GO did nothing prejudicial or harmful to him professionally. Instead, the tussle between the GO and ER turned into a slugfest. Hence, the ER caused the transfer of the GO once.

Nevertheless, the GO returned after some months because he belonged to the locality and clansman and submitted his joining, which the ER delayed or refused to accept.

After remaining lull, the GO got his joining accepted by the HER (Higher Elected Representative) of the Legislative Assembly.

Meanwhile, the senior of the GO transferred; now, the charge should go to the GO only on the recommendation of the ER to HER, who was the final accepting authority. But alas, the ER suggested the name of ER's junior. The junior official was also the ER's clansman but needed a sense of being and belonging and would do whatever the ER wanted.

After the Junior Official took over the charge of GO, the ER did whatever he liked. The ER had an intense longing for money and luxury. So, he contested and won an election. Afterwards, he victimised the GO to realise his objective, amassing wealth and properties and misusing his power, embezzling money from the public exchequer. Thus, without vision and mission, the ER got the chance to head the department, which seems riddled with corruption and non-functionalism!

Similar is the balkanisation of Tripura. Nobody outside their State balkanised the State; the people of the same State did it.

CHAPTER-VII

Traditional and Religious Perceptions

Contribution and conversion; The practice of worshiping deities; Some Brahmanical Traditions; Dimasa traditions & rituals; The spiritual development in retrospection;

Contributions after Conversion

Though the British usurped power in India, they introduced modern administration. They first established medical facilities, pioneered building markets and roads, and sent children to educational institutions in English. The establishment of the educational institution virtually sealed the fate of the Guru Kula system in the Plains.

In tribal areas, the Christian Missionaries rendered yeoman services to educate the people, apart from carrying out religious conversions in the entire Northeastern region of India.

Mentionable, until the Christian missionaries entered India, the spiritual masters, popularly known as Gurus, used to teach the students under their respective Kula. The word "Kula" represents "Life Force" and "Master's School or Life Energy", on which we shall dwell in the following few lines.

The British taught how to realize revenues from the people. In addition, the method helped the Government and people come close together, ensuring social cohesion in the region under the imposition of prayer in church on Sunday. As a result, almost all smaller tribe members are today Christians.

For instance, Jeme-Zeme Naga, Hmar, Baite, Hrangkhol & Kuki tribe members are churchgoers.

Among all tribe members, the Dimasas, who hold a majority in the Dima Hasao, are mainly Hindus. Though some Dimasa intellectuals from the Christian Group like Palon Chandra Langthasa inwardly wanted the mass conversion of the tribe members to ensure unity and development of the community, there is now a slim chance of any religious conversion, with the RSS, VHP and BJP making inroads into the Dima Hasao and politics.

Moreover, the establishment of the educational institutions in English, Hind, Assamese and Bengali media, coupled with the growth of literacy among the tribe members, sharpened the tribe guardians' minds and intellect, apart from helping them know how best they could achieve a better quality of life for their children by educating which educational institutions, and not joining or changing which religious groups!

The practice of worshipping deities

The Faith in the Almighty does not fade away from the minds of the believers who believe in religion and God.

Only the Providence and His believers or worshipers know who is what, nobody else. So, the relationship between the two entities – man and heavenly body always stick out as the whit of belief for all eyewitnesses.

Thus, the synthesis of religion turns out to be an outward belief for a thinking mind, nothing much else, for the relationship is describable in the truest sense of the term. But, on the contrary, it is the feeling that tastes the mystery between two or more persons.

Further, the relationship is so vast that it is difficult to define within a few words. The more we define it from different angles, the more it appears as a part of the whole.

Likewise, the Dimasas used to worship different deities. Sivrai (equivalent to Lord Siva) seems to be their principal one in modern times, and some of them bow down before Him as a 'formless' (Nirankar) deity. However, all Dimasa tribe members do not follow the worship of a particular ancestral god. Instead, there are not less than twelve deities the Dimasa people worship – namely, Ranachandi, Daman, Alu, Banglaima,

Hamri/Hirimdi, Longmailai, Manja, Misim, Mongrang, Riao, Wao and Waibra. They worship each of these twelve deities in "Daikho" (equivalent to "temple") through a separate priest known by Zonthai from each of their particular clans. So, there are twelve numbers: Zonthai and Gishiya are the religious chiefs of all.

According to a knowledgeable source, the temporal world existed following the conception of "a divine bird and the god of earthquake". The name of the heavenly bird is Airikidima, and the King is Bangla Raja. The place on the earth where the intercourse of Dilao and Sangi takes place was Dilaobra and Sangibra.

At the outset, the divine bird lays seven eggs, of which Sabarai comes into this world. Next Alu Raja, then Naikhu Raja. Afterwards, Owa Raja, Gunyung, Brayung and Hamyadao were born sequentially. They said the hatching of the seven eggs by Hamyadao led to the birth and spread of evil spirits in every nook and corner of the Dimasa Kingdom, which their Sivrai saved from His healing power.

Commenting on the system of worship, which seems expensive, one of the intellectuals of the tribe, Ramesh Thaosen, once said: "If possible, the Dimasa community as a whole may use the Daikhos for religious purpose into a specific system of worship Sabarai as per social requirement under the present circumstances."

The Dima Hasao Autonomous Council arranged the establishment of a Ranachandi Temple Park in Maibang, the Sub-Division of the Dima Hasao.

All stocks of Dimasa tribe members do not follow the worship of Ranachandi. Instead, there are eleven other deities the Dimasa people worship as above. They adore each of these twelve deities in "Daikho" (equivalent to "temple") through a separate priest from their particular social clan.

On the other hand, no Government of the Council ever celebrated such a deity in the past. They said the tribe members also have such gods in their traditional belief who want nothing to get executed without their permission.

The Chief Executive Member of the Council inaugurated the temple above, holding a two-day programme on the 14th and 15th of January, 2023. Mentionable, Maibang was the ancient capital of the Dimasa kingdom.

There is also a report about the worship of Maharani Chandraprava, the queen of King Tamradhvaj, in her glory among some Dimasa tribe members.

Some of the tribe members worship Hirimdi, which is next to Ranachandi. According to a reliable source, Hirimdi is the principal source of Tantra in the tribe. The same source said she spent her later life practising Tantra in Northern India, where some people worship her footprints at Mohali.

By the way, the worship of Ranachandi by the Dimasa is reminiscent of the Kul Devi worshipped by the people in some parts of India. The word "Kul" is synonymous with "Life Force" as stated already. It is a catalogue of all kinds of life energy produced from the daily foodstuff people consume in their bodies. So, going by the syllogism, Ranachandi is the Goddess looking after the life and well-being of the Dimasa tribe members.

Some said that even if there is nobody present in the garden where one requires plucking up fruit, they should ask the tree or address the open place, "Hello, I am XYZ, and I have the requirement of this fruit. So, please note I am taking it from your garden".

The declaration stands as permission sought for carrying specific exercises in somebody's gardens. Thus, such deities are stricter than others. Because they said the gods could get the unauthorized pluckers insane if they carried out any activities without sanction from the owners concerned.

I have a story drawn from the Khasi tribe. To one's surprise, an incident happened in the case of a friend's relative in Shillong. An unauthorized person plucked some oranges from a garden, and his neck got crooked. Afterwards, he had to apologize to the owner of the park, who pardoned the unauthorized plucker.

In some parts of India, such deities belong to a larger group of people adopted. For example, some people in Himachal Pradesh, Bihar and Uttar Pradesh also worship such divinities.

Worthy, there was a debate over the tribe members being what they called superstitious. If following such traditions and customs defines superstition, the Hindus in India who follow their rituals must join the bandwagon of superstitions.

On the other hand, the growth of philosophy, logic and science originates from following different traditions and beliefs. The tribe members have not hitherto stuck out any fatalistic attitudes that may logically prove to be full of superstition. On the contrary, they have kept some traditional beliefs without rejecting the course of logic and science.

Mentionable, until the United Nations accepted Yoga as the physical well-being of the human race, it continued to be the superstitious product of India. Likewise, where Yoga has not permeated the anal of social health, the traditional belief restricts crimes in some groups of people. Hence, the practice of the Dimasa tribe members seems healthy. Now, let me turn to the Brahmanical traditions drawn from the Aryan group of Gorkhas who used to follow in the past, and the practice is still in vogue in some places.

Brahmanical Traditions

Man is born to die, but they adopt different activities, fulfilling their longevity fixed by the unseen and unknown. In some traditions, including the Hindu Brahmanical ones, they appease the soul of the dead so that the departed soul gets on the path to the Pearly Gates. Whatever may be the method of worshipping the soul, it reflects the appeasement of the dead, which sprouts from love. Barring that, I have reservations about accepting the veracity of facts because the issue is foreign to me and will continue to be the same until I die and experience it. Anyway, there is no question of supporting or opposing such an issue because it is the only way the Aryan Gorkhas accept it as the truth. So, they practise it.

Even if some oppose performing rituals, some strictly follow the tradition after the demise of an individual. Hence, they perform rituals for thirteen days. Treating the period as mourning, the son(s) of the deceased performs the sraddha ceremony. During this period, the son is to make a Thala (*Pinda Kund*), where he worships the departed soul as Pitra and offers flowers, pies and other confectionary articles as permitted by their tradition. Besides, he requires lighting incense sticks or pouring ghee into the coal made of firewood, a purifying place where the *Pinda Kund* gets prepared from the clean soil.

Having completed all kinds of rituals, apart from the already mentioned ones, to the departed soul, he now takes a bath and prepares a meal, which he is to take every day once during the period. His voj (meal) consists of rice mixed with cow ghee. The tradition allows him to take ginger, lemon, and some fruits during mourning. The diet remains free from milk, pulse and salt. A religious pundit performs all these rituals. On the last day, some people engage several pundits to narrate several rites, including reading out Bhagavat Puran.

Those who follow the tradition retain the mourning period for one year. But there is an option after thirteen days, beginning with the occasion, fifteen days, forty-five days, six months or one year of the date of death of an individual.

According to the Gorkha tradition, the departed soul gets united with the heavenly bodies when the son of the dead performs the above rituals.

The rituals above are the most popular among the Aryan group, though non-Aryan groups perform their rituals differently.

I do not know how the rituals came into existence in the Gorkha custom, nor anybody I requested to dwell on the issue succeeded in convincing me. Hence, I stopped talking on the subject, thinking it had the potential to bring about an inevitable controversy, which I don't like to indulge in, because I feel it gives a bumpy time to everybody.

Now let's examine the Dimasa traditions and rituals from one example; as,

Dimasa tradition & rituals

The Dimasa tribe members' tradition is somewhat similar to the Brahmanical one:

For instance, some Dimas follow slightly different traditions. I came across the Nunisa clan of the tribe. The family constructs their deceased's Mangkholong and perform Maimutharba. "Mangkholong" is equivalent to "Pinda Kund", while "Maimutharba" (aka Maimu Tharma) refers to "shraddha".

Mentionable, having constructed a bamboo structure resembling the funeral pyre of the Dimasa tribe members, it now symbolises the departed soul securing their holy place in Heaven. Until they perform the sraddha ceremony, the bereaved family offer food daily prepared by it in the name of the lifeless in their kitchen.

The Dijuwasha Dimasa tribe members make the Mangkholong inside the compound of the diseased, while the tribe members hail from the Dima Hasao in the cemetery, said Dr Monali Longmailai, who teaches at Assam University, Silchar.

However, they also allow the food prepared by the old ladies outside their home to the dead after the erection of Mangkholong, which they consign to flames on the occasion of Saradha.

According to the tribe members, the lighting of the constructed structure in the name of the dead signifies severing the ties between the living and the dead.

Birth and death are the two aspects of human life staged by Nature in their vast existence. Between these two, the hidden reason for the creation stages a show of illusion in which both good and evil go alike. However, the civility of the soul always gets idolised as the love that ensures peace, which stands next to unity, progress, prosperity and beauty as one of the best and universal traditions to foster in the given society.

A Roman lyric poet, Horace, said, "I shall not altogether die" in his Odes. Contextually, what remains after demise? It is the reflection of love concerning the transactional relationship between the deceased and alive, nothing much else, according to this ordinary conscience!

The spiritual development in retrospection

Having gone through the traditional practices of Guru Kul in this chapter, let me dwell on how the followers of Guru Kul believed in the spiritual development of humans in the past by regaling a story.

In a village, there lived two families belonging to the Rishi School (Seer School), popularly known as Gurukul - Upamanyu and Bhardwaj. There was a visible competition between the two. Upamanyu had grown-up sons known by Dhakals; Bhardwaj, too, had children who matured late. With Dhakals not getting married, they turned overage and did not find a match for even one of Upamanyu's sons.

Upamanyu thought it necessary to get one of his sons married before his demise. Though he wanted to get his sons to tie their nuptial knots with Bhardwaj's daughters who grew up, he could not succeed in it. Because Upamanyu knew Bhardwaj would not consent to marry the former's sons with the latter's daughters. So, Upamanyu sought the help of some prominent persons from the Bhardwaj allied clan members to get it done successfully.

Finally, Upamanyu married one son to Bhardwaj's daughter. He played the game of tricks and persuasions well.

After the marriage, Upamanyu transferred his Pranic Shakti to Bhardwaj's brother, known as Pokhrel-1, causing hallucinations and resulting in the loss of his job, memory and family. The birth of the disease substantiated lacking original existence of such a disease in Pokhrel-1. Moreover, the insanity was the creation of vested interests.

Next, following one son's marriage with Bhardwaj's daughter, Upamanyu again eyed another son's marriage with his daughter-in-law's sister, which did not materialize.

However, Upamanyu's sons vowed to take revenge. How? They now followed their father's trade so that they would be able to teach a lesson to Bhardwaj's kin. Having specialized in controlling the disciples with their Pranic Sakti (life force) and finished off Bhardwaj, Dhakals caused one of Pokhrels to lose his job and two families! The other two did not create any family, or, if married, one soured the relationship with his spouse under the influence of Upamanyu's evil Pranic Sakti.

Not satisfied with ruining several kins of Bhardwaj, Upamanyu's two sons, popularly known as Dhakals, resolved to pave the way for obstructing education, marriage and relationship with all mattering them, planning a slow and steady extinction of the whole family of Bhardwaj.

Indeed, Bhardwaj felt hurt deeply when he got wind of it. Though Pokhrels did not meddle with Dhakals, the vengeful and greedy attitude of the latter spoilt the former's familial and heavenly choices and pleasures, respectively.

The cause of deprivation exhibited between the two groups above resulted from ignorance and mean-spiritedness. Somewhat, Dhakals satisfied their pent-up anger and frustration by ruining the lives of innocent Pokhrels, who cut off their relationship with Dhakals instead of frequenting them and indulging in revenge.

In the Guru-Kul system, one who is fortunate used to come across not revengeful but compassionate Gurus or Masters who, in turn, got respect even after them, and their disciples prospered because of the virtue, which was synonymous with an individual's DNA. Many achievements of disciples came from the Bhardwaj clan of Rishi Bhardwaj's devotion to spreading moral education, and the people also respected him, though he would not long for it, thinking it was a temporary satisfaction.

As a visitor, man should do something to benefit others as their legacy. In those days, by citing several examples, Bhardwaj's disciples emphasized possessing a high sense of being and belonging to the locality, intellectual ability, compassion, justice, equality, tolerance, frankness, and sincerity in dealing with human issues.

There is an immortal tale in which the most famous King of Nepal, Prithibhi Narayan Shah, who ruled the country from 1723-75, once went to the ancient Indian city of Banaras where he changed his Gotra from Bhardwaj to Kashyap. Why? Because he belonged to the Bhardwaj Rishi, who would never commit any sin or crime in his Kula. Being a monarch, he had to punish the guilty in his country, which can not be free from criminals. But the King could not do it because his Kula had no permission to carry out the hatya (slay/crime) of the people belonging to his Gotra during the unification of Nepal. But the change of Gotra did not help the King remain endearing forever, for nobody loves the killer.

Rishi Bhardwaj changed his Gotra as above. In Kashyap Gotra, it seemed murder or crime acceptable. Likewise, Dhakals' inflictions, which consisted of causing separation from Pokhrels spouses, betrayal and doing to death upon Bhardwaj, and punishing Pokhrels and Bhardwaj's daughter-in-law, reflected heinous crimes.

The interpretation also aims to subtly tell the truth about how the hereditary came into existence. Supposing the father as a businessman is vindictive, and his sons, who take up the dad's profession, indulge in severe crimes. In that case, it can not be the instinct of growth of the hereditary disease in human beings, for the offspring can be a better human if not influenced by the evils of their parents, subject to the available provision for enlightenment about the essentiality of the original spirit of human to be the messenger of beauty, unity, peace, prosperity and progress in the society. Hence, hereditary is the creation of man out of their gluttony.

Considering the preceding discussion, one feels safe to say if the Guru happens to be noble-hearted, his nobility spread after him far and wide, for the Gurukul's Master's virtuous qualities used to get treated as the DNA of an individual, even in the modern scientific world. The prosperity of an individual group depended much upon the source from which their origins started.

By the way, some elderly Dimasa tribe members in the past got the blessings of such prominent masters or gurus' different schools. For instance, some family members got the blessing of Sri Sri Ravi Shankar, Anukul, Prabhat Ranjan Sarkar, Rama Krishna, Ram Thakur, Sat Gurus, Bhakti Pada Vedanta, and so on. Their disciples have achieved worldly prosperity.

As everybody knows, every accomplishment of human beings results from the growth of awareness in them. Contextually, some founding members of the erstwhile North Cachar Hills who belonged to the disciples of some gurus above proved themselves to benefit from the teaching of their masters.

For instance, their broad-minded activities during the formation of the erstwhile North Cachar Hills amply reflected their beings as ambassador of peace and unity in diversity. Today, the founder members of the North Cachar Hills Autonomous Council stand as an umbrella of how the different groups of people can live together by feeling protected and shadowed under the autonomy granted by the Sixth Schedule to the Constitution of India.

CHAPTER-VIII

Strategic Development

Denizens' footstep; Yearning workforce; Propelling the Kopili River; Cross-examination; Luring efforts; Entrusted Subjects' Administrative Establishments; Ornamental & Tunnel Tree Plantations; Religious and Cultural Tourism; Post-Harvest Bonanza to lure Tourists; Different Development Entities' functional approaches; Other approaches towards the development; An egalitarian structure of Development proposition; Handloom potentials; Strategizing further Development of Dima Hasao; Administrative future of Dima Hasao; Development Plan extension; All about the self-sufficiency cord; Tap Ethnic power, Ensure peace by Awards; Towards a Bi-cameral Solution; In support of scrapping SIU & Others; A Nostalgic Account

Denizens' footstep

Amidst the growth of population of a region represented by about thirteen tribesmen and other non-tribals, followed by the enhanced percentage of literacy among the settlers, the life in Dima Hasao is increasingly becoming competitive, with each group competing against others because of the conspicuous race to excel or ensure success.

The advent of education brought about an inevitable expansion of knowledge, inducing many motives to enter into competition. In the struggle for a better tomorrow, nobody is friend; everybody, whether rich or poor, fights for their survival. Every day, the desire to possess more increases in the people, regardless of whether the supply or growth matches with their daily requirement. Without fulfilment, there is no satisfaction.

As long as the effort to grow more for fulfilling the demand remains limited, the shortage in supply leads to an inevitable dissatisfaction among the ones who feel or remain deprived of their want. When the displeasure turns violent, even a mistaken spilled drop flames.

Naturally, even a trifling issue gets quickly sensationalised because of the potential threat of scarcity. Along the post insufficiency, there exists gluttony in every man, which paves the way for the growth of evils in different guises.

Further, the greed followed by the desire to earn money, name or fame, many a time induces an individual into being a Sheep in Wolf's clothing. In the race for power, they always look for an issue to lead their respective societal units in particular and their society as a whole.

The urge to rule in the prospective participants tends to exaggerate trivial issues to win the game of power. In the guise of representing their respective communities, some make their presence felt by bringing the people under their fold. The necessity seems to give an impetus to the birth of various communal outfits, bringing different groups of people under their particular social units, pretending to work for some special causes.

Agreeing it or not, the integration of people with their respective social units paves the way for the growth of suspicion against one another groups by taking not only little interest in others, but also it ignites the feeling of subtle insecurity in one group over others. Thus, it prompts to the exhibition of a conditional life of human on this part of the world.

Considering the situation, the concept of community-wise representations in the Dima Hasao Autonomous Council seems to have developed in the hilly region of Assam. However, the development of a community under the leadership of an individual from a particular ethnic entity seems impracticable if the people themselves don't participate in improving their lots. On the other hand, how far the leader of a social unit has succeeded in fulfilling the aspiration of their people is there to judge them.

Nevertheless, the division of people on ethnic consideration, coupled with their subtly longing to remain foreign to each other many a time, seems to sprout from the hidden feeling of insecurity in integration with each other. Should such a situation warrant, I am afraid, it might show off the people under the banner of their respective communal outfits to support individual wrong doers, saying they belong to their respective groups. Such a situation only panders to the subtle growth of intolerance and sectarian outlook. Hence, there is a need for all community leaders to adopt an integrated approach not to mess in the affairs of the State. That will go a long way in taming any obsolete feelings, let alone helping the State to enforce the law and order under the territorial jurisdiction of the Dima Hasao Autonomous Council, apart from ensuring safety and security to the lives and properties of the people without any fear and favour.

Before any unseemly incident takes place, it is incumbent upon all groups of people to think over twice before issuing any statement supporting or representing anybody.

Let me now invite your attention to cast a glance at how I enjoyed being in Haflong as a young man!

Yearning Workforce

When I was a young boy of fifteen to sixteen years, I used to frequent the former Assistant Engineer's office of the N.F. Railway, Haflong, situated on the western side of the present Ram Thakur Mandir, above the beautiful Haflong Lake. I would go to this office because my dad was an employee of the Indian Railway, and worked in this establishment from where he superannuated in 1986 after serving about thirty-three years to the N.F. Railway. During his presence, I would avail of the privilege to sit nearby the clerks and Inspectors of Works. They always held long and tedious discussions on different topics. Except one Hazarika, all were Ghosh, Dey, Majumdar, Chanda, Das, Bhattacharjee, Chetri (Bom Bahadur Chetri and Ron Bahadur Chetri) and one Upadhaya (Pitambar Upadhya), some of who used to be very position conscious and would not talk with but love me. I would take an advantage to associate with some of them by correcting their grammatical mistakes, which I would politely point out and correct them. I would get their heart-felt appreciation, but I still think there is room for development in the language!

A few Babus and Sahibs were arrogant enough, and would not speak and smile ever! Among them, one was a strange uncle Subrata Ghosh (aka *Khukaa Babu*), who did not ever chuckle, let alone laugh. He was but a kind-hearted man, although. His short replies to my queries would make me uncomfortable! One of his sisters used to work in the District Council, other at the erstwhile Deputy Commissionerate, Haflong. They were good and helpful, but mindful of their positions. However, I would manage to get all replies to my queries, slowly and steadily.

After their retirement, some died, others left for Kolkata, Lumding or Cachar district. Very few settled in Dima Hasao. Similarly, after their superannuation, most of the non-tribal work force dominated in the State Government establishments in Haflong and elsewhere office establishments slowly disappeared. Most of the non-tribal grades-III & IV staff shifted their families to Silchar, Karimganj, Guwahati or Kolkata. Some even sold off their immovable properties gained to settle here in their later years of life and left for their community populated areas in Plains district after the political tension in the former North Cachar Hills and Karbi Anglong.

Having felt left in lurch, after their departure, I gained my new friends who hailed from this locality. The local association with my classmates turned exciting. As they supported the more power movement, I joined my hands with them by reporting their day-to-day activities. The agitation surfaced in the aftermath of the Asom Gana Parishad's failure in sharing powers with the people of these hill regions – North Cachar Hills and Karbi

Anglong. In the movement, I also appeared to be one of the active participants. So, the erstwhile Congress Government punished me. The movement was for an Autonomous State comprising these two hilly regions of Assam above.

After the Autonomous State Demand Committee (ASDC) movement for more power was over, the party led by Prokanta Warisa and Samarjit Haflongbar captured power in the North Cachar Hills Autonomous Council elections. In ruling the autonomous body, some of their colleagues did not, however, examine their lives and indulged in evils to such an extent that their involvement turned out to be a big scam, subsequently.

Until the regional party came to power, we could see some beautiful plots of land having potential to extend tourists' spot available around the town where we would play football. Today, it exhibits the loss of beauty. The short-sighted power caused the disposal of every small plot of land in the surrounding areas of Haflong Lake and Railway colony in Haflongtown. The need of the ruling class for homes and avenues narrowed the space of vacant land, apart from the growth of hidden feeling of greed. There was no difference between the tribals and non-tribals who are the permanent residents of Dima Hasao in the Government offices. Undeniably, there is still flail work-force of non-tribal in some educational institutions.

Frankly, the intelligentsia would have done well not to systematically seal the fate of the local non-tribal workforce in the category of grades III and IV forces in office establishments for the last decade. The rejection in recruitment only ensured tickling no tribals' vanity forever, which they'll experience at appropriate moment. The elders (especially from the majority Dimasa tribe members of the erstwhile North Cachar Hills) were not ignorant or stupid that led them to engage non-tribals in Government office establishments there. In recruiting some non-tribals to perform white colour jobs, the elders exhibited their ample sagacity, were far-sighted and full of wisdom like the intellectual of the modern western world where several people of Indian origins have ruled some States without diluting the cultural and social values of their respective States. A place becomes redundant when an individual does not respect its original beauty.

As for other adverse effect of development, even the passage of the run-off water has become congested, one can spot water-logging during rainy season due to the growth of human settlements in the above area, where erosion of the Lake bed will throw light from the tunnel of darkness in years to come.

If my memory does not mislead me, similar situation cropped up in Guwahati and Dibrugarh and other places when the people constructed random structures in Assam where the wound of foreigners' movement used to infect the whole Assamese society. As the virus of aliens spread like wild-fire and the people started getting foreign to one another, some intellectuals of Assam saved it by bridging the communication gap between the Hindu Assamese and others. Subsequently, good sense prevailed.

Today, every group of people feels secured and privileged in the Brahmaputra valley. Likewise, the tribal intelligentsia of Dima Hasao would do well to take a leaf from the majority Hindu Assamese *Danguria* of the Brahmaputra valley and wipe out the difference which got stuck out between the tribals and non-tribals by the vested interests in Government offices, not at par with other smaller tribal groups. It would for sure foster the Growth of our legacy of the past. The initiative to wipe out the difference must come from the majority Dimasa tribe members, because they top in my estimation of being one of the front-ranking secular and enlightened tribal groups in the entire Northeastern region.

By the way, the prevailing peace in the whole Northeastern region paved the way for the Government's power to increase the satisfaction graph by extending happiness to others who had hitherto felt deprived of their legitimate share of privileges. But, on the other hand, some vested interests occasionally try to fuss over the trivial issue; they feel swamped by any ruling party sharing benefits to anybody outside their domain. Though it would not repeat the history of Tripura, where the tribals got booted out of power in the State by the Bangladeshis.

Today, tribals are more intelligent than the non-tribals in ruling some Northeastern States. So, the fear of some conscientious tribe members getting victimised by the whims of some tribal leaders in collaboration with the non-Tribal ones in this region seems unfounded and politically motivated. Moreover, the apprehension seems groundless amidst the existing Provision for the tribals of the Northeastern region under India's Constitutional Sixth Schedule. They can enforce reservation in which every permanent resident of all sixth scheduled areas feels secured and treated well.

Similar fear leads the tribal intelligentsia in some parts of the Northeastern region to unfairly treat the non-tribals, who have settled within the jurisdictional boundary of the Councils for two to three generations. And occasionally, some tribal bodies talk about the disfranchising of the non-tribals in the council elections. But alas, some entities migrated to the council areas from other states of the Northeast and got better privileges than the permanent resident non-tribals. So, it sticks out an immature ruling of the autonomous councils in the twenty-first century.

There is room for streamlining the employment generation sectors in Dima Hasao. The authority of the Council will be sensible if it works out a clear-cut reservation policy, which seems essential in line with the Government of India's Reservation Rules, preserving the local, political and economic interest of all groups of people, who are the *permanent residents* of the jurisdictional areas of the council on a percentage basis. The Recruitment Board, when set up by the Dima Hasao Autonomous Council as per the Clause 3.5 of the Memorandum of Settlement, will have to dwell on how the employees of its Transferred & Inherent Subjects should work under the administrative control of the Dima Hasao Autonomous Council. Apart from that, the Rules of the Dima Hasao Autonomous Council, which the Executive Committee will have to frame as per order No. PIU/13/2019 dated:23.05.2022 of the Hon'ble High Court of Guwahati, and the political body has reportedly invited suggestions from all stakeholders already, the task may apply to selecting the beneficiaries (of the government schemes) having their individual registrations, granting privileges to them as per the Voters' List of the Dima Hasao Autonomous Council election.

A separate Election Cell/Commission aiming to carry out the whole exercise of preparation, inclusion, deletion of names of voters and election of the Autonomous Councils is in the list of demand of the Sixth Schedule Protection Committee. Perhaps, some modalities will have to get worked out between the Election Cell of the Council and State Election Commission.

By the way, any legislations framed by the Executive Committee of the Council must, by procedure, have to obtain the Governor's approval as per the recommendation of the Hill Areas Development Ministry of the Government of Assam.

Having got familiar with the employment issue, I now turn to dwell on the perennial problem of water in Haflong

Propelling the Kopili River!

"When Desondao Hojai was the Chairman of the Haflong Town Committee, and Nityalal Daulagupu was the Principal Secretary of the Normal Sector of the North Cachar Hills Autonomous Council, they caused the implementation of the farsighted "Water Supply Scheme to pump up water from the Didaola stream" to the district headquarters of the erstwhile North Cachar Hills (now Dima Hasao) in the sixties. Nobody can now compare the population of the sixties. Today, Haflong is in 2024. While one must appreciate all elders' planned scheme, which hitherto managed the requirements of the people, can they not now expect a similar type of new scheme serving humanity during this time?

Agreeing on it or not, with the ever-increasing growth of the local population due to rural migration, water consumption has increased because of water scarcity in the urban areas. So, they should stop dreaming of managing the water supply for the urban area of today's Haflong from the Didaola stream or other small water bodies. Besides resolving the introduction of a house-tap connection covering all citizens under the Haflong Municipal Board areas, there is a need to work out a viable plan towards meeting the water requirement in the locality. There are several places in Haflong where people have been consuming unfiltered water. There is a need to find a permanent source where the growth of the water body is strong. Nobody can depend upon small river sources like Rabi Nallah and Diyung, where the development of water sources is dwindling daily following the haphazard use of the region's natural resources.

Though it sounds high, Haflong should work out a scheme in the line of how the water pumped out of the Brahmaputra River, near Tezpur town's Ferry Ghat, quenches the thirst of the whole city. Going by the success story of the water supply scheme adopted by the authority in Tezpur Town, the policy or plan makers may well study the feasibility of pumping up water from the river Kopili. It is a long-term beneficial scheme, gearing up the fund-crunched Municipal Board to realise tax, apart from catering to the citizenry's needs within its jurisdictional areas."

By the way, the new establishment of the Public Health Engineering created a stir in the Town Committee's whole office establishment. Some needed help to speak with whom to get what they wanted. During the changes that take place, such hiccups surface. However, there was a little problem with setting all establishments under B.K. Dey was the first Executive Engineer of public health engineering. The establishment of his office, followed by the recruitment of staff when Chanda was the head of the office, increased the number of visitors and their movement in the Sarkari Bagan areas. Frankly, during his tenure, the establishment of the Department at Sarkari Bagan was in the eye of the public.

Till such time, the surroundings of the Engineer's establishments were full of thorns and thick shrubs. The setting up of Forests, Veterinary, Industries, and Public Works establishments upgraded to the cosmopolitan characters.

By the way, many staff of the Town Committee (now Haflong Municipal Board) could not exercise the option due to the lack of knowledge about how secure their future would be if they joined Public Health Engineering. There needed to be a communication gap. Those who did not join the Public Health Department remained with the Town Committee and, when they superannuated, did not get the retirement packages. In contrast, the State Public Health Department employees who bonded with it from the Town Committee got pensionary benefits after their superannuation.

Mention worthy, the staff of the Town Committee would, hitherto, get their regular wages. The random recruitment of staff with the change of every succeeding Chairman of the Municipality led to the growth of outstanding dues of the organisation's staff. However, A. Daulagupu restrained the recruitment. During his Chairmanship, he did not allow the recruitment of staff. It is now Haflong Municipal Board. By the way, the authority of the North Cachar Hills extends a helping hand by causing all the Transferred Subjects to liquidate their dues off and on.

After the three prominent faces of the Department as above, Bijoylal Thaosen became prominent in my mind's eye. How? He was my sister's and brother's classmate – all District Council Colony Lower Primary School pupils. His brother also happened to come in close contact with me for some years when he worked as a Junior Engineer of some Development entity of the erstwhile North Cachar Hills but passed away prematurely. He was also a good guy.

As the inception of the water supply scheme in Haflongtown crops up, one cannot forget the Town Committee of those days.

Under the Chairmanship of Desandao Hojai, they executed the plan above per the approval and instruction of Nityalal Daulagupu, the first Principal Secretary of the North Cachar Hills District Council.

Executing and planning are two different heads of work. Only a farsighted and honest official or leader can carry out these exercises better than other persons who draw their monthly salaries for being the employees of the entity that recruits them. Nityalal Daulagupu and Desandao Hojai were the brainchildren behind the successful execution of the central scheme of those days. Though the people who use the water of Jatinga may have yet to learn who planned and executed the distribution of house tap connection, they would thank planners and executors when the value of their services rendered to the people becomes known. It was not a small project because the allocation was meagre, and getting such a big project as the supply of Water to Haflong sanctioned for distribution among the Town Committee's clients on a door-to-door basis was undoubtedly a gigantic exercise. But the two sons of Haflong's efforts paid off.

Of course, there were many people behind their backs. For instance, the Engineer in charge of implementing the scheme was Sadananda Das. He was one of the kins of the first elected Member of the North Cachar Hills District Council, Harimoy Das Barman. He was the Overseer of the Town Committee, and reportedly responsible for establishing a Thakur Bari (Palace of a heavenly body), which subsequently got recognised as the Lord Jagannath Temple, on which I have dwelt in other details in my other published title.

Having dwelt on the house-tape connection, let me talk about Haflong Lake. There was also a proposal to convert the lake water into a consumable one. Honestly, the Dima Hasao Autonomous Council's ruling party has been trying to beautify it. The British initially dug Haflong Lake in the heart of Haflongtown. Apart from it, there is another Fishery Lake. I am still determining who searched for it, but it is beautiful. Undoubtedly, there is room for developing it, and the district's planners must have conceived how to execute their tasks. The more they beautify it, the more the place is likely to attract tourists.

However, how they will tackle the encroachment problem, in the long run, is an unsolved question. Considering the encroachment problem, I wrote a few poetic lines as:

THORNS IN GALORE

Reject if you like
I've no sight
Not to be on your side;
But there's fight
Where to get it right,
In my mind eye,
And I said the idea's bright,
We've lot of guides
But those've got the Knight
They've spotted a beautiful eye sight,
In which they said
There's beauty in thorny plants
Which bloom roses;
So, every time,
Every soul
Is not hard-hearted;
Somewhere,
They may've hidden hearts

Those receive your Cart;
There lies the actual art!
Both poetry and prose sprout;
I've yet to trace it out,
Because it seems deep,
Like the Mahadev Tilla pit!
The greedy spoilt its Might,
Throwing flow from high,
Beauty, they saw in their living right,
Not the archaeological pride;
The century of valour
It's injected sins in the societal skin of galore!

Given the growth of human settlements beside the Lake, there will be a rush of dirt. One hopes they will not cite an example of the river Ganga. If the town planners passed the law preventing the erection of structures within a certain meter distance fixed by them, it would have helped the implementing agency to insist on adhering to it. However, there is perhaps no such law preventing the erection of the residential structure. The Haflong Municipal Board has yet to be a watchdog. Beautiful sights, once created, should remain preserved. Nobody wants the pumping of public money for short-term beautification. On the other hand, any expenditure planned for the Lake's long-term beautification would be good exercise and ensure joy forever.

Next, there is a need to pass the Council's legislation, which only allows some people to cut down the trees around the town with written permission from the Haflong Municipal Board.

Cross-examination

Water scarcity is the top of solving the fundamental day-to-day problem of amenities for the hill people from both urban and rural areas in the district; the Council gears up Public Health Engineering and other development departments to meet the challenge.

If the scarcity of water continues in Haflongtown and its adjoining areas, the North Cachar Hills Autonomous Council will have to examine the feasibility of pumping the river water from Panimur or Dehangi areas. Though the project appears big, it will be the most viable one considering the growth of population.

Next, the village people practice shifting cultivation, popularly known as "*Jhum kheti*".

So, the administration of the Council has emphasised rooting out the age-old habit by involving the State departments like Agriculture, Fishery, Forest, Soil Conservation, Sericulture, Rural Development, Veterinary, Social Welfare, Industries, Handloom and Textiles, and allied agencies concerned.

In implementing their respective departmental schemes, the Council enforces them regularly. The concerned departments introduce their separate plans in pursuance of the Government's approval at the Centre and State. Each department's schemes aim to raise the hill people's economic standard.

By the way, there is a need to cross-examine the official record on the total areas of plantations created by the different development entities every year so that their creations do not bizarrely cover the entire geographical area of the Dima Hasao!

Luring efforts

Mentionable, the District of Dima Hasao is an abode of various groups of people, and the Council's inherent aim is to make the commoners aware of their cultural heritage. So, the District Museum under the aegis Cultural Department and other central development departments, including Town and Country Planning, has been functioning in line with the prevailing need.

In addition, the Dima Hasao Autonomous Council has emphasised the development of hill tourism to absorb unemployed youths in this sector. Since the last eight years, the Council has made efforts to improve the roads of every nook and corner. The endeavour is to ensure benefit to the tourists who can travel around the district where the PWD roads hitherto remained severely shaped. However, they improved the road and transport sectors. In that case, the tourism sector of the Council can only expect guests from within the hilly region, including abroad, and they can lure anybody to visit the Dima Hasao.

Entrusted Subjects' Administrative Establishment

Under the Sixth Schedule of the Constitution, there are two types of administrative establishment of the Transferred Subjects of the Dima Hasao Autonomous Council – Headquarters and Subordinate Establishments. The former belongs to the District Head of Department (DHOD), and the latter is the institution's Divisional or Executive Engineer level.

The district-level functionary is the leading work-implementing agency of the Government of Assam under the administrative control of the autonomous body.

The DHOD acts as the second administrative head of the Government, the first being the Secretariate of the Council headed by the Principal Secretary of the Transferred Departments as per the standing agreement between the two entities – Government and Council.

Like the above two types of official establishment, the workforce under these administrative units seems classified into two categories – one that concerns the DHOD; the other helps the divisional head of the establishment in implementing the Government schemes.

The promotion and transfer of the workforce of the DHOD rest with the Head of Department (HOD) of the State, whose establishment is in Guwahati. Though the HOD carries out these two functions regarding the workforce of the DHOD, the service of the two categories of force – namely, Grades III and IV staff – remains placed under the disposal of the Dima Hasao Autonomous Territorial Council.

The services of both Grades –I and II workforces of all establishments of the Entrusted Subjects of the Council get placed under the administrative control of the above autonomous body. These two categories of services of even the Normal Sector of administration of the Dima Hasao Autonomous Council have been paid their monthly Salary under the State Grants-in-Aid package to the Council, following the recent decision of the ruling Party Government at Dispur to bear their monthly pay.

However, there is a need to frame the Council Service Rules in line with the State Government Service Rules, which will pave the way for ensuring the Services Assured Progression Scheme.

By the way, even with the maintenance of the Seniority List of Grades III & IV staff and the establishment of the DHOD by the HOD, there needs to be more clarity in following the Services Rules.

For instance, the service particulars of the Grades III and IV staff recruited by the DHOD as per the recommendation of the first administrative authority of the Transferred Subjects needed recording correctly. Even the junior staff recruited by the HOD overtakes the senior team appointed by the DHOD in granting promotional benefits.

Ornamental & Tunnel Tree Plantations; Religious and Cultural Tourism

Every year, the Dimasa tribe members take a holy bath at the Panimur Falls. They regard it as *Kopili Tirtha* (Kopili Pilgrimage), which they hold on the occasion of Maghi Purnima. The place where they take the religious bath is on the Umrongso-Lanka Road in the Dima Hasao district. Umrongso is about forty-five kilometres from the district headquarters – Haflong.

The place known as Panimur Waterfall has become popular ever since the last Dimasa King of Maibang reportedly took his bath there. Besides, when he was the Deputy Leader of the Congress Legislature Party and Hill Areas Development Minister, holding among other portfolios, in the Cabinet of the former Chief Ministers of Assam – Hiteswar Saikia and Tarun Gogoi – Gobinda Chandra Langthasa used to participate in the Community Bath. The present Executive Member of the North Cachar Hills Autonomous Council, Debolal Gorlosa, also participated in the community ceremony.

Given that most Dimasas worshipped the Lord Siva (aka Sibarai), I proposed establishing a temple in the middle of the Haflong Lake, in the heart of Haflongtown.

Lord Siva, mentionable according to some Hindu traditions in India, is also an incarnation of Lord Vishnu and Brahma. Let it be clear why I initially happened to propose Lord Vishnu's temple.

My proposition to establish a place of worship in the waterbody without disturbing the existing environment emerged from the location of Kanya Kumari as per Swami Vivekananda's wish. The place, surrounded by the Ram Thakur Mandir, is on the east side of the recently installed statue of Mahatma Gandhi at the North Cachar Hills Autonomous Council Rotary. The residential complex of the former Chief Executive Member of the autonomous body, Shyam Chand Hojai, is on the South, and the Dimasa Mahila Samiti Office building on the North will add to a new Tourist' Spot. If the site does not suit the plan, we can work out a new one towards implementing similar mechanisms in the Lake somewhere else.

When the political will is strong, it can also work out tunnel tree with ornamental plants in between Sainza Raji Road Tinali and Council Gate and around Haflong Lake, and Tourists' Lodge to Jatinga. Likewise, mass participation in the community bath, apart from establishing a place of worship for Sibarai (Lord Siva) in Panimur, will be an attractive suggestion for luring tourists outside Assam's hilly region.

Likewise, we can work out cultural events highlighting the celebration of the paddy-harvest festivals of different ethnic groups. Such celebration ensures a similar streak of unity in diversity.

With the present North Cachar Hills Autonomous Council working on preserving the culture and traditions of the tribe members of the Dima Hasao, the proposal, when implemented, will pave the way for beginning religious tourism in the countryside.

Post-Harvest Bonanza to lure tourists

Beginning in January, the people of Dima Hasao celebrate their Bihu festival. By the individual name of such festival, each ethnic group has given its name with an ethnic tone.

For instance, the major Dimasa call it Busu, the Zeme, Kuki, Hmar, Baite, Karbi, Hrangkhol, Khasi-Jaintia, Khelma celebrate the festival as Hega-Ngigi, Chavang Kut, Sikpui Ruoi, Nuldim Kut, Hacha Kekan & Ok Kepru, Rualsafak, Sngi Lumlang and Parsem Kut respectively.

Each group of people in its cultural attire looks colourful. However, one notices that the individual celebration of their respective festivals ensures a unique identity.

If I am right, each group celebrates the uniqueness of its particular social unit. However, everybody's participation in rejoicing would look better without diluting the objective of the carnival.

We could work out its celebration in line with the Annual Falcons Festival in Dima Hasao.

For example, in Upper Assam, the people participate in Bihu dance, wearing the cultural Assamese Dress, regardless of which group a dancer belongs. Likewise, in Dima Hasao, the people led by the majority could well encourage other groups' participation in such competitions.

Agreeing on it or not, such competition would not only ensure unity in diversity, but also it would virtually be a sporty event. Everybody knows sport never pulls up spectators if it goes by any communal consideration. Further, the sport may not prosper without getting it scrupulously projected and rewarded.

What is the harm if we appreciate a winner's success in terms of multi-participation? The communal participation in a game is narrower than that of various groups in a heterogeneous society. If we continue encouraging only communal celebration, it fosters the growth of rigidity towards the difference, which seems diabolical. It helps the indirect development of fissiparous elements.

Unless we encourage the flexible concept as above by holding a multi-participation event sooner than ever, it would be problematic to foster the growth of unity in a society inhabited by various groups of stakeholders.

Mark the word, politics accessibly tuned to ethnicity, thereby encouraging a subtle majority-versus-minority amidst the potential of various groups, does not seem favourable to the health of the hilly region of Assam–Dima Hasao.

With time, there is a need for modern celebration, keeping the concept of cementing the relationship with one another groups alive, without weakening the basic idea of Busu or Dima Hasao Bihu.

Perhaps, Dima Hasao will have to engage some consultants who can work out such an ambitious plan foreseeing fostering the growth of unity in diversity.

Should we conceptualise such a standard celebration once a year within the territorial jurisdiction of the Dima Hasao

Autonomous Council, it would help the Tourism Department under the administrative control of the Dima Hasao lure tourists outside the hilly region.

The above proposition is not averse to the greater interest of Dima Hasao society, which is an abode of various groups of people, including non-tribals.

Different development entities' functional approaches

The adoption of specific schemes by the district villagers in growing, reaping or harvesting, the Departments of Agriculture, Sericulture, Soil Conservation, Handloom and Textiles and other allied agencies extend such facilities because these are some of the significant development departments allied with agricultural activities. All adopted and implemented schemes substitute for shifting cultivation practised by the cultivators. They feel only *jhum kheti* helps them ensure food for their livelihood.

On the other hand, development entities like the Departments of Co-operation, Industry and Commerce dispose of the village produce in the markets.

In uplifting the people's economy, the Council also gives importance to the Education Sector towards skill development. Apart from that, it insists on collecting and preserving cultural objects like records, textiles, ornaments, musical instruments, and ethnographic items belonging to the different communities.

However, there is a perennial problem in executing the National Highway passing through Dima Hasao.

Next to the railway line that passes through the Dima Hasao, the National Highway bridges important communication between these regions – North and South Cachar districts of the State Assam.

The people of these localities would not be fortunate enough to enjoy it if Atal Bihari Vajpayee did not dream of the East-West Corridor project. It was the dream project of the erstwhile visionary Prime Minister of India. He was the first to dream of the project connecting Silchar and Porbandar in Gujarat. However, he could not see it executed with his physical eyes when he was alive.

He publicised the project on 10th October 1999.

Due to administrative intricacies, the Forest Department did not issue any green signal to construct the Road, especially from Balacherra to Dima Hasao. However, the area did not fall within any Wildlife Sanctuary.

It is a stretch of about 31 kilometres of construction that has been having a hard time for the National Highway Authority of India. You will be in awe of the cutting of the earth if you go and see the ongoing work of the project. But, unfortunately, during the rainy season, there is no guarantee the runoff water will not wash away all the cut earth.

Even in the dry season, traffic movement between Silchar and Haflong is risky and not hygienic for humans because of dust and the available loading and unloading of heavy vehicles.

The irony is that some intellectuals of the Cachar district term it as a stumbling block for developing Barak Valley.

The actual work of the project, taken up by Sushi Infra and Mining Infrastructure Ltd, began in December 2017 at Balacherra.

Nevertheless, the company could not smoothly execute it once. Because some villagers reportedly did not get any compensation entitled to them after the road construction authority remained callous towards their genuine grievances, they surrounded the company's office above and asked for payment.

Afterwards, the NHAI showed documents permitting them to execute the project in the particular areas before the villagers withdrew all agitations. However, things began to go wrong between Harangajao and Durbintilla when the villagers raised similar issues above and started obstructing the execution of works.

The trouble allegedly led to the non-returning of some staff to the work site or others resigning from their company's jobs under the above circumstances.

On the other hand, the sporadic interference coupled with the indiscriminate earth cutting and loosening of soil led to the frequent suspension of traffic between Silchar and Haflong.

Thus, the story about how the National Highway Infrastructure and Development Corporation Limited got delayed in executing the dreamt project of the former poet Prime Minister, Atal Bihari Vajpayee.

The success of any Government's Tourism and other Development Departments rests with the activation of the Public Relations Department. Though the expenditure involved in disseminating Government information sometimes gets higher, the department always enjoys the status of a mouthpiece.

Above are the functional approaches adopted by the different entities of the State towards development.

Other approaches towards the development

As for their developing vision of the hilly region, some tribal intelligentsia want to concentrate on socio-economic development to create long-term welfare and benefits that ensure resource potential. They need to chalk out plans to bring about an automatic agreement with the Government of India, besides improving things to realise the objective above. In addition, the group focuses on these goals by maintaining a healthy relationship with their traditional neighbours - subtly advocating a non-communal attitude towards realising the above objectives.

Some advocate an effective and efficient waste disposal mechanism. As a step towards managing it, the tourism department may charge a reasonable amount for homestays, restaurants, and small hotels. But, of course, only those involved in tourist hospitals should get the privilege. There is also scope for utilising organic waste like foodstuff, plates, paper, glass, and so on for making manure. Regarding inorganic wastes like plastic bottles, recycling seems best for its management—some waste.

The Municipal Board may utilise organic waste, like foodstuff, paper, and so on, for making manure. It may also arrange to dispose of some waste by installing incineration chambers outside the town.

The Dima Hasao Autonomous Council encourages the local youths to execute different tasks to ensure good governance and proper public service. The administration of the autonomous body has already established more than sixteen facilitation centres across the district to render online portal service through the Right to Public Service (RTPS). It aims to provide better and quicker services in issuing Jamabandhi (Land Holdings) Copy, Permanent Residential Certificate, and No Objection Certificate for immovable properties; Income Tax Certificate for farmers; Income Tax Exemption Certificates and Trading License.

The Dima Hasao Adventure Association organised the White-Water Rafting Expedition on 21st July 2022. Efforts are going to explore the Diyung and Kopili Rivers and manage rock-climbing, zip-lining, rappelling and trekking

An egalitarian structure of development proposition

There is also one school of thought which says the adoption of individual development is repugnant to the social units of the Dima Hasao. It wants the community's progress. Because there is no shortage of resources - forests, minerals, rivers - the need for human skill to wisely use these is essential, for which all groups are to develop, subtly opposing individual development. Given the emergence of the school of thought from the fear of losing socialism, the supposition seems unfounded because it supports community participation, which is narrower than individualism.

Frankly, the essence of development must be rooted in the growth of the mental horizon, which, in turn, paves the way for involving an individual in the competition for a better tomorrow. On the other hand, many people cannot achieve consciousness because it requires much effort, and on the other hand, an entity can only accomplish it singly. In such a situation, encouraging individual participation is highly acceptable, for it helps man adjust to different conditions towards growth and development.

An Individual's growth or development ensures perfection in their transactional business, privileging knowing good and evil, which, in turn, helps them restrain the random use of their resources. But, on the other hand, strong support for the participation of the community may lead to the birth of some politicians' poodles –forming gangs to indulge in more corrupt practices for money, pleasure and power, thereby paving the way for a systematic uprooting of the natural resources, let alone lacking the sanctity of secular spirit of the community.

There is no guarantee a group of people will achieve the same enthusiasm and energy an individual possesses at a time. Given the proposition, it amounts to treating an entity as a commodity. It seems impossible for an individual to take society in their hand because it is a byzantine exercise.

Further, the community is not a product an individual can take wherever they like. Of course, if somebody wishes to change the mindset of the people, they are to encourage the growth of consciousness in the masses' minds. A more significant increase in mass participation involves a long or time-consuming process without guarantee.

Hence, we cannot deal with awareness in anticipation of vigorous growth to the extent that individualism guarantees success with a hundred per cent application of efforts.

Contextually, there is no place for socialism to ensure development to the wise expectation of the people; it dampens the spirit of an individual's progress due to the wrong systematization of the human mind, saying no one can do anything worthwhile in life without the support of their people or community or group. But in practicality, growth has remained in the initial participation of the individual.

On the contrary, agreeing on it or not, the more significant participation of people ensures the political success of the leaders, contrary to the maxim of man's growth or development perching on following individualism.

For instance, we oppose the Caste system, but how can we contain the division growth based on stocks? In every political development, there is a subtle birth of disunity. The discord brings about the changes. Ultimately, history repeats itself in different forms.

Tribals have yet to succeed in some areas of growth and development because they have a limited chance to participate in the life of competition. And the privileges to them have ensured success for their selected groups of people.

Regarding compatibility, some tribals are superior and more competent than the non-tribals. Hence, the responsibility to guide their clan members or stocks to adopt the model of indigenous non-tribals of the Brahmaputra and Barak Valleys while retaining their culture and identities of particular social units rest with their intelligentsia.

Handloom potentials

Next to agriculture, the handloom sector has enough potential to generate employment opportunities in Dima Hasao, where the womenfolk of different groups produce high-value clothes in the hilly region.

Proper public relations exercises would have popularised the products.

The erstwhile Chief Executive Member of the Dima Hasao Autonomous Council, Debojeet Thaosen, inaugurated a showroom of handloom products in Kolkata.

The establishment of the outlet aimed at online selling of products like handkerchiefs, jackets and mekhela from Dima Hasao and Karbi Anglong abroad, for which the Council targeted destinations were in the United States of America, Switzerland, Canada and Japan.

After the store's inauguration, there were reports of the sale of forty thousand rupees in three days. Then, however, the change of government after a series of violent events erupted in the territorial jurisdiction of the locality led to the dampening of the spirit of the trade.

Though some designs hitherto adopted by the weavers may only attract some prospective buyers, such methods need upgrading to suit the changing world's daily needs. The Handloom industry is the cottage one, and weaving is a way of life for the tribes' women.

Strategizing further Development of Dima Hasao

If I were to strategize the development of Dima Hasao, my introspective moves would be inclusive progress.

In the thirteenth election, several candidates who contested on different parties' tickets promised to chalk out some programmes relating to development when voted to power. Their promises are worth considering for the prospective ruling party Members of the North Cachar Hills Autonomous Council to work out implementing all bright ideas towards bettering future planning and monitoring, apart from ensuring development within the jurisdictional areas of the autonomous body.

Dima Hasao requires invariably allotting major Transferred Subjects to the capable, honest and devoted elected members chosen to act as Executive Members.

They should not encourage the Government Departments to implement schemes departmentally; they can engage the local contractors with the requisite sense of being and belonging.

The contractors from the locality deserve to implement all works duly supported by the technically skilled departmental officials.

In the event of the shortage of such contractors as above, preferably without political affiliations, there should be no objection against allotting such works to those deserving members of the ruling party who do not get elected, or they can allot contract works to any party members' kith and kin who have proven record about having responsibly executed the works on previous occasions.

There is a need to chalk out better fund distribution and utilization, equalizing the percentage of allotment among all divisional and sub-divisional establishments of the Entrusted Subjects to ensure transparency and development.

On the other hand, there were several protests over the fielding of candidates outside of the relevant constituencies, though it was perhaps not illegal. If the candidate hails from the jurisdictional areas of the Council, nobody should prevent them from contesting in the election. The protest should not have gone to such an extent as bringing about a physical fight between the supporting and opposing groups. What would I suggest? Those voters who do not like any candidates chosen by their party outside their constituencies could have rejected them, and the chosen one could have got their favour in exercising their choice. Everybody needs to be a bit sympathetic towards redressing such an issue because running a party is not that easy; different strategies require adopting and accommodating the aspirations of different important blued boys of the party, for everybody is not fit for a job in nurturing such an outfit in a locality.

Agreeing on it or not, the lack of farsightedness results from the communication gap between the party's high command and their political functionaries. The party could have done well to allow the local candidates to contest on Independent Symbols, apart from indirectly supporting them, which minimizes the chance of opposition between the supporters of local and outsider groups of candidates. Further, it would continue preserving the stronghold of the party concerned.

Likewise, Dima Hasao can never give lukewarm support to the digital revenue receipts or payment of the contractors' and or beneficiaries' bills if they wish to curb the evils of greed. There is an urgent need to streamline the online registration of PRC, Professional Taxes Clearnce Certificate, Annual Income Certificate and so on.

In the end, everlasting peace coupled with rapid progress in the jurisdictional areas of the Autonomous Council seems possible if they consider preserving the legacy of the past in terms of environment, among other things. Then, there will be the need to crash all adverse forces. The North Cachar Hills Autonomous Council will have to resolve not to seek the service of fund swindlers in the guise of local hoodlums.

Ensuring development should be a joint effort, not necessarily perching on any particular elected Member. All the best!

Administrative future of Dima Hasao

The actual position in getting recruited could be better. Those who enjoy political, administrative or financial clout get jobs in Government establishments (unrelated to Dima Hasao). In private institutions, they want efficient or less remunerative workforces. Moreover, some people's low economic condition prevents them from attending better educational institutions, which charge higher fees than low-income earners 'affordability. So, they have to depend upon the government's highly paid teaching staff, some of whom, in most cases, do not care about the future of the student community. Why? Their Salary is handsome and regular; their teaching or attendance does not matter - whether they belong to the employees of educational or other Government establishments.

The lesser-fated workforces have no bread. In such a situation, the problem of the whole State becomes chronic. A man with the required skill does not get the matching job, so education remains a literary type with no success in convincing anybody at the helm of affairs. Further, moneyless people cannot succeed in a democracy where the ruling class speaks louder than work. With the people having power and enjoying all privileges, they also use some media houses to control their minds.

When the unemployed lose hope for jobs in the temporal world, they try for these through God's blessings if they are believers in their respective religions. Contextually, the Courts of their Bhagwan, Iswar, Khuda, Ruub, Allah, God, Goddess and Lord seem to be full of Cases consisting of unrelenting prayers for a job every one of them.

The unemployed do not get justice from their representatives—both ruling and opposition. In contrast with the ruling class, the opposing one sometimes acts as if it has no sense of being and belonging. When the game of power turns wild, it fires the framework of democracy. Though the people's government scheme does not subscribe to "Might is Right" in theory, Prosperity does not ever build a castle in the Feeble. I do not see much difference between Doom and Crazy, contextually. Nor can a conscientious man waste their energy thinking of goldening it – How can an individual's contribution alone make it so? Though heaven would not fall from a short contribution toward the unity and integrity of the country, the light of it is possible if everybody participates in the right earnest. So, the problem to tackle is: How do we convince the human race? Everybody is superior; nobody is equal, either. But the effort to dictate terms to others already remains present in all!

So, on the trip to control one another among men, there is a similar employment problem because it concerns societal living status. Everybody who is unemployed feels dissatisfied in life. They always feel deprived of what they think they deserve. So, any discrimination in the grant of privilege by one to the other ignites anger and emotion. Moreover, it requires diplomatic dealing in some States – including Assam – of the Indian Union, whose inhabitants are of various ethnic origins. Recently, there was a hue and cry over recruitment in some parts of the State, including the Cachar district.

Though the opposition to recruiting and posting of the unemployed in the same State from one part to another does not augur well, the issue is sensitive and deserves a soul-searching solution. Somewhere, there is subtle justification for the opposition. How? Where will we take, or what immediate opportunity will we give the unemployed of the same potential area of the State if we wish to arrange the new hands outside it? As long as there is darkness in the tunnel, there is no interest in locating the sight of light. Such an issue may snowball into a major controversy if not appropriately handled.

We may cite an example of the decision to roll back the merging order of the Hill Areas Development Ministry of the Assam State Government into a Sixth Schedule Areas Development Department. The objective behind the amalgamation was to be free from any evil motivation. However, since the Sarbananda Sonowal Government did not take the leaders of Dima Hasao and Karbi Anglong into confidence before moving to form the proposed department, it had to bow down upon their pressure.

Similarly, before the circulation of the Government Notification on the creation of a Mini Secretariate, Barak Valley, at Silchar, the recruitment of a large number of employees from Lower and Upper Assam without taking the leaders of the Southern Assam into confidence led to the seething of the people of the potential areas with dissent. Of course, the appointment's objective aimed to bridge a significant communication gap between Assam's Dispur and Cachar districts.

Strategically, it's worth justifying Dispur's point of view, which even ordered the organizational unit's establishment on the 19th day of February 2021. Mr M.S. Manivannan, IAS, the Commissioner and Secretary to the Government of Assam, General Administration Department, Dispur, signed the order. Establishing the State's administrative unit in the Cachar district is a welcome step in a strategic administration. It would go a long way in containing the evil effect of a similar lingua franca between the intruders from the neighbouring countries and misguided people of India – Bangladesh, and Myanmar.

On the other hand, the establishment of a Mini Secretariate will better nourish the bond between the people of Dima Hasao and Cachar if we order establishing transactional relationships of all departments of the Dima Hasao with the newly created administrative unit at Silchar, in Barak Valley. Besides narrowing the distance of communication between Silchar and Haflong compared to Dispur Secretariate, Guwahati and Dima Hasao Autonomous Council, Haflong, it enhances a more accessible administrative link between the two entities.

By the way, unlike other parts of Assam, an administrator who carries out their given assignments in all Cachar districts – namely, Silchar, Hailakandi and Karimganj – must have felt satisfied with the respect the people of these administrative areas of the State tendered to them. Though care is conditional, it is worth mentioning when serving in Southern Assam, which has many similarities in the Bongaigaon and Dhubri districts. These places are closely associated with the people of the Jalpaiguri district of West Bengal.

The original Bengali Bhadralok or their descendants of Cachar districts are indisputably Indian-spirited. Still, they may only be able to maintain their existence if they contain the influence of intruders who easily mix up with the local people by taking advantage of the same lingua franca between the two groups.

Some may oppose it, but those who seriously think about their locality's future, including the need for avenues toward the succeeding generations, can not downplay it if they don't indulge in politics by coalescing people from the same language for political success.

One understands that language originates from the heart, which cements the relationship with the clan members deeper than strangers. Hence, even the original conscientious inhabitants may develop a soft attitude towards foreigners (Bangladeshis). However, I wouldn't say I like to charge anybody with indifference because the heart's chemistry is magical, making it challenging to exercise limitation.

I honestly think the Bengali Bhadralok may not be a loser if they work out a better give-and-take formula with the people of the Brahmaputra Valley to ensure a better future for their birthplace. The original Bhadralok will deprive bread of their children if they now ignore the above issue. Hence, they must realize it: they have a history of sacrifice for the country's cause of freedom. So, they can do better than others.

Development plan extension

The growth of evils becomes visible when we observe the uneven population distribution in a State. The history of humans speaks of the birth of the wicked out of greed. The non-fulfilment of their wants brings about the birth of an attitude filled with the bankruptcy of ideology. Such an individual may feel that power with position is the ultimate resort to life, thinking it ensures everlasting peace and dignity. The unlimited desire to acquire wealth undercuts the moral resource in man. The sight of unequal distribution of wealth amidst the presence of competitors paves the birth of anti-social elements.

Hence, places like Haflong, Maibang, Umrongso and Harangajao should get singled out, concentrating on producing jobs apart from ensuring facilities.

There is a need to work out a mechanism for adopting an extension of the development plan toward Harangajao, Mahur, Diyungmukh, Gunjung, and Langting. The proposal will arrest the population's rise in urban areas when implemented. Agreeing on it or not, in most cases, the mindset of humans tends to undermine the ethical value of their wants because of the uncanny growth of competition in them for a better living than others.

Considering the above, the development makers would do well to emphasise electrifying villages, increasing the number of market congregations, ensuring better education and entrepreneurial skills, and setting up health units, water supply and sanitation in rural areas.

Joy Bhadra Hagjer was the first Member of Parliament from the erstwhile North Cachar Hills, which all of us know.

The movement for an Autonomous State led by the Autonomous State Demand Committee ensured the increased intensity of the subtle division of people. However, the division did not ensure disunity in the hilly region of Assam,. The founders of the erstwhile North Cachar Hills best planned and developed the countryside.

It is time we got a direct representation from the Dima Hasao in Lok Sabha. The standing picture covering three hilly districts of Assam – Dima Hasao, Karbi Anglong & West Karbi Anglong – with one Parliament member has not met the people's expectations.

Hence, there is every reason to argue that the backwardness of the hilly region of Assam – Dima Hasao – has resulted from the lack of scope to properly submit the people's grievances by their representative in Parliament.

We will further get to know about the issue in Chapter III, where Cabinet Mission, Advisory, and Bordoloi Sub Committees' reports have also found a prominent place.

All about the self-sufficiency cord

The use of insecticides and pesticides, among other things, in the cultivation of the leafy and other vegetables has posed a serious health hazard. Reports emanating say some people have started injecting fruits and vegetables with poisonous substances to ripen these has been increasing. There is no answer: where is the destination of the man's greed? By harming their fellowmen, an individual is getting harmed themselves due to the ideological bankruptcy. The gluttony to earn more does not die down with no trouble.

Before the evils above spread their wings, every conscientious citizen must make the harms featherless. For there is nothing man can not make or break in the temporal world, the will to contain the wicked is the need of the hour. It should begin with the village on where the spirit of our India perches.

The people of Dima Hasao may join hands with the proponents of other localities of India in the organic farming, which will give no chance to the evils. There will be the need to increase the productivity of various crops through proper regulation in organic farming, apart from extending irrigation facilities, price count and post-harvest running.

In this hilly region of Assam, there is scope to adopt the method of agriculture, which is the mainstay of the tribe members in the rural areas, which have no favourable geographical place and problematic land, the development of such places under wet cultivation is limited.

The borough is hilly, unlike Karbi Anglong; I don't know how far we can go for the organic farming. Nor do I know how justified it is to think of it in terms of self-sufficiency along with our food production in Dima Hasao where the production of rice is not sufficient.

Likewise, the sufficiency of water is not visible in the Dima Hasao's rivers, which are getting depleted day-by-day. Because the stakeholders have been haphazard in the use of their natural resources, right from the extraction of boulders, sand to the felling of trees and bamboos, it seems bound to happen.

Honestly, if the Dima Hasao will ever succeed in preserving the pride in the possession of the natural resources and beauties. As for the countryside's participation in achieving hundred percent food security, it needs to make the Agriculture and allied development Departments responsible for it.

Though there is a feeling in which the presence of local technical and non-technical skills ensures better justice, due to which it has given a lukewarm support to the establishment of a university and other institutions, it is not adequate. So, there will be the need to hire trained personnels from the various fields, right from the educational to developmental sectors, such as Soil to Sericulture to Animal Husbandry. Those who have got the requisite talent can enhance the local youths' mental horizons. Apart from that, they must have the potential to suggest suitable and multiple cropping to our farming community.

Keeping the objective in view, the Dima Hasao requires suggesting which type of officials they require posting in the office establishments of the Government Departments. The proposed Dima Hasao Territorial Autonomous Council will have the power to exercise over it as per the standing agreement with the Government. At the same time, the personnels so hired from outside the locality expect better treatment as the locals extend to their near and dear ones.

Tap Ethnic Power, Ensure Peace by Awards!

Every year, the Dima Hasao celebrates our country's freedom, remembering the sacrifices made by the national and state levels freedom fighters. They hardly think of how the district level people participated in rooting the British out from India. How hard we earned our freedom or independence from the British?

Many of us know most of our national and state level participants in the country's struggle against the British. Very few of us lay emphasis on inculcating the spirit of patriotism our local elders exhibited in today's youths.

The spread of education has expanded the mental horizons when properly preserved and utilised simultaneously, will pave the way for ensuring a perennial peace and tranquility in the assorted society.

Whether it is the 26th day of January or the 15th day of August, we celebrate both occasions every year very auspiciously. Nationalism seems best defined in terms of peace, progress and prosperity. The contribution of masses, right from the village to district, State to Centre level, caused the British leave India. The country, as we all know, is a multi-ethnic and religious country. Thus, as we earned our freedom by applying different strategies, so we should preserve peace by squeezing out our creative energies from the different groups of people.

Contextually, it is time we instituted awards to crush our different methods sticking out an interest in maintaining peace, remembering all freedom fighters, including prominent founders of Dima Hasao. Because some of them deserve recognitions, others do not get their share of contributions in different fields, at par with their national and state counterparts, recognised.

Based on the quality or, for that matter, quantum of contributions the elders of Dima Hasao made, the North Cachar Hills Autonomous Council could work out awards in memory of those who sacrificed their lives for good of the locality, to present such awards on the auspicious occasions above. Every celebration becomes meaningful when the partakers make it so.

Some of the prominent participants in ousting the British at the district level were – Hamdhan Mohan Haflongbar, Joy Bhadra Hagjer, Veer Sambudhan Phonglo; Dimalik Kemprai; Senapati Tularam Thaosen, Joya Thaosen, Disru, Rani Gaindinliu.

There may be others like Nityalal Daulagupu, Desondao Hojai and Jatindra Lal Thaosen who seem more projecting in their chosen fields than those freedom fighters, which the countryside would do well to decide including their names in the decent proposition.

As we all know, the greater Dima Hasao society is heterogeneous and always tends to get united on ethnic line, requiring to focus on tapping the different segments of creativity toward ensuring unity in diversity. When instituted, the awards will go a long way in realising the objective above.

Towards a Bi-cameral solution

You may agree on it or not, the present ruling dispensation of the State honoured the sentiment of the people of the Dima Hasao which ensured maintaining a unique identity. For instance, the people of the countryside got a ministerial berth in the Himanta Biswa Sharma cabinet, though they are a single Member from the locality to represent the Assam Legislative Assembly, and that the quantum of privileges get perhaps determined depending on the physical presence of the strength of members in standard political calculation.

What I contextually mean is the hilly region of Assam has no comparison with Karbi Anglong in terms of its numerical strength of their representation in the Assam Legislative Assembly. Karbi Anglong sends several elected representatives every term in the Legislative Assembly. In contrast, the Dima Hasao has the voice of 1(one) elected Member of Legislative in the house.

Thus, the difference has led the people of the erstwhile North Cachar Hills to always feel the integration of Karbi Anglong (East) and Karbi Anglong (West) with the present Dima Hasao in Parliament has brought about an inevitable injustice to them. Because not a single case for Dima Hasao has ever come up for discussion in Parliament since the formation of the Autonomous region in 1952, the people of the countryside genuinely want the presence of their voice in Lok Sabha.

Even the lion's share of fund allocation entitled to the Member of Parliament every five year goes to Karbi Anglong. Hence the people of Dima Hasao feel step motherly treated. Given the feeling of deprivation, Dima Hasao submitted its demand in which they serialised their demands, which the Government did not concede.

On the contrary, there is now reported planning to introduce the 125ᵗʰ Constitutional amendment, in which the people of the Dima Hasao have the feeling the Government has been trying to dilute the autonomy of the North Cachar Hills Autonomous Council/Dima Hasao Autonomous Council. How? The allegation is that the Government has reportedly been trying to implement some schemes under the Department of Panchayat and Rural Development in the jurisdictional areas of the Dima Hasao Autonomous Council. In contrast, the people have been sticking out their demand for an Autonomous State, Parliamentary Seat, along with their representation to enhance two more seats of Member of Legislative Constituencies. Seeing the people expecting a good gesture of the Government, the Home Ministry has already constituted a committee to examine the issue. The indifference attitude seemed to have been seeding an uncanny apprehension upon what they called the systematic encroachment of their land and the autonomy granted to the Council under the Sixth Schedule to the Constitution.

Mentionable, on the pretext of the implementation of the Panchayat Raj as per the Memorandum of Settlement signed between the Governments – State and Central – and the representatives of the proscribed Dima Halam Daoga, some ethnic group leaders accused their counterparts of the Government of the erstwhile ruling party of Assam about indulging in chauvinism.

The allegation and counter allegations traded on both ruling and opposition parties in the State politics when the former Assam Gana Parishad Government led by Prafulla Kumar Mahanta and Bhrigu Phukan were in power. The two Danguria of the Brahmaputra valley seemed misled by their advisers. Thanks to the phenomenon, the rise of ethnic politics surfaced, and the movement for division of the State Assam posed a serious threat to the age-old relationship of one group with another.

As the ethnic division turned into a slugfest between the Hindu Assamese and tribals, the Congress party happened to defeat the AGP and ruled the State. Afterwards, the three consecutive terms victory of the Congress led by Tarun Gogoi in Assam ensured confidence and once again, the party rule slowly but steadily lit the light from the tunnel of darkness in the history of the State. Despite being the Savoir of the society, the Tarun Gogoi Government in the State riddled in corruption, inefficiency and factionalism in the eyes of the people. Subsequently, the State power went to the Bharatiya Janata Party, which restored peace.

Considering the rise of the ethnic smokescreen in Assam's politics, directly or indirectly backed by the opposition of the ruling class, the spirit of the Sixth Schedule to the Constitution appears haunted by the bogey of Panchayat Raj. With the Sixth Schedule Protection Committee slowly but steadily integrating with all political forces, which are against the ruling classes of all the autonomous councils' areas, the movement against the Panchayat Raj is likely to bring about some changes in the Sixth Schedule to the Constitution in months or years to come, because some clauses in the Constitution provide for the political enthusiasts to increase their political graph. Hence, the issue stands as a complex problem.

Nevertheless, if we cite an example by thinking of introducing a Bi-cameral legislature in Assam, where the potential rise of fissiparous tendency continues, amidst the conspicuous presence of certain constitutional clauses extending political safeguard to the various groups of people, the political leaderships of Assam only need to be highly responsible for ensuring unity in diversity. All aspirations sprouted from the growth of political consciousness rooted in the advancement of the educational system in all the social units of the State may squarely perch on working out ethnic representation in the above political institutions once for all. Agreeing on it or not, transparency to accommodate the ethnic representation by adopting a Bi-cameral legislature must pave the way for fulfilling the distinctive aspiration arising out of the constitutional loopholes in the multi-lingual States. The authority might well set up an Expert Committee or Commission to go into the details.

At present, the States of Telangana, Maharashtra, Uttar Pradesh, Andhra Pradesh and Bihar have their respective Bi-cameral legislatures.

In support of scrapping SIU and other.

In the Sixth Schedule areas of Assam, the Autonomous Councils exercise their power over the local recruitment of grades-III and IV posts, whether technical or non-technical categories. In the Assam's hilly regions, there was a shortage of technically skilled workforce. Hence, the State used to fill up the type of technical posts. The growth of education ensured the availability of adequate technical workforce, there is now no problem in the local recruitment of such categories of staff.

After the Government of Assam passed an order, imposing necessary restriction on the staffing of unproductive workforces about – or more than – a decade back, an SIU (Staff Inspection

Unit) came into existence to streamline it. The State restricted filling up of the posts of the driver, film operator, handyman, sweeper in grades III and IV categories in some Departments.

In the case of their territorial areas, the autonomous councils recruit staff based on the original sanctioned strength in the above categories. One can say SIU got substituted for the First Salary in Dima Hasao, in which the new appointees are to obtain approbation from the Finance Department.

The need for the submission of the Finance Depatment's approval towards the payment of regular monthly salary aimed to cross-examine the requirement. The introduction of the First Salary aimed at scrutinizing the validity of sanction or retention order of the post against which the State Subjects hold recruitment from time to time in pursuance of the approval and instruction of the Autonomous Councils.

With the commencement of the online salary payment, all entered data of the staff, including the sanctioned strength against which the staff get recruited, the Treasury can get all such engagement details cross-checked before passing the new appointees' salary bill. A strict instruction to the Treasuries itself ensures transparency – Why does the Finance Department insist on the new appointees producing the original sanction for disbursement of their first salary? I feel the presence of data with the bill passing authority (read Treasury) to detect and object in case of any discrepancies in their engagement seems sufficient for the payment of salary to the new hands.

One would like to reiterate that there is no scope for the Autonomous Councils to hold any recruitment of staff in the State Subjects without possessinga valid sanctioned strength of posts. Hence, all recruitments carried out by the Councils seem always legally binding. I sincerely feel the new appointees of the State Subjects could have felt relieved from the hassle of the First Salary if the Government relaxed its insistence imposed upon them, especially in Assam's hill councils' territorial areas in the interest of public service.

Further, with the Principal Secretaries of the Councils requiring consenting and recommending the grant of GPF Final drawal of an employee of the State to the Principal Accountant General, Guwahati on line, the insistence on the countersigning of the AG's sanctioned bills by the District Commissioners of the Hill Areas of Assam to get them paid by the Treasuries is nothing sort of the creation of delay or inconvenience to the applicants for getting their saved or earned money.

With the Government already started the devolution of power to the gras-root by establishing mini secretariats, I think scrapping of the SIU along with other difficulties above only ensures transparency in the Councils' areas because the mini-secretariate is similar to Autonomous State, the status of which both hill Councils already enjoy.

On the other hand, towards bettering administrative management, there is a vital issue relating to the Council's preparing its annual budget and the State Government approving its grant. However, close monitoring of expenditure from the annual allocation due to the conspicuous absence of the branch office of the Accountant General in each autonomous region is widely visible. The establishment of Accountant General has no monitoring unit in the area mentioned above. It has also not allowed the depreciation of the existing hindrances in the speedy disposal of Pension and General Provident Fund Withdrawal Cases of State employees working under the administrative control of the autonomous Council many a time.

For example, the power to liquidate the Medical Reimbursement Bills within its jurisdictional control rests with the Council, over which it does not get any chance to exercise authority.

Secondly, some heads of the Departments of the Transferred Subjects of the Council undermine its autonomy by recommending the employees' promotion and voluntary retirement to their respective State Heads of Departments.

Likewise, some employees apply to their State Heads of Departments for Study Leave, No Objection Certificate for appearing in Competitive Examinations, etc.

In this context, the North Cachar Hills Autonomous Council may well issue necessary tips, tagging a Welcome Note carrying essential points to follow on how to serve as a government official under the administrative control of the autonomous body when an official of the Transferred Subject assumes the charge of their departmental establishment to act as or serve at the establishment of the Council Head of Department. That will go a long way in wiping out the intricate communication gap between the State and Council.

An Account of Distasteful Support

Humans have a fundamental right to select something suitable for them. To this end, I had to exercise choice in recommending one Ganesh Joshi's name as a representative of the Gorkhas by insisting on his nomination when the ASDC (Autonomous State Demand Committee) leaders were against it. My conscience dictated I support Joishi because he was at the party and did not like to accept the offer.

The nomination of a Member of the Autonomous Council is just an eyewash. A nominated non-tribal does not ever get the chair of Executive Member. The designated member still dreams of getting such hospitability from the Executive Committee headed by the Chief Executive Member, even if the nomination belongs to a veteran politician.

Hence, I beg to point out that even if the world's outlook has changed toward excellence – a lady of Indian origin became Vice President of the United States of America, who is now campaigning for the position of the President, a gentleman from this country's head became the Prime Minister of the United Kingdom. Our tribal leaders are more sophisticated or capable than non-tribals in some contexts. Nevertheless, they are still not sharing such a political privilege as contesting in the Dima Hasao Autonomous Council's elections with one or two non-tribal political aspirants.

Let the tribal intelligentsia of the hilly region of Assam decide if the issue raised deserves consideration. But I have no professional interest in it, nor do I personally like any participation in the game of power, nor do I, at this moment, raise the issue given the presence of my clansman. Moreover, even I don't fit for it!

In arguing for privileging one or two seats to contest in Council elections, I recall when I had to recommend a person's name for nominating Member of the Autonomous Council during the Autonomous State Demand Committee's rule. Before I suggested the above name, I wanted to know if Somnath Sasthri (Upadhaya) had any interest in accepting the offer. Still, I did not get to talk with him because of his absence from headquarters.

Then, of course, one Madhuram Joishi wanted it, but I found it better to suggest the name of Ganesh because he had been working for the Autonomous State Demand Committee long. Though I wouldn't say I liked dabbling in politics, I had to carry out the exercise as above because I needed to flatly refuse Prokanta Warisa and Samarjit Haflongbar, who wanted me to hold it. My conscience dictated me to show an eligible person before they took up the assignment; they wanted to give to make it justified to leave them in the lurch.

Further, it was my responsibility to carry out the exercise because the movement over the issue of an Autonomous State sweated us all, directly or indirectly.

Additionally, some people suspected my *distasteful* support of the Autonomous State movement.

For instance, even a man came on the pretext of offering his daughter's hand and stayed two nights at my home so that he could detect if I had led any party and leaders would come to my residence to seek my advice! I could suspect him of not being a genuine man, so I took the liberty to search his bag, in which I saw his dress and a revolver as he went to the bathroom.

Moreover, in one of my enquiries about some people of Kokrajhar, there was no man named Hari Prasad having a marriageable daughter and that I would fit to be her Prince Charming.

Afterwards, I concluded it was a ploy to detect my exercises because some told the lie that I mainly advised the Autonomous State Movement leaders to indulge in violence, which I stoutly denied, for I do not ever support evils that take the life of an individual or ruin them for the sake of power or position of somebody. So, I did not ill-behave with that visitor or make many queries.

However, I said, "It will take time to enter any matrimonial errands!" He even wanted me to tell him why I kept my beard, about which I said I just liked growing it up in my cheeks. I remember sharing with him that some people suspect ulterior motives for nourishing it. But then, he instantly said it did not matter to him when I was at no fault.

Instantly, I sensed the rat after his last powerful statement.

I did not take it seriously because I knew that power corrupts man. But then, he was comparatively a gentleman. He could have well harmed me at midnight and fled away. Instead, he slept in a bed adjacent to my room, which always remained open. Why did he not commit any crimes when all members were asleep fast?

I believe nobody stands for killing any innocent without specific reasons, which I did not have any of these and proudly said after the incident. Every Government employee does not misuse the power conferred upon them.

But some babus in Government establishments may indulge in corrupt practices, I added, as I once experienced it after the outcome of my brother's interview in the APSC Examination at Silchar Circuit House.

Following his feeling of deprivation, I decided not to ever compete in the Assam Civil Services Examination, for I felt I would hardly get any justice, saying: "Even J.K. Thaosen, one of the Members of the APSC was sure my brother would get a job.

Hence, he asked him to opt for allied services. But he has not got it". If one was wrong or right, there was no direction to life in which I lost my employment age fixed by the Government of Assam.

The APSC did not select my brother for the Civil Services; only people from the selective groups got recruited in the State Civil Services, not without indulging in drawer dealing. Further, the corrupt practices were hydra-headed in the Public Services Commission until the Sarbananda Sonowal led the Bharatiya Janata Party Government to Assam's power. So, the good now follows.

We now turn to conclude the book with one more chapter.

CHAPTER-IX

Culture & Creases

A Cultural Icon-Princes Disru; Alaidao Khersa; Negotiating the Social changes; Post Harvest Bonanza; Busu; Chavang Kut; Hega-Ngigi; Hacha Kekan & Ok Kempru; Nulding Kut; Parsem Kut; Rualsafak; Sikpui Ruoi; Sngi Lumlang

Negotiating the social changes

The Dimasa Mothers' Association has done a proper job. Creating awareness among the people is a must. It is also the responsibility of the higher educated class to ignite consciousness among the less educated one without causing a misunderstanding between the two stakeholders of society.

Suppose there are traditions and customs in some social groups that require upgradation. In that case, social organisations should resolve such issues to rescue society from unjustified superstitions, on which we require dwelling in respect of other community.

For instance, some rituals in the Gorkha community require carrying out during the mourning of the deceased. Hence, the Assam Gorkha Samelan has recently instituted a committee to go through such complicated customs and traditions in detail and suggest some remedial measures. It is a welcome step towards rescuing busy persons from the grip of unenlightened social stakeholders. The so-formed committee can make some issues optional. Honestly, where the interpretation of traditions and customs continues to rest on the people who are not enlightened, society can not expect to walk on the wheel of the twenty-first century.

Under the above circumstances, one would like to recall the words of a noted female intellectual, namely, Tapoti Daulagupu (Langthasa) of Dima Hasao:

"The modern Dimasa women of Haflong may start demanding equality of status based on their economic independence, which their male counterparts may be unwilling to grant, resulting in clashes. Moreover, the changes in the women of Haflong also affect the women of the neighbouring areas. Hence, until and unless we give some painful thoughts over the question of women's rights, thereby creating trust and respect between men and women, these clashes of trials will drastically affect the overall Dimasa community."

Let us also study the issue of women, recalling the view of another Dimasa Women activist cum Public Relationist, Purabi Phonglo Bodo, here:

Dimasa Women are given a position and status in society, though they may not be at par with men; the rituals, traditions and by-laws followed within the community broadly show the influence and vital existence of this gender recognition compared to many others in the mainstream populace. We regard the surname (jaadi) inheritance matrilineally as no less than the patriarchal surname (shengphong). Just as a girl, when married to a boy, adopts her husband's surname, the husband must regard and take responsibility for his wife's lineage. It was a pleasure to be part of the meeting cum get-together of our Jaadi held(yesterday) at Haflong. Unfortunately, many couldn't make it due to bad weather in the morning, but hopefully, there'll be more such heart-warming programmes in days to come(sic).

Let the abovementioned issues ignite enthusiasm among all groups of settlers and wipe out all loopholes in their respective social units of Dima Hasao, refraining from brewing any misunderstanding.

Post-Harvest Bonanza

Dima Hasao is an abode of different groups of people with other cultural habits. But all have one common want: To become better than yesterday, even if it seems impossible for some, regarding the standard of living. However, every group tries to improve their communities' way of living, which has become competitive, from footing to speaking to eating, both overtly and covertly. "Overtly" refers to their community people meeting places, where they dwell on specific issues, while "covertly" refers to behaving in public places based on the obnoxious tips of the vested interest. Every prospective leader turns tall as they consider both good and evil aspects of social life and move towards ensuring peace and unity. The advantage of guiding society in proper perspective is to ensure safety, security, harmony and peace. So, everyone who feels responsible for leading their club must invariably think of it in an appropriate perception. Human history teaches us everybody is breaking the old thread of unity in diversity for petty personal gains.

Agreeing on it or not, man's selfishness is the leading cause of their concern. I bet if there is any disorder sans greed in man. Even the fear or sectarian outlook developed due to gluttony. But, of course, everybody is not conscious enough, so weakness drives a man into committing wrong, which is synonymous with sin or crime in society. The greater society of Dima Hasao is always secular. How? Most of us have individual festivals and holidays simultaneously.

For instance, Busu for the Dimasa; Hega Ngi for Zeme Naga; Sngi Lumlang (Behdeinkhlam) for the Jaintias; Nulding Kut for the Baite; Rualsafak for the Hrangkhol, Chavangkut stands for the Kuki, Sikpui Ruoi belongs to the Hmar; Hacha Kekan & Ok Kepru belongs to the Karbis; and Parsem Kut is for the Khelmas. Contextually, every citizenry should feel proud of the secular character of the greater Dima Hasao society. Therefore, they may introduce a provision for celebrating every group's participation in their post-harvest festival.

Mentionable, all tribes, such as Jeme, Hmar, Kuki, Baite and Hrangkhol, end their respective post-harvest celebrations in one day-long programme. But the Dimasa tribe members have three types of Busu – G-daap, Surem and Hangseu. Every family can celebrate the G-daap Busu because it is a one-day scheme. The second one, namely, Surem, requires celebration for three consecutive days. Finally, the last Hangseu festival ends in seven days, about which you will get in detail somewhere in the narrative.

It appears the second and third Nos. Busu aim for more significant participation of the community. So, most Dimasas only celebrate these singly; they party with a group from their community.

The Dima Hasao Autonomous Council has declared a Busu holiday on 27th January.

One of the exciting features of the Surem or Hangseu celebration is the people continue to get these festivals commemorated without any disturbance. For example, if death occurs during these celebrations in the village or locality, it does not affect the merriment, which has the social sanction of the community.

Busu

Of the three numbers of Busu (Busu Jidap, Surem Baino and Hangseu Manaoba) of the Dimasa tribe members, "Hangseu Manaoba", which they celebrate for seven days, is the most prominent. The tribe members celebrate Busu Jidap for three days and Surem Baino for five. During the celebrations, men wear dresses: Risha, Rikhaosa, Pagri, Rimshau, Ritab and Rimshaorimai. The tribe women wear dresses like Rigu,

Rijamphain, Rijamphainberen and Rikhausa. The ladies also wear different ornaments, namely, kaudima, khadu, kamaotai, longbar, pantaubar, chandrwal, rangborsha, engrasha, jongsama, ligzau, jingjri and yausidam. Also, other tribes of Dima Hasao celebrate the post-harvest festival.

To commemorate the seven-day celebration, the Dimasa tribe members prepare a big budget and collect cash or donations from the people. They do not celebrate the festival at a particular place every year. Like the literary festival of Assam, namely, Assam Sahitya Sabha, which the people of the State, especially those who live in Brahmaputra Valley, celebrate at different places, the Dimasa tribe members hold the post-harvest festival. Of course, the Busu does not relate to the Assam Sahitya Sabha; it is just a contextual reference, not to undercut any entity's importance.

The celebration of the seven-day festival helps the youth unite together. It motivates the children to work better and produce more food grains from their paddy fields. The higher growth allows them to spend more towards feeding the whole society, which participates in celebrating it for seven consecutive days.

Besides, the celebration inspires the youth to give importance to the festival and garners support from all people in grooming new "leaders" from the "young boys" and "young girls" known as "Nagahoja" and "Malahoja" respectively, towards celebrating the Hangseu Busu. Besides, they are to select "Gajaibao" (the house's owner where the Hangsong Busu takes place). Moreover, one of the unique features of the Busu is the tribe members play on their flutes, called "Muri", in their dialect non-stop for seven days.

The entire area gets excited or mesmerised during the flute playing. The sound of the *Muri* is similar to that of the snake catcher. So, the flautist remains strictly meditative in praise of the holy name of Sibarai (equivalent to the Lord Siva).

Under no circumstance should their concentration on the flute play be disturbed as per the rule.

Commenting on the celebration, Dr Mahanta Langthasa said, "The Dimasa tribe members celebrate Busu Dima during peak winters, also between new moon to the full moon, coinciding on auspicious days, ending either on Saturday or Tuesday, as the Dimasas feel, these two days are inauspicious. Unlike other communities, they do not hold the carnival on a fixed date. The villagers fix the date & days according to their respective convenience so that all members, from far & away together, along with their near and dear ones, get a chance to participate, pay respects or homage to their close departed souls, let alone elders before their full Busu starts. Every household, including nearby villagers, joins to celebrate.

Everyone tries to wear their best traditional attire and visit one another to share joy and festivities. Rich or poor prepare Judima (local wine made of rice) to offer to whosoever visits them, only to share amongst community members, not alone; that's outside of Dimasa tradition.

Every day ends with a cultural programme of Dimasa Traditional Dance. Distant Villagers with marriageable sons visit their relatives during Busu to find suitable future brides for their sons. The Dimasas follow a traditional, social arranged marriage system. The biggest tragedy of the present is the fixed date. The single-day Busu Celebration in Dima Hasao Dimasa village has had an adverse social impact on selecting the future bride for a Dimasa family. As hardly there is an occasion to participate in such a meeting or select a suitable bribe for their young son.

Matter to ponder over!".

Chavang Kut

The Kuki tribe members mainly celebrate Chavang Kut and Chapchar Kut, out of several post-autumn harvest festivals, which give a break from the whole year of hard work in the field by the farming people. The other important festivals of the Kukis are- Chon, Chang-ai, Sa-ai, Gal-ai, Lom-ki, Avah, Toh-phat Kut, Muchi-lhah Kut, Anchuh-kut, Gamsa-Kut, Mim-kut. The tribe members have a good time in November every year. These events aim to ensure harmony, wealth and peace in the place, State or district where they live.

Not only has the Dima Hasao Autonomous Council declared a holiday to celebrate the festival on November 1st, but Manipur also declared a state holiday because the State has a sizeable population of tribe members. On this occasion, even the business establishments remain closed in Manipur.

As mentioned, the Kuki tribe members used to follow Animism or Nature. The entry of Christianity into their fief seemed to create a rift between two groups – pro and against Christians. At first, those Kuki tribesmen who belonged to the Christians discarded these Kuts that supposedly originated during the worship of Nature or animism. However, they subsequently started celebrating them as a highly emotional cultural event.

The word "Kut" refers to "harvest", and one can see the use of the term in naming the post-harvest celebration of several tribe members from the Kuki-Chin group of the North-eastern region of India. "Chavang" is equivalent to "autumn".

Hega-Ngi

Zeliangrong people who follow the Heraka Movement propounded by Haipou Jadunang, hitherto led by Ramkuiwangbe Jeme ever since the death of Rani Gaidinliu, celebrate Hega-Ngi for three consecutive days in December. But they have several post-harvest festivals: Helei-ngi, Nchang-ngi, Puakpat-ngi and Nsim-ngi

The Hega-Ngi is a post-harvest festival, offering and praying for their best jhum product to Tin Wang (similar to the Hindu or Christian Trinity) at the Prayer Hall (popularly known as Kelumki) on the first day.

On the second day, the Zeliangrong tribe members celebrate by playing traditional dance and sports.

The third day is to tie the thread on the wrist of those who seek elders' blessings and offer meat and rice beer to the guests.

The Dima Hasao Autonomous Council has declared a holiday on December 24th.

Though the Christians among the Jeme tribe members rejected celebrating the traditional festivals in the past, the realisation of having lost custom and tradition has prompted some of them to adopt the celebration.

The sight of youths in traditional and colourful shawls and mufflers on the occasion of the celebration mesmerises the onlookers at the village Lodiram.

Hacha Kekan & Ok Kepru

In the past, according to a knowledgeable source, the Karbi tribe members in Karbi Anglong would select youths to carry out crops harvesting. Then, they would form a committee and carry out the entire operation to save their community from the danger of famine. So, every household was to represent the exercise. The group comprised both males and females, and most participants used to be energetic. Hence, it was an exciting task. Next, they would select land on which they carried outcropping for the livelihood of the whole community of their particular village.

After completing the cropping exercise, they would chalk out a Group Exercise called Jir Kedam. The method of celebration is somewhat similar to those of the past Dimasa tribe members who selected an owner of a home where they celebrated Busudima called Hangseu Busu for seven days. Then, the Karbis would ready "terank" – A joint camp hut where the tribesmen would select and live until they completed farming. Afterwards, of course, the entire operation consisted of uprooting stums from the burnt field, clearing debris, sowing, and ensuring the protection of the crops. So, it was a big project jointly organised by the community people.

Soon after completing the farming, the tribe members would celebrate Hacha Kekan. It is an annual or post-harvest festival in which merriments, including dance, as sanctioned in their traditional way, get commemorated.

The Karbi Anglong Autonomous Council has declared a one-day holiday on January 14th as the Karbi carnival is called Hacha Kekan.

In Dima Hasao, the Karbi tribe members celebrate Ok Kepru, an age-old Community Fishing festival. So, the Dima Hasao Autonomous Council has declared a holiday on April 6th. All Government establishments under its administrative control remain closed. The festival symbolises all youth tribe members harvesting together, which they call "Ritnongchingdi" for the benefit of the community, though the method is a bit different. Some of them even tie their knots on occasion.

One of the prominent features of their fishing is the tribesmen place a plate-like stone to hammer, on which they keep a poisonous fruit called "Ruthe" together with the roots known as Rumet. Afterwards, they mix the juice into the river water, which turns into a white clay-like liquid. When the fish consumes the poisonous substance mixed with water, it dies instantly floating on the water. Then and then, the tribe members collect the lifeless floating fish, boil them, and enjoy the curry. There is no report of any food poisoning following the consumption of fish killed by the poisonous substance.

Nulding Kut

Nulding Kut is one of the most popular festivals of the Baite tribe members. They hold it in January every year by following certain rituals. The celebration marks the beginning of a new year.

In celebrating it, the Baites observe the event by performing cultural and folk songs. Their traditional attires (Nampuan) wear a festive look on the day of the celebration, regarding it as the Festival of Life's Renewals.

The merriment is also a resolution to start new activities like cultivating and constructing dwelling houses. It renews their strength and determination to forget and forgive all shortcomings, including sorrows and discontentment arising from their past deeds. They pray in the glory of their God, Puihitm, seeking forgiveness for all their past sins and granting prosperity in the coming year.

So, the Dima Hasao Autonomous Council has declared a holiday on January 11th.

Parsem Kut

No other tribe members celebrate such a festival as the Khelmas or Sakacheps do in Dima Hasao. It is Parsem Kut, during the celebration of which the tribe members, often boys and girls of marriageable age, get blessings from their elders. The consecration speaks of a happy and prosperous life throughout the New Year they welcome. Nor does it not augur the bond between two opposite sexes belonging to the above groups.

Because the male members offer flowers to the female ones in the commemoration, the Khelmas also recognise it as the "Flower Offering Festival", symbolising the token of care and respect to the female members.

The plucker should not break the branch of the flower meant by the male to offer the female. Nor can the plucker fall down the flowers once plucked and are in their hands.

Any falling flower or loss of it from their hands invites punishment, forfeiting the wrongdoer to serve rice beer (local wine) among the people, or the offender is to seize their shirt or turban. The celebration also paves the way for teenage girls to get into adulthood.

The Dima Hasao Autonomous Council has declared a holiday on April 11th.

Besides, the celebration paves the way for youngsters to have a funny moment between two mature opposite sexes amidst the presence of elders or seniors. The company of seniors ensures restriction on any anti-social activities. The festival begins with a prayer by the village priest, who sacrifices a hen and offers a rice bear in the name of their Tarpa God.

Ruolsafak

The Hrangkhol tribe members celebrate Ruolsafak in February. In celebrating the festival, the tribe members spent the earnings of the youth. So, it is a post-harvest carnival. They commemorate it for two consecutive days.

On the first day of the fiesta, the tribe members' priest and co-elders hold fast and carry out certain rituals, besides sacrificing cock and hen and cooking the meat with rice called Nempok. They also make a short speech before the villagers on why they must hold the festival.

The Dima Hasao Autonomous Council has declared a holiday on February 2nd.

On the second day, they hold traditional games and sports apart from singing and dancing. One has not heard about any restriction imposed in the event of death, unlike the Hmar tribe members. Instead, the Hrangkhol people celebrate it with traditional zeal and fun fare. The objective behind celebrating the fiesta is to record the Hrangkhols' satisfaction over the successful harvest season.

The celebration marks the beginning of a New Year for the tribe members, apart from bidding farewell to the outgoing year.

Sikpui Ruoi

Sikpui Ruoi is the grand festival of the Hmar tribe members. They celebrate it after their weeding operation and early autumn harvest. The respective festival is to give respite to the farming tribe members. Every family is to participate in the fair, which they can continue for one month, depending upon the favourable environment.

The Dima Hasao Autonomous Council has declared a holiday on December 5th.

During the festival celebration, the tribe members do not allow any hostility. Only they continue celebrating the fiesta if anybody dies within the selected celebration area. They maintain strict discipline.

Like a red rug shown to the bull, they hang two big ropes on either side of their reception gate to where they hold the festival venue, also known as Sikpui Zawl, warning to bind with these if anybody creates trouble. The carnival begins with their priest performing some rites. They end their fiesta in a day-long programme because of the cumbersome exercises involved in observing it for a long. They traditionally kept it only once in 1956 at Khawhmunlien, Cachar District, Assam, said one of the tribe members.

Sngi Lumlang

When the Jaintias embraced Christianity, they felt it was sheer wear and tear of their precious time to celebrate their SNGI LUMLANG festival. But they used to commemorate the post-harvest celebration till 1936. Then, given the self-imposed inhibition, they virtually lost their existence.

Suddenly, an idea for reviving their culture, customs and tradition emerged from one Howell Rupsi, an English teacher at the erstwhile Government Boys' High School, Haflong. Only then did their festival get celebrated. Afterwards, in the year 1999, the teacher-turned-social worker from the tribe member alerted the further impending loss of their identity.

Still, he needed help celebrating the festival. During this period, Moril Massa, an active community member who was also a Member of the North Cachar Hills District Council, took the initiative. In reviving their lost glory, Moril Massa got the support of the then Chief Executive Member of the autonomous body, Debojeet Thaosen, who caused the declaration of a Holiday (on January 7th) of all offices under the administrative control of the council.

The Jaintias held the festival for the first time in January 1999 by holding a feast called Bamja. It aimed to unite all stokes of the tribe members and share their views on reviving the Jaintias' culture, customs and traditions in the erstwhile North Cachar Hills (now Dima Hasao).

Epilogue

What the people of Dima Hasao could not imagine is happening now there. So, it rightly defines the uncertainty of the future. Whatever the future holds, it remains uncertain. However, what is certain is if the people of the locality learn to turn the positive side of changes rapidly taking place, it will ensure peace. Tranquillity brings about development, without which the countryside cannot exist.

There is nothing to falter about the present dispensation's performance in the hilly Assam area; the previous Government could not benefit from the highlight of the media.

At the same time, one cannot deny the improvement of the conditions of roads, footpaths and water supply in the present time. The Council has also taken up skill development, improving the quality of education, tourism and health sectors. Apart from that, it has been successful in ensuring the preservation of cultures and traditions more than ever before.

The improvement of law and order, road and water supply, both in rural and urban areas, has ushered the new spirits of development, of which all right-thinking people of the hilly region of Assam must take note.

However, this is not to say there was no single development activity noticeable in our past elders-ruled party Governments, but the present one is better.

Likewise, joining some officials with outside deputed assignments to draw their pay and allowances from the Council's exchequer is tantamount to rendering no services to the people of its jurisdictional areas. Hence, it undermines the position of the autonomous body when it accepts the disposal of benefits of such officials.

Be that as it may, one must be without any qualms to say achievement or accomplishment is possible if there is peace, which has prevailed in the countryside ever since the surrender of underground militants. Moreover, every success sprouts from peace and unity among all the stakeholders of the locality.

On the other hand, division or disunity is the cause of deprivation. It may be the power or privilege responsible for creating unrest in people's minds. So, every fight results from the urge to get individual desires fulfilled. Some suggestions offered herein in the book are worth considering.

The last seven to eight years have seen development in the hilly region of Assam. Indeed, how the people have accepted the changes in the countryside became visible after the result of the thirteenth council election.

Further, the recent release of Mohet Hojai, Joel Gorlosa and Niranjan Hojai was a significant achievement, apart from the proposition to establish a Sainik School at Mahur; the inking of an agreement with the Dimasa National Liberation Army, visualising; the elevation of the present Maibang Degree College to a Campus of Gauhati University; a Hiramba Students' Hostel at Guwahati; a Sports Authority of India Centre in Dima Hasao; a Medical College at Maibang; an Agriculture College at Langting; a Veterinary College at Gunjung; an Ayush Medical College and Hospital at Hatikhali; a Hiramba Temple at Hathikhali and boundary wall around Dimasa historical sites; a Dimasa Kachari Royal Museum in memory of Veer Senapati Tularam Hasnusa in Dima Hasao; a Statue of Senapati Tularam Hasnusa at an appropriate location in consultation with the State Government; a Dimasa Cultural Complex and auditorium in Dima Hasao district; two lane roads from Diyungbra Tinali to Manderdisa via Digandu and Nayapurpur in Dima Hasao; Dhansiri in Karbi Anglong to Dima Khoroh (Dima Hasao); single lane roads from Darunbra to Semkhor; Khepre to Daoreb Haja in Dima Hasao district; Lodhi-Kacharibasti (bordering Cachar and Dima Hasao districts) near Joypur Shibosthan to Polylapur(Poilapur) (Manipur National Highway Road); Madhu bazar PWD road to Kumbhirgram Airport.

Besides, there are plans to construct some Tourist development structures at Dimasa historical sites, for which we can work out mechanisms towards adopting religious tourism.

At the same time, there is good news for the student community of Haflong Government College, for the premier educational institution of higher learning of Dima Hasao is getting autonomous, which is a long felt one.

Though there are140, 873 literates in the Dima Hasao, where the percentage of males and females' literacy ranges 83.29 and 71.33 respectively, there is no scope for the student community to exercise their option for pursuing their chosen post-graduation courses in the educational institutions of the countryside where no University, Engineering, Law and Fine Arts, exist, but the need of which the people have felt a long.

Notwithstanding the demand for a university or a campus of Assam University at Haflong, followed by occasional assurance of some political leaders, nothing has yet come into existence. According to a reliable source, the State Government has agreed to convert Haflong Government College into an Autonomous educational institution. As per the report, it was to depute the incumbent Principal of Nogaon College (Autonomous) Haflong to help the counterpart of Haflong Government College work out modalities by which the former has already accomplished the task.

The proposed autonomy will perhaps ensure power to recommend or recruit faculties, which might redress the deprivation of local recruitment. If the opportunity does not get misused by indulging in politics and nepotism, it will be a big gain for the proposed Dima Hasao Autonomous Territorial Council to process streamlining the educational sector in its jurisdictional areas.

In the end, the Memorandum of Settlement signed between Governments – central and state – and Dimasa National Liberation Army/Dimasa People's Supreme Council (DNLA/DPSC) on the 27th of April 2023, which brought about a light in the tunnel of darkness, seems to pose a hazy look now. The issue of an Autonomous State for the Dima Hasao under Art.244 (A) is getting rapidly recharged by the Sixth Schedule Protection Committee. May the Dima Hasao always be blessed with a good omen! I'll say it!

Selected Bibliographies

1. A History of Assam — Edward Gait
2. Ethnography — E.T. Delton
3. The Early History of India — Vincent Arthur Smith
4. The Problems of Change — Balmiki Prasad Singh
5. Introduction to the Constitution of India — Durga Das Basu
6. Footfalls of Indian History — Margaret E. Noble
7. Topography of Assam — John McCosh
8. The Challenge of the Northeast — Sudhakar Bhat
9. Sixth Schedule — Gobinda Chandra Langthasa
10. Revisiting Dima Hasao In Search of a rhythm — Tanmay Bhattacharjee
11. An Ancestry of Dimasa Social Customs Through the Ages — Sanjib Parbosa
12. Festivals of N.C. Hills - DIPRO publication Compiled by — Z.A. Tapadar
13. Dima Hasao G.K & Current Affairs — A. K. Paul
14. The Hrangkhol — Sumneibul Hrangkhol.
15. Centenary Commemorative Souvenir — Dy. Commissionerate, Haflong
16. Wikipedia
18. Assam Government website
19. Queens of Cachar and the History of Kachhari — N.K. Barman

Other published works of the same author:

A Landless Alien: Where Heart Lay

Trial & Errors

Sight of Vision

Parody

Revelation

Endearing Species

Penalty & Pardon

Assam's Dima Hasao: Pearls of Big River

e-mail: ramu.upadhaya19@gmail.com

facebook.com/RamuUpadhayaBooks